National
Service
Exploits

Brian Davison

DAVISON

3

First published in 2011 by

Brian Davison

ISBN 978-0-9569271-0-1

Printed and bound in Great Britain by Orbital Print Limited.

CONTENTS

ACKNOWLEDGEMENTS

To my lovely wife Hazel, for putting up with my compulsive obsession for writing this book these last two and a half years, as well as helping with the proof reading.

Also to my son Ian, for his IT skills, technical expertise and help in all printing matters, and Caryn and Adrian and the rest of my family, for their support and general interest in what I was doing.

Finally, a big thank-you to all those wonderful ex-National Servicemen who took the time and trouble to listen to what I wanted, and willingly gave me their stories and loaned me their precious photographs.

INTRODUCTION

After Britain had defeated Hitler's Nazi Germany, alongside America and Russia in 1945, the country was on her knees economically, and peace in Europe had come at a price, in the shape of a massive financial debt to America through loans, which have only in recent years been paid back.

Clement Attlee's Labour Party had defeated Winston Churchill's Conservative Party in the General Election held in that year, but the new Prime Minister was finding the victory something of a poisoned chalice, with more problems to deal with than had been the case in the entire six-years war. To deal with those problems Attlee would soon have to do something which had never been done in Britain before – the introduction of compulsory military service in peacetime, in the form of conscription, even though he and his party had opposed it when it was introduced in wartime 1939. The only other time Britain had used this was halfway through the First World War, in 1916, when recruitment had dried up, and men had to be found to replace the soldiers being killed on the front line in France.

Communism was showing its ugly head in parts of Europe after the war, and British troops were needed to restore order in Italy and Greece, where the Communist resistance movement had grown in strength in opposing Hitler in those countries. Now they wanted to prevent the return of the monarchy in Greece, and form a socialist state instead.

One of the two most pressing issues however was in India, where religious friction and hatred between the Hindus and Muslims over a long period of time brought about a civil war between 1946 and 1947; only the world war, in which they fought against Germany and Japan creating a pause.

The Labour government were under pressure to replace the wartime soldiers, who were fed up with being in the Army for six years and wanted to go home to their families; so in March 1947 they introduced a National Service Bill, intended to be for males between 18 and 26, for a period of 18 months. The opposition to this was so intense that a few days later the government reduced the length of service to 12 months, followed by six years on a part-time basis, and this became law in May 1947. The only exemptions were the blind and mentally ill, police, coal miners and merchant seamen.

As soon as they realised that the British intended to relinquish their hold on India in the near future, Hindus and Muslims started killing each other by the tens of thousands. Britain had intended to phase themselves out gradually over a period of time, but the British Army could not keep control any more, and left in undignified haste in July 1948, leaving India partitioned into two countries; India being mostly Hindu, and Pakistan mostly Muslim.

Palestine was the other huge problem that Britain faced, having being given a mandate to oversee the country after the First World War by the then League of Nations. The predicament that Britain faced was that they had promised self-governance to the Arabs, but were also helping to set up a new Jewish homeland there, which was a recipe for disaster. Arab attacks on Jewish settlements went on until 1939, and continued again in 1945, when boatloads of Jewish survivors of Hitler wanted to settle in Palestine. In desperation Britain restricted the flow of immigrants to a manageable level and set up holding camps in Cyprus, such as at Xylotimbu, holding around 20,000, where they oversaw the overflow as a half-way house, which the Jews then tried to escape from, in their resolve to reach their new homeland.

Determined to force the creation of a new state as quickly and by any means possible, extremists organised wholesale acts of sabotage, blowing up just about everything British they could find, including trains carrying soldiers, buildings, RAF aircraft on the ground, paratroopers sleeping in their tents, etc. Two British sergeants were hanged in an olive grove and their bodies booby-trapped, which killed an officer when he attempted to cut them down, and 91 people died when the King David Hotel in Jerusalem was blown up in 1946.[1]

By 1948 Britain had endured enough, gave up the mandate and left the Palestine problem to the United Nations, having suffered over 300 troops killed by the terrorists. The state of Israel was created, and the first of many Israeli-Arab wars began, and tensions between the two countries continue to this very day.

Egypt was regarded as the worst possible posting for any National Serviceman, having been granted independence in 1936, yet still allowing Britain a garrison there to guard the Suez Canal. The real reason for Britain being in Egypt was to look after her holdings in the Far East, and the Suez Canal was the quickest and best route to get there.

During the Second World War Egypt had been an important military centre for the war in the Middle East and North Africa, but by 1945 the Egyptians wanted the British to leave their country. Some British Servicemen were killed by terrorists in Cairo and elsewhere, to hurry them out, but the British retaliated by just leaving the cities and moving to the Suez Canal Zone, establishing their HQ at Fayed. British garrisons were locked into the Canal Zone by 1950, still guarding the Suez Canal, but really protecting British possessions from Egyptian attacks, and over 50 British servicemen were killed there between 1950 and 1956.

Aware of not being able to keep a 70,000 garrison in Egypt, the Conservative government negotiated a hand-over of British power, and in March 1956 the Grenadier Guards left Port Said forever, and plans were afoot to change the British military presence in the Middle-East to Cyprus.

The War Office looked upon Cyprus as a strategic base in the East Mediterranean, but very soon after Britain had announced that her Middle-East base was to be moved to Cyprus, the Servicemen there became involved in another terrorist war against the Greek Cypriots living there, who were determined to have union with Greece, or *Enosis*.

Between 1955 and 1959 Greek Cypriot activists called themselves EOKA Cyprus freedom fighters under the leadership of Bishop Makarios and Colonel Grivas, and during this period over 450 British servicemen and policemen were killed by them, as well over 200 civilians. In due course this terrorism spread between the Island's Greek and Turkish inhabitants, at which point Britain handed the whole problem over to the United Nations.

Britain kept an Army and Air Force in Libya until 1970, and their bases such as Tripoli and Tobruk were used mainly as training areas, but towards the end military units helped King Idris to keep control.

The British government, thwarted in their aim to use Cyprus as a base in the Middle-East, then thought of Kenya as that base, but decided not to, as it was clear that our position in that part of the world was becoming untenable [2]. By 1970 Britain no longer had a presence in the Middle East.

Besides the major problems in India, Pakistan and Palestine in 1948 the British government had to contend with a fourth, in the shape of the Malayan Emergency. During the Second World War the Japanese had heavily defeated the British Army at Singapore, taking over 100,000 prisoners, despite a previous promise of protection to the Malayan population by the British. Resistance to the Japanese came from the Malayan Communist Party (MCP), who then turned against the British after the Japanese were defeated in 1945. However, they came up against some determined opposition from the British Army of Regulars and National Servicemen, who finally defeated them in 1960, after 12 years of fighting. This being the only successful British anti-insurgency operation after the Second World War.

Lt.-General Sir Harold Briggs had a plan, which incorporated the efforts of the military, police and intelligence sections, to give him information about terrorist movements. The infantry then moved into the jungle, secured bases and drove the Communist Terrorists (CTs) deeper into the jungle. At first the Chinese villagers gave the CTs food, because they were terrified of them, so the answer was to resettle the villagers well away from the jungle, into newly built villages, thus denying the CTs their supply of food.

Infantry patrols usually consisted of a National Service officer with a Regular sergeant nearby, plus another two experienced corporals and maybe another ten or eleven mostly National Servicemen. This included the radio operator, plus one or two native scouts who were then used to find and kill the CTs in the jungle, if possible. The young officers had been superbly trained by experienced Australian officers at the School of Jungle Warfare at Johore, who made sure that their pupil officers were well ready for the jungle by the time they left them. This in turn meant that the infantry platoons were well led, which kept their own casualties down to a minimum, while keeping the number of CTs killed high.

To emphasize the dangerous job they were doing however, 12 Royal West Kents and three Iban scouts were killed in the North Selangore jungle in 1951, victims of a clever ambush, while there were many other incidents involving loss of life of both National Servicemen and Regular soldiers alike [3].

Again in 1948 came another major, but thankfully short-lived problem. The Russians cut all railway and road access from the west into the sectors of Berlin under Allied control in June, in a move to make the Allies' presence in Berlin untenable. This was answered by the RAF and USAF flying in 7,000 tons of food and supplies every day on round-the-clock missions, which became known as the Berlin Airlift.

Concern over Communist intentions in Europe, (and Germany in particular), as well as elsewhere in the world, made the government realise that 12 months National Service was just not creating enough manpower, and in December 1948 the National Service Amendment Act became law, reverting back to 18 months service again, with four years in reserve.

The blockade lasted for 318 days, and during this time the Berliners only had dried potatoes, powdered eggs and tins of meatballs to live on, and the capital city needed at least 6,000 tons of supplies every day to survive. However, the British and Americans carried on relentlessly landing supplies every three minutes, every day, and by the time Spring arrived in 1949 it was obvious even to the Russians that the airlift was succeeding, and they lifted the blockade in May. This resulted in two German states being formed; the Federal Republic of Germany, known as West Germany, and the German Democratic Republic, known as East Germany, which divided Germany up into two parts [4]. In 1961 the Russians constructed the Berlin Wall to prevent the massive exodus of East Germans going into West Germany, and this stayed up until 1989, when it was broken down.

In 1950 over 20,000 British Servicemen were sent to Korea as part of a United Nations force, after North Korea invaded South Korea. This caused the length of National Service to be increased again up to two years, with three-and-a-half years in reserve, and was destined to stay the same until the last man left in 1963. During the three years long war National Servicemen played a vital part in Korea, forming just over 50% of the British Servicemen serving there. In some infantry battalions such as the Duke of Wellingtons, Green Howards, Durham Light Infantry and the King's Own Scottish Borderers, the percentage was even higher.

They had to contend with bitterly cold winters, where the temperature was often as low as –40 degrees centigrade, with the dangers of frostbite, and very hot and clammy summers, with the temperature rising to +40 degrees, and having to survive being constantly bitten by thousands of mosquitoes, with the danger of contracting malaria later. Those infantry lads had to live out in the open in hoochies, cut out of trenches, living on indifferent food, and sharing their accommodation with giant rats.

Two battles stand out from the many fought by British Army Regiments during the three years of the Korean war. The Battle of the Imjin River in April 1951, where the

Gloucestershire Regiment defended Hill 235, and where they made their famous last stand, cut off, and facing overwhelming odds. The second battle was named the Third Battle of the Hook in May 1953, which was in a strategic position vital to both sides, lasting for three weeks, and being preceded by the most intense barrage of enemy shells since the Battle of the Somme in 1916. The 1st Battalion of the Duke of Wellingtons Regiment held on during the ensuing ferocious attack, but 28 of them were killed. However, they eventually defeated and routed a fanatical Chinese Army.

After the Korean war finished in 1953 until 1963 when conscription ended, there were plenty of occasions when National Servicemen were called upon to keep the peace, in various parts of the world. The ongoing IRA troubles in Northern Ireland needed attention between 1952 and 1956; in Kenya the Mau Mau terrorists were causing severe unrest between 1952 and 1956; British troops had to sort out the rioting in both Hong Kong and Singapore in 1956; the Malayan war which had started in 1948 took until 1960 before the British Army finally defeated them; the unrest in the Suez Canal Zone between 1950 and 1956 had the opposite result, being told by America to leave in undignified style in 1956; in Cyprus the EOKA activists caused many British deaths in the civil unrest between 1955 and 1959.

It seemed that there was unrest everywhere after the end of the Second World War, where the long awaited 'peace' was plagued by rioting and civil unrest, and British troops were also called out to settle conflicts in such unlikely places as Jamaica, Barbados, British Guiana, the Cameroons and Zanzibar.

The RAF were called upon to attack terrorist camps during the period of Mau Mau atrocities in Kenya, between 1952 and 1955, and were used in Malaya during that 12-year war, to attack the Communist Terrorists when directed to their positions in the jungle, and also to drop much needed supplies to the infantry engaged in flushing the terrorists out. The RAF were also involved in Oman against rebel tribesmen in 1953, and during the Suez crisis of 1956 they were also heavily committed.

The Royal Navy still used its major overseas bases at Gibraltar, Malta and Singapore in the early Fifties, because it was thought necessary to keep them there to maintain Britain's influence in the Middle and Far East. Although the Royal Navy had a strong presence in Korean waters during that three-year war, the ageing fleets used in the Second World War were soon to be scrapped, and naval strength cut to the bone, in a series of savage cuts in both manpower and ships. It was not surprising therefore, that Naval National Servicemen were few in number, with very few indeed going overseas, and they were employed in the main just on maintenance work in home waters. The Royal Navy became the first of the three Services to dispense with National Servicemen in the late Fifties.

In the next part of the book the reader will find 121 stories of young men conscripted mainly between 18-21 years of age, but occasionally a little older. Some of those stories are amusing, some are sad, and others highly unusual, because no two National Servicemen's experiences were the same. While thousands of National Servicemen served in England, patiently crossing off the days on a demob chart, thousands more served abroad in far off places of the fast receding British Empire, making the most of the free travel to, in some cases, exotic locations in the Caribbean or to Hong Kong. Some had the good fortune to serve in two or even three different countries, as George Rogers, Barrie Shepherdson and Rex Strawson did.

The book is divided up into chapters, representing the main areas of the world in which the British forces operated between 1945 and 1963. All three Services are represented, but as the Royal Navy required fewer men for National Service, this is reflected in far fewer contributions, while the Army has 30 Regiments represented. There are stories from 30 different countries, and there are 30 pages of photographs from those countries. Some familiar names will keep cropping up, if they have served in several countries during their two years. The last few pages entitled National Service Index, show the National Service details of the stories' authors.

Finally, this book is dedicated to the many hundreds of young National Servicemen who died for their country in far-off places, inaccessible for most relatives in those days before cheap chartered flights. This was because their bodies stayed where they were killed, for example in India, Korea and Malaya, many thousands of miles from home.

CHAPTER ONE

How National Service Started

National Service or conscription has only ever been used three times in Britain during the last 95 years; the first during war time in 1916, the second whilst preparing for war in 1939, and on the last occasion, in peacetime, at the end of 1945.

At the start of the First World War in 1914 Britain's Army numbered less than a quarter of a million men, well short of what was regarded as an official complement, but as most people thought it would be all over by that first Christmas, perhaps enough. In any case Britain at that time had the most powerful Navy in the world, and most of our war leaders thought that the war would be won at sea by the superior quality of our Royal Navy.

Secretary of State for war, Lord Kitchener did not share that optimism, because of his successful military experiences in Khartoum and in the Boer War, starting in the final years of the previous century. He knew that the Army as it stood was vastly undermanned, and totally unprepared for war, and he told the rest of the Cabinet that the war would go on for at least three years, and we would need well over a million more men to fight it. They gave him authorization to recruit them.

Kitchener's Volunteer Army was about to be formed, and posters were pasted up everywhere, exhorting young men to go and fight for their country. Even today there are very few people unaware of that most famous of all posters, depicting Kitchener as a recruiting sergeant with the commanding message being: *'Your Country Needs YOU!'* [1]

This had a dramatic effect on Britain's men folk, and by the end of 1914 nearly one-and-a-quarter million of them were recruited, with friends making up 'pals' units, consisting of groups of policemen (although exempt), carpenters, teachers, printers, butchers, etc, all willing to fight for King and country, and to protect their families from the possibility of foreign invasion.

However, after those heady early days of 1914 came the ever increasing death toll of British soldiers, having being repeatedly badly led in battle after battle by Generals Haig and Rawlinson into senseless repeated frontal attacks on the German front lines in France, and being mown down in their tens of thousands by the German machine gunners. The reality was dawning on the British public that this was going to be an extremely long war indeed, and that there was no glory involved at all, especially as the latest deaths were being published by the morning newspapers every day. This of course had a dramatic effect on recruitment, and by the end of 1915 it had virtually dried up.

Something had to be done to make up for the huge losses being experienced on the front line, and to somehow find replacements for them. That came in the form of the National

Military Service Act in May 1916, which conscripted all fit men aged between 18 and 41 to go and serve their country. For the very first time every family in Britain was involved and affected in some way in an overseas war. Previously Britain had sent an Army to fight an incursion abroad and the public at home had shown very little interest in the outcome, as happened in the Crimean and Boer Wars. All this now changed, and even women were recruited into the Auxiliary Service as nurses and drivers, etc. [2]

Eventually, with a belated appearance by the American Army into the war, the Germans were defeated in 1918, and the surviving Forces returned home to an impoverished Britain, and not as had been promised, to a land fit for heroes, but in many cases, unemployment, and some even had to resort to begging on the streets. They were however, determined that they were never going to be involved in anything like that ever again; but even this indomitable spirit was about to be dashed less than twenty years later by Adolf Hitler. Devoid of hindsight the British Army was very soon much reduced in size, and the National Military Service Act repealed, thus ending conscription. [3]

Despite Winston Churchill's exhortations in the 1930s to rearm quickly because of the ever-increasing threat of war from Germany, his warnings went unheeded, because the memories of the First World War were still fresh in the recollections of those government officials in charge of the country. Pacifism and appeasement were exhausted though, when Prime Minister Neville Chamberlain returned from his Munich meeting with Hitler in September 1939, brandishing his piece of paper, supposedly guaranteeing 'peace' with Nazi Germany, but shown to be false when Germany invaded Prague shortly afterwards in the following March.

Faced with the knowledge that war with Germany was now certain, and the fact that Anglo-French guarantees of support to Poland would mean forming a large Army at short notice, Chamberlain announced in the House of Commons the re-introduction of National Military Service in April for men aged between 20 and 21. Surprisingly, over three-quarters-of-a-million men responded to the call by Christmas 1939, and two years later the numbers had increased to over four million, after subsequent National Service Acts had widened the net to include all those men between 18 and 41. [4]

Six long years of bloodshed later, with millions killed and with most of Europe laid waste after the Allied victory over Germany in May 1945, all the British servicemen wanted was to get home to their wives and families as soon as possible, even though they were spread out all over the world at the time. Attitudes had changed too, and the men who had been away for six years or more were fed up with war and discipline, and began to demand that their rights be observed. The British Government realised that it would be impossible now to maintain wartime conscription.

However, due to a misconception of Britain still being a world power, and despite being financially bankrupt and dependent on America for aid, as was the rest of Europe, the government still had responsibilities overseas, such as occupational duties in a divided Germany, maintaining security in a rapidly shrinking Empire, and maintaining influence in various parts of the world.

This perceived need for a large peacetime military force led the Labour government to pass the National Service Act in 1947, but with much opposition within its own party. This required one year to be served in the Armed Forces, followed by five more in reserve. Due to the Malayan crisis and the Cold War with Russia, the National Service Amendment Act was passed in 1948, which increased the length of service to 18 months. [5]

The 1950s began with the advent of the Korean War, when it was felt necessary to increase the length of National Service to two years duration, which for the majority – but not all, as will be shown later – remained at that level until ending in May 1963.

CHAPTER TWO

What Was It All About?

Most of the two-and-a-quarter million men conscripted into National Service between 1945 and 1963 went into the Army, with about half a million going into the Royal Air Force, and very few indeed into the Royal Navy, which roughly equates to the number of stories for each Service in this book.

For the vast majority this came as a tremendous shock to the life they had become used to, leaving their homes, families and loved ones for the very first time. For a few, such as those who had been Army Cadets, Sea Cadets, etc., it was not so great. Bonds were quickly formed among the young men from greatly differing backgrounds while doing their basic training, and some of those National Service friendships formed during those years would last a lifetime.

The Fifties provided many problems for our armed forces, with National Servicemen fighting alongside Regulars in a full-scale war in Korea, and providing nearly 60% of the men involved. They were also heavily involved in such trouble spots as taking on Communist insurgents in Malaya, EOKA terrorists in Cyprus, terrorists in Palestine, Mau Mau terrorists in Kenya, not to mention the unfortunate Suez Canal episode in Egypt. The young conscripts were thrown into those combat situations with minimal training. They were then expected to fight in Korea - living and fighting in trenches, and engage in jungle warfare - as in Malaya, and cope with riots and civil war situations all over the world.

The price to be paid for all this military involvement came in the form of just under an estimated 600 National Service deaths on active service, together with around 300 accidental deaths, from late 1945 until its end in 1963.

In theory all men attaining the age of 18 had to register for National Service at their local Ministry of Labour. The would-be conscript would then be sent a letter a few weeks later telling him to attend a medical examination to see if he was fit enough for military service. Prospective conscripts could be traced through their National Health records to make sure that no-one was missed. Successful conscripts were those who passed a full medical including an X-ray, and graded 1-3; they were then interviewed by an officer to see which Service suited their skills. In reality the vast majority went into the Army anyway.

Those conscripts who had no trade usually went into one of the Services at the age of 18, while tradesmen were mostly deferred until their apprenticeships were completed at the age of 21, and University students even longer, after obtaining their degrees.

Six weeks later a conscript would be sent an enlistment notice telling him where to report for basic training, and a rail warrant for that destination. Unless they were married, conscripts were sent as far away as possible from their home town to do this six to ten weeks basic training.

Upon arrival at the nearest railway station to their camp, mostly on a Thursday afternoon for some obscure reason, the new recruits were met at their destination by two or three of the roughest and most foul-mouthed NCOs they had ever seen. In no time at all after they were deposited inside their new 'home' they had been given their AB 64 part one service book, and part two, pay book, which had to be kept for the duration of their service. They then had their two-minute shower, regulation very short crew haircut, and issued (thrown at them) with the most ill-fitting uniforms possible.

New recruits were generally issued with a best uniform and a second-best uniform, composed of a BD blouse and BD trousers with both usually badly fitting. Next came best boots and second best boots, the necessary underwear, web belt and gaiters, greatcoat, beret and badge, together with physical training kit, rifle, bed linen and eating utensils.

After this they would be assigned to a Company and a particular barrack room, where swaps took place, to get as near as possible to somewhere near a fit for all the gear they had just been issued with, which acted as an ice-breaker for most of them. They were then told to parcel up their civilian clothes in brown paper and send them home – thus severing all connection with their former civilian life for the next 730 days.

That first night would be spent 'bulling up' their ill-fitting boots, which meant removing the pimples on the toecaps with a spoon heated by a candle flame, and then polishing for hours, going round and round in little circles with boot polish until they could see their reflections. Belt and gaiters had to be rubbed with green Blanco, and all cap badges and buttons had to be polished with Brasso until they were immaculate. This was all done to supposedly change civilians into soldiers – a part of discipline in those days.

The next morning, day two, a new recruit could expect to be awakened by an NCO shouting at them to get up, around 5.30 a.m. A quick wash and shave in cold water would be followed by breakfast and then back to the barrack room for a room inspection. Any serviceman with dirty or untidy kit could expect to be put on Company Orders, and if there was no drastic improvement, then CB (confined to barracks) for a number of days would follow. Room and kit inspections would be held usually every day during basic training. As part of the kit inspection the new recruit had to make a blanket box of his bedding, which was made up of a folded sheet, folded blanket, folded sheet, with a further blanket wrapped round them all neatly.

Many hours were spent on the parade ground usually in the mornings, doing intensive drilling with a drill corporal and a drill sergeant, which some found rewarding, while the majority of new recruits certainly did not. Most afternoons were used for weapons training and six-mile runs, while the evenings were taken up with cleaning their barrack rooms, rifles, boots, belt and gaiters, etc., a procedure well known as 'bull.' To most conscripts basic training consisted of incessant drill practice, with lots of marching, parading and weapons training.

Some conscripts were put into old rundown barracks, with little or no heating, ancient toilets and very poor and inadequate washing facilities. Later on conditions improved and occasionally conscripts had new brick barracks with central heating. National Servicemen sent abroad found that accommodation varied greatly depending on where they were. In Germany the Army barracks were usually luxurious compared to anything in Britain, but abroad it could be very poor. In Korea thousands of infantrymen slept in hoochies cut out of trenches and lived outside for the duration of their posting, where it ranged from –40 degrees centigrade in winter to + 40 degrees in summer, and lived with giant rats and mosquitoes. Those posted to Malaya had to use mosquito nets to avoid malaria and toilet facilities could be a bucket or just a dug trench, and here too, infantrymen had to sleep outside in many cases.

Any new recruit who had experience of camping out with the Boy Scouts, or had been in any of the military cadets found the first few days unremarkable, and adapted to anything the Army could throw at them. Those who had never been away from home before however, suffered most, and struggled dreadfully to cope with all these new demands from bullying NCOs, and occasionally, even from a fellow recruit.

During that first week Service numbers were issued; six-digit numbers in the Navy, seven in the Royal Air Force, and eight digit numbers in the Army, which had to be stamped on everything they had been issued with. Fifty to sixty years later what all those Servicemen have in common is the ability to be able to recite their own particular number at will, as if forever indelibly stamped on their minds. Another ritual to be followed was to be marched to the medical centre to be given various inoculations, two of which were for smallpox and TAB, anti-typhoid, and administered on the first Saturday. In those days they seemed to use only the one needle, and by the time the last ones were inoculated it was inevitably blunted, which explained why big fit lads used to fall down like ninepins. The following day the new recruits could hardly lift their arms up, let alone enjoy their free day off!

Towards the end of basic training recruits had to take their turn in doing guard duty, which most if not all recruits hated doing because of a lack of sleep. From 6.15 p.m. until 6.15 a.m. they had to do two two-hour patrols, with four hours rest in between them, sleeping on a very hard bed. The only way of avoiding this was to become the 'stick-man' out of the seven men listed for guard duty; being awarded for this by the duty officer to the best turned out man. Guard duty was boring and seemed to last forever, with usually one posted on the main gate and the rest circling the camp during their tour of duty.

National Servicemen were given 14 days leave for every eight months service, and they were paid around £1 per week to start with for a home posting in 1958, considerably less than the average weekly civilian wage of £14 at that time. Out of that £1 they had to buy shaving gear, boot polish, and Brasso for polishing brass metal badges. If any of their kit went 'missing' they had to pay for it twice, once to replace it, and once as a fine. Any trips home had to undertaken by hitching lifts with lorry drivers or private car drivers, who were usually sympathetic to their plight, and happily shared their vehicles for part or all of the journeys.

Around this time there were always several ingenious attempts at getting a discharge, and a passport back to the paradise of normal life. Some recruits used to try and stay in bed and refuse to get up at Reveille, others blancoed their boots and blacked their belt and gaiters with Cherry Blossom boot polish, (the opposite of what was needed), and a few even urinated in their beds every night. The desperate tried to shoot themselves in the foot during weapons training, and the most desperate of all even committed suicide, rather than go through any more basic training at the more brutal training camps. [1]

A much better way of easing National Service life was to be good at sport. All the Services encouraged sport because it kept the men fit, and was thought to encourage leadership and teamwork skills needed. Young recruits found that if they boxed or were good at athletics, football or cricket, they were often excused guard duties and drills, to give more time for training in their particular sport, and as a consequence there was never any shortage of volunteers for any sport. Bobby and Jack Charlton and Brian Clough are just three of many household names to have completed their National Service during those years.

Because of the usual acute shortage of money the NAAFI (Navy, Army and Air Force Institute) was the main source of recreation, providing food, non-alcoholic drinks, games, newspapers, music, and sometimes pretty young girls behind the counter. For those with money to spend, and wanting to get as far as possible away from the camp for a while, local dance halls and public houses were very popular, and for many young men it was their first experience of drinking alcohol and getting drunk.

When their basic training was finished the National Servicemen were either given a home posting, or were posted all over the world, to Europe, the Middle East, Far East, Africa, Australia (for nuclear testing), or the Caribbean.

Conscripts going into the Royal Air Force usually had a better time, regarding accommodation and with a lesser emphasis on bull. Most of them went to RAF Padgate and RAF Hednesford for their kit and then basic training, before being posted to their various units either at home or across the world.

The RAF Regiment on the other hand was every bit as hard in basic training as the Army in general, excepting the Guards, while Royal Navy National Servicemen were far and few between, being sent to either Portsmouth or Plymouth for their training, and very rarely being posted abroad. Conscription finished in the Royal Navy in the late 1950s, because they considered that two years was an insufficient time to train conscripts up to the standards necessary for the new advanced equipment coming in before they completed their two years service. The Royal Navy could afford to do that because their recruitment was going far better than was the case in the other two Services.

CHAPTER THREE

Europe

ENGLAND

If a National Serviceman did not manage to be sent to one of the most popular postings abroad, such as Hong Kong, Austria, Bermuda, or SHAPE in Paris, there were always a few desirable places in England in which to spend the next 730 days. Those who excelled at sport, such as professional footballers, golfers and athletes rarely went abroad, but spent their time honing up their skills somewhere in England. Some lucky conscripts were sent to the War Office and never wore a uniform, while others were posted to out of the way depots where there were no drills or duties. A few even managed to be posted just a few miles from home and went there every night. For the majority of postings in Britain however, it was just boring repetition day after day, especially in the latter days after 1958, and it was a case of ticking off the days on a demob. chart, and waiting for it all to end.

JOHN PRENTICE

Royal Warwickshire Regiment, 1958-60

On his first day of National Service, joining the Royal Warwickshire Regiment, based at Warwick, in 1958, John said goodbye to his mum and girlfriend next door (now his wife). His hair was in a big quiff, and he was wearing his drapes and everything, and carrying his Brooke Bond paper carrier bag. He told his mum he would be home that same night, but of course he wasn't able to. Nevertheless, after being in the Army a couple of weeks John decided that he liked it so much that he would sign on for an extra year, which he did. After a couple more days however, he decided that he didn't like it anymore. So he telephoned his mother back home and she wrote to his CO, saying that: *'Her Johnnie didn't like doing this Army thing now,'* etc., and he actually got off it! (*See Pic. No. 6*).

John did his basic training at Warwick before being posted to Northern Ireland, near the Mourne mountains, and spent 10 months there, and was then sent to Worcester, before his posting to Aden. There was a rule of the Warwick camp during those first few weeks of training that if you had a pair of shoes you could go out on a night with them on. Someone suggested that John should ask the sergeant for a loan of his shoes, for a dare. John took him up on it, because he was very keen to get home to see his girlfriend, and went along to the sergeant and asked him for a loan of his shoes. 'Borrow my shoes, *borrow my shoes*, he exploded! Here, take them for your cheek.'

John didn't see any action in Northern Ireland, but he was glad to leave there for Aden. While he was in Ireland he had to do a cadre for driving. There was a Sergeant Fisher sat next to John as he was doing his driving test. All of a sudden he shouted: 'Stop, *Stop!* Where did you learn to drive like that'*?* John thought he was happy with his driving, but when he told the sergeant that he learned to drive with the Co-op, he exploded into telling John that he was driving like a maniac. (John is still working and driving to this day, getting up at 3.30 a.m. every morning - at the age of 74!)

At the Passing Out Parade at Worcester Barracks, Field Marshall Montgomery, hero of El Alamein in the Second World War, came down the ranks giving his inspection. As John was only 5ft 2in. tall he went down on his knees to him to get eye-to-eye contact, just smiled at him, and got back up again without saying a word. (*See Pic. No. 25*). *(See also, Aden)*.

BRIAN CLOUGH OBE, MA

Royal Air Force, 1953-55

Brian was called up for his National Service in 1953, and spent the next two years in the RAF. According to his autobiography in 1994 he hated the thought of leaving his family home for two years, but the uniform he wore during that time actually generated a strange sense of pride, the moment he put it on.

Cloughie's basic training was at RAF Padgate, and he was then posted to RAF Watchet in Somerset, where he spent most of the remainder of his service marching, standing to attention, swimming, running and playing football. Brian's second love in sport after his beloved football, was cricket, and he would often sneak off to listen to a Test Match commentary on the radio.

Cloughie was quite content to be a Leading Aircraftsman, not being interested in promotion, finding the camaraderie much more important than rank. He played lots of football whilst in the RAF, 'but they couldn't see the talent right under their noses, very much like the FA in later years.' Amazingly, considering his later successes as a prolific scoring centre forward, for Middlesbrough and Sunderland, as well as playing for England, he was never chosen for the RAF national team!

MALCOLM MacGREGOR

Royal Engineers, 1958-60

Malcolm's National Service basic training for the Royal Engineers in 1958 was at Aldershot, where he had a young green soldier called Neil Mills sharing his double bunk, and he told him to go onto the top bunk. On the first night he fell out and landed on the floor next to Malcolm. Now Neil used to get huge food parcels sent regularly from home filled with Cornish pasties and fruit cakes, sweets, cigarettes, etc, which he shared with Malcolm. However, Neil had difficulty with everything, and Malcolm had to strip his rifle and sten gun down for him, and other simple tasks, as he did not want the supplies of goodies to dry up. On Passing Out Parade day Neil's parents thanked Malcolm for looking out for their little boy! Someone was definitely looking out for this lad because he finished up playing golf with the CO every Wednesday!

Malcolm recalls one lad called 'Scrawny' McDonald, who was excused from wearing Army shirts because they irritated his skin, excused boots, because he had bad feet, excused drill on the parade ground, for the same reason, and excused from carrying a rifle, because it was too heavy for him. He lived just a few miles from Aldershot, and made the most of the situation by spending more time at home than at the barracks. However, he had something the other lads did not have, being so well endowed in the nether regions that the rest of the lads turned to the wall in the shower area in shame whenever he came in. Ironically, he was eventually discharged on medical grounds, because he *'couldn't carry heavy equipment.'*

Malcolm was later posted to the Royal Engineers 33 field squadron, based at Ripon. They were sent to build a road at Otterburn artillery range in the middle of a very harsh winter, and billeted four to a tent, waking up at night with their breath frozen and the top blanket covered in ice. It often snowed heavily and they had to push the snow out of the way to exit the tent. They had to build a road in arctic conditions, and wear arctic suits, all-weather. The cook wagon came out to them, and every day it was one dollop of stew and one dollop of rice in their mess tin, plus a cup of tea. Someone got in touch with the *'Sunday Pictorial,'* a popular newspaper in those days, to inform them of the conditions these young lads were working under, and shortly after a brigadier came along, and asked them what the trouble was. They complained about everything, so he offered to improve the food and to give them a daily rum ration, which was instantly accepted. The road was finished on time, and they returned to Ripon.

The Ripon pubs were glad to see their return, because they had a Scots lad in their group whose party trick was to down a pint of beer in less than two seconds. He would bet anyone for a small wager that he could down the pint while the person turned their head away and turned straight back again. The man had no swallow, a large mouth, and he simply picked it up and poured it straight down, and then collected his winnings! (*See Pic. No. 11*).

The next job was in Hampshire, to build a heavy girder bridge across Hawley Lake. As military equipment had grown in size, a Bailey bridge as used in World War Two was not adequate – so this new bridge had to be built, tried and tested. Finally, the bridge was ready, and tanks, rocket launchers, etc. were rolled onto the bridge. However, one of the pins securing the bridge to one of the pontoons sheared, which created a domino effect, and the bridge and everything on it all went into the lake. Three months work had all gone in under three minutes! Heavy cranes were called in to lift everything out of the water – and then they had to start to rebuild the bridge again, which of course took another three months.

While at Hawley, under canvas, the surrounding woods were full of wildlife. One day one of the lads found a very young fox cub, which appeared to have been abandoned. It was brought back to camp, fed and watered, until strong enough to survive on its own. During its time with them it devoured boots, webbing, socks and almost anything else it could get its teeth into! (*See Pic. No. 11*).

With just a few months of his National Service to go Malcolm became an officer's batman at Ripon, which was very much easier than anything else he had ever done before. He just had to lay out the officer's uniform the afternoon before, for him to put on the next day. Duties also included cutting lawns and babysitting. When he was doing this duty he used the officer's hi-fi equipment, had supper in the kitchen, and just had to look in at the little girl upstairs occasionally. Then

Malcolm had a phone call one night to go home as his wife Anne was ill – the officer's wife told him just to go home and she would sort it, which she did, resulting in seven days compassionate leave.

On his return to duty as a batman, Malcolm discovered that he now had another officer to look after, who had a five-year-old daughter. One day, on seeing Malcolm working in the officer's garden, she asked him if he was *Mister MacGregor* the gardener from the Beatrix Potter stories. She was very sad when the time came for Malcolm to leave, but he told her that he had to go home to look after Mrs. MacGregor, and his own garden, and this seemed to be acceptable to her.

Malcolm does not regret doing his National Service, and feels that his time spent in the Army helped to develop his character for the better. *(See also, Last Thoughts).*

MALCOLM SCRATCHERD

Royal Air Force, 1947-49

An early memory of his RAF National Service for Malcolm is of joining Station Flight Horsham St. Faith, near Norwich, with 245 Fighter Squadron in 1947. He was alone one day in the office when the phone rang which Malcolm answered, while the corporal and other members were not there. The person on the other end asked for the corporal, and Malcolm said that he was unavailable, and he was the only person there; but he was told to get himself out on the pad, as there was an incoming aircraft with a VIP on board. As Malcolm had never brought an aircraft in before because his job was being a flight mechanic, he was very nervous, but nevertheless went out to do just that. He brought it in, turned it round into the wind, absolutely perfect.

The doors of the aircraft opened and out came the top brass. The first one with lots of gold braid on his shoulder was a Squadron Leader. He came down the steps, and following him was a Wing Commander. Behind him was a chap with a lot of 'scrambled egg' on his cap, and bars on his arm and up to his elbow. All of this time Malcolm was standing with the bats under his arm and saluting. The Squadron Leader, acting as aide-de-camp, but extremely scruffy himself, with long hair over his collar, Malcolm noted, gave the order to: *'Put this man on a charge for being improperly dressed.'* Later, Malcolm was called into his own flight office and told that the person he had upset was none other than Lord Tedder, Air Chief Marshall of the Royal Air Force!

It was realised that Malcolm had saved a lot of people's bacon that day, being the only one there, but he had to be put on a charge, because the Squadron Leader needed to know that his order had been carried out. So Malcolm had to serve his three weeks sentence in the officers' mess, supposedly cleaning up after their meals, but he was also getting officers' food and receiving all the perks that were there, because he was a *cause celebre* for what he had done.

A duty officer approached him one day and asked him to work late at night behind the bar on a special night when Joe Louis lost his world heavyweight boxing crown. The officers were all listening in to the fight at 2 a.m. in the morning, and buying Malcolm all the drinks he wanted, and even gave him a bottle of rum to take back to his barrack room. Malcolm met more sergeants and officers in that short time than anyone else would do in two years.

On another occasion he was asked to do the same again, and everyone was laughing and joking. Malcolm went out to the toilet and out there was a young pilot on a ladder, full of life, singing at the top of his voice. The following day he went up in a Beaufighter and hit high tension cables and was killed, and his young wife and baby daughter came to see him at the funeral. She asked to see her husband's body, but was persuaded not to as the body was not suitable for her to see.

(See also, Germany).

BILL HUBBARD

Royal Army Ordnance Corps, 1958-60

Basic and trade training for Bill, joining the RAOC in 1958 was at Hilsea Barracks, Southsea, and Blackdown, Aldershot, before arriving at his final posting at Donnington, in Shropshire. During basic training the fellow in the next bed urinated in his bed every night, and he confided to Bill that he was 'working his ticket' back home. It turned out that he had been doing this non-stop for some time, and during several intakes. Bill told him that he did not fancy his chances of ever getting out just doing that, but one night he went over to Bill to tell him that he was being discharged the following day, and he whispered to Bill: *'Who's the mug now then?'* (*See Pic. No. 17*).

A similar story concerned old Ernie, who had been in the Army for over 20 years, and was still a private. Every night he went to the pub and got bladdered. He had a bed right next to Bill, and this particular night he came back very late and couldn't find the light switch, because they had been put out at 22.00 hours, and he was very drunk. All of a sudden Bill heard Ernie relieving himself on the floor next to his bed, and his bedside mat was floating on top! As there was a room inspection the next morning everyone had to help to get it all cleaned up – but poor old Ernie was never seen again.

Sergeant Smith one of the drill instructors at Hilsea Barracks, Portsmouth and the worst by far, was kicked out of the Army in early 1959, because of his brutality shown towards young National Service soldiers. Many of his victims wished that they had been there to have seen it.

When Bill had been at Donnington for a few weeks, he was told that he was going to join a team doing printing work for the War Office in London, and from then on he would be working night shifts for the duration of his service. One day they had a room inspection, and a sergeant came into the room and went ballistic at the state of it. As Bill stood there he heard one of the officers whisper the words: '*War Office.*' All at once the sergeant's attitude changed completely, saying: '*OK chaps, carry on.*' They were never bothered again for the remainder of the two years. From then on those magic words were used again and again, at every available opportunity, as they obviously carried enormous weight. (*See Pic. Nos. 28, 31, 32*).

After a week-end leave Bill hitch-hiked back to camp on Monday mornings between 10 and 11 a.m. starting from a certain spot on the Edgware Road in central London. While waiting for a lift two men came along and asked what he was doing. He explained he was going back to his Army camp, and they asked about his pay book, but Bill explained he did not have it on him. As he did night shift work starting at 6 p.m. there was no need to be going back earlier. They asked for the camp telephone number, and said that it sounded more like a holiday camp than an Army camp. They searched his bag and reluctantly let him go. When he got back to camp his fellow room mates said that these two fellows were just having a laugh, and to just forget it. Two weeks later, at the same spot, at the same time, the same two men approached him, and said the same things to him all over again, and looked inside his bag, etc. Bill asked them to: *'Hold on, what's it got to do with you?'* They reached inside their pockets and produced Metropolitan police cards, and told him not to start getting aggressive with them or else ... When he got back to camp he told his room mates that they had dropped him right in it! The following week Bill changed his position, rather than go through all that again.

When demob. day approached it was a recognised thing for those working in the War Office team to request a testimonial from their senior officer in the War Office in London, Captain S. ...... They were told to write out their own testimonials, put in whatever they wanted, and he would sign them. Suffice to say, he did not look at what he was signing, and the outrageously favourable wording helped them all considerably in their job seeking after National Service!

(See also, Last Thoughts).

BRIAN DAVISON

Royal Army Ordnance Corps, 1958-60

The author did his basic training at Hilsea Barracks, Southsea in 1958, and suffered an horrendous start to his National Service career. After going through the usual 'welcoming' party at the railway station, and the 30-second shower, the No. 1 haircut and having any old thing thrown at him in the guise of a uniform, he went along, with all the other new recruits, to the introductory lecture by the CO. He was just getting into his stride with the lecture, when someone whispered something to him. He then announced that: *'Private Davison must report to the cookhouse for duty immediately.'* As that person was the author, and having led a very sheltered life, and being terribly naïve, he did just that, and cleaned and scrubbed horrible greasy pots and pans for the next four hours.

Meanwhile, when the lecture had finished, about 6 p.m., the rest of the new recruits had been told to spend the rest of the night 'bulling up' their new boots, and ironing their uniforms, etc., which took until about 10p.m. That was about the time that the author staggered into his new billet, and discovered what was in store for him, which kept him occupied for the next few hours, and incurred the wrath of his new comrades in the next beds, trying to get some sleep.

On finding out the next day that he was not the Private Davison that was meant to do the punishment, the author determined to even the score with the Army somehow – and this he did, handsomely, but not unfortunately at Hilsea.

The next posting was to Blackdown Barracks in Aldershot, and one day it was announced by the CO that as it was the Queen's Birthday on the Saturday, no one would be allowed to leave camp that weekend, for any reason whatsoever. Knowing that eating one orange and one tomato on the Thursday night would bring out disgusting looking red blotches and transparent blebs all over his body, including hands and face, on the Friday morning, the author decided to make a good job of it – and ate two of each, just to make certain. Sure enough, on the Friday morning he awoke and, a glance in the mirror told him that he had done a great job; the very large, angry looking red rash and white blebs just about covering the whole of his body. (*See Pic. Nos. 29, 30*).

Ignoring the alarmed looks and derogatory remarks from his room mates, he made a bee-line for the Medical Officer's room. The young MO had never seen anything quite like it before in his life – was it some sort of plague that had descended on Blackdown? Backing off, he did not want to discuss the ins and outs of whatever was wrong. 'Just go and get some medical attention at home,' he demanded. 'But Sir ...' '*No buts, just go,*' he shouted, and the author obeyed the order to the letter. Out of 1,000 men in camp that weekend, only one got away! And that was just the start ... *(See also, Last Thoughts)*.

BERNARD COZENS
Royal Navy, 1954-56

Starting his National Service in the Navy at Victoria Barracks, Portsmouth in 1954, Bernard did not do his basic training; going straight from there to Collingwood in Fareham, where he had 12 weeks not in uniform, to pass his Skill of Hands course, and he then passed his trade test. He went back to Victoria Barracks for his Passing In Parade as a Petty Officer, then returned to Collingwood for nine months, specialising in fire control. Next came Chatham Barracks on Reserve Fleet, for another seven months, then with six months to go, he was sent to a concrete battleship, HMS *Diligence* at Hythe in May, and was married just after this in June on an extended long weekend in Sunderland.

Previously Bernard was on £30 a month while working for the Admiralty at Bath, he then went down to 29 shillings a week, as a National Serviceman. Cheap £1 a week accommodation was denied him because of being National Service, and he and his wife had to get accommodation in a Country Club at over three times this price. So they had to go everywhere by tandem as a result, to and from ship to accommodation, but it was a superb place to be, near the New Forest. His wife worked alongside the camp, and he used to go out to lunch with her, but one day the RO said that he was on a charge for talking to a female at an improper time and improper place. Bernard explained she was his wife, and the Chief came in just then and told the RO not to be so stupid, case closed.

Bernard got stopped for speeding in the barracks one day, and he had arranged to see a young lady and pick her up in Portsmouth harbour to go sailing. However, the officer of the watch held him at the gates for doing 40 mph, keeping him there just long enough for him to miss his date!

He had no problem with being National Service among the Regular sailors, even though he was more skilled, studying for his Higher National at the time, and there was no animosity from them at all. His rank was an acting EA4, artificer 4th class, and he wore a peaked cap instead of a milkchurn hat, about the same level as an Army sergeant. He was on his own there, as there were no other National Servicemen with him. After basic training at Collingwood they were sent all over the place, some to sea on minesweepers.

According to Bernard National Service was not a waste of time. He learned a lot, became more self-sufficient, and got used to the strong discipline, after finding it hard initially, and has no regrets. *(See also, Last Thoughts)*.

BRYAN HIRST

Royal Air Force, 1946-48

Posted to ten different RAF camps during his two years three months National Service, Bryan was kitted out at Padgate, and posted to West Kirby, Liverpool for his square bashing. After the unit passed out they were all sent to different camps and he spent his first few weeks blowing up surplus and out of date detonators and incendiary bombs. These were all put into large holes dug by German POWs on the Yorkshire Wolds above Cottam, shortly after the end of World War Two, in September, 1946.

Whilst he was there Bryan had been home on a weekend pass, and had been given a cake to take back with him. For a few evenings he enjoyed the cake, until one night he went for a piece for his supper, and a mouse jumped out of his kitbag. Only then did he realise that he had been sharing his cake with a mouse! His next move was to Kirkham for his trade training, where he became a u/t armourer for six months.

Bryan's favourite posting was to RAF Duxford, where he became a member of No. 56 Fighter Squadron, working as an armourer. The last aircraft that Bryan worked on was a Meteor 7, which is now on show in one of the hangars at Duxford Imperial War Museum, still showing its squadron markings and colours. *(See Pic. No. 35)*.

(See also, Germany).

RAYMOND TAYLOR

Royal Air Force, 1956-58

RAF basic training at Hednesford in 1956 was hard for Raymond, but he was very fit when he left. He then went on to Melksham, Wiltshire, for his instrumentation training. Whilst he was there Ray was training also for aerial photography, and became heavily involved with cameras. It was a new set-up in Bomber Command, and he spent most of his time involved in aerial photography. His final posting was to RAF Wyton, Huntingdonshire, and was based there, but he did occasional overseas detachments to Singapore, where he serviced the cameras used in the aerial surveys of Borneo and Thailand in Canberra aircraft, and also aerial surveys of the Far East in general. While he was in Singapore Ray went to the usual tourist places, like the Brittania club, Raffles, Happy and New World Parks.

Ray also assisted in extensive aerial ordnance surveys in parts of England. Some of the crew however were filming on Christmas Island, but Ray was quite content to just fly over on a leisure trip.

One day a Valiant bomber blew up in a hangar. It was pay parade, and Ray had just collected his pay, and went to the toilet with a friend and they stood talking outside for a while, before going their separate ways. On his way back, Ray opened the hangar door into the section, and there was a big *whoosh*! and the Valiant caught fire with a dull explosion. The hangar door was open, and Ray was blown through it, and opposite to the door into the hangar there was an open door to the outside, and he flew through there as well. Someone had made a mistake in the servicing of the aircraft, but fortunately, there were only a few 'bods' working on the aircraft at the time, due to it being a NAAFI break.

A sergeant picked up a couple of fire extinguishers and mentioned the fact that there were about 3,000 gallons of kerosene in that aircraft, at which point the pilot officer shouted: *'Better to be live cowards than dead heroes,'* and he left quickly, and Ray and the rest did likewise. The US fire brigade, six miles away at RAF Alconbury, was sent for, as well as their own brigade – and the US brigade got there first! But the Valiant was a write-off. There was a roll call after the accident and Jim, the person with Ray going to the toilet, was missing. Just then he was spotted dashing round the corner with his trousers hanging around his ankles!

Ray's unit had image compensation lenses, where the camera was synchronised so that at any given time the film was going across the lens, which appeared to make the earth stationary, while going over it at a very fast speed. This was most advanced technology in those days.

Ray went back to his trade as an instrument maker, but after being in the open air for two years he did not take kindly to being inside, so he left for about six years and then went back again. After that he took out management and engineering degrees to enable him to go into management.

Ray thought that National Service gave him two of the most informative years that he had ever had, such as teaching him the value of money, respect for others, and authority. In fact, why on earth is it not operating today he wonders? *(See also, Last Thoughts).*

HUGHIE McGOURAN
Green Howards, 1953-56

Hughie was in the Green Howards from July, 1953 to July, 1956, but as he was a sergeant, he was back in the Army within five weeks, because of the Suez crisis. He was called into the Yorks. and Lancs. because he was a weapons instructor; so he went on a course to Hythe, and was teaching all the new intakes who had joined the battalion in Cyprus. Consequently, when they had finished in Cyprus, and the battalion was disbanded, Hughie treated himself to new clothes, billiards cue, etc., but when he arrived home there was a brown envelope waiting for him, telling him to report to the Yorks. and Lancs. Regiment.

Before Hughie went into the Green Howards he was in the Army Cadets, and was Green Howards through and through, going through the ranks to become one rank above RSM. He got an award from Sir William Worsley, a compass, for being the outstanding cadet in England. Hughie was also the last soldier in Britain to get on the King's Birthday Honours List, as a sergeant major in the cadets, finishing up as under officer.

The sergeant major of 'B' Company had had a good drink in the sergeants' mess one night, and came to the lines very much the worse for wear, and the OC of 'B' Company was Major Powell. When he arrived he said to the officer that the Company was present and ready for inspection, and he was definitely a bit shaky. So the officer had a quick look at the men, and saw that everything was OK.

Major Powell had a batman whose name was Hall. The sergeant major was standing there and Major Powell wanted his batman to go to his tent with him to get his revolver, whistles, compass, maps, etc. He then said: 'Hall, follow me,' meaning his batman, of course. But the sergeant major, completely inebriated by now, misheard, and told the men to: '**all** follow the Major to his tent.' So Hughie dashed over to the sergeant major, explaining that the Major didn't want **all** of the 100 men to follow him – just his batman, **Hall**. The consequences if everyone had followed the officer don't bear thinking about – all of 'B' Company, just over 100 men, would have finished up in Major Powell's tent!

LAWRENCE BELL

Royal Navy, 1950-52

Lawrence started his National Service in June 1950, and was lucky, going in with four others from ICI, all aged 21, delayed for three years doing an Engineering Apprenticeship, and wanting to be in the RAF. They were taken down to Middlesbrough Town Hall and an Army sergeant told them to sit down and fill in some Army forms, but he later came back and told them to tear them up because they were all going into the Navy. They didn't argue, they just signed up. The four of them helped each other, because they knew one other, and they all went down to Southsea, Portsmouth, to Victoria Barracks, where they did their six weeks square bashing.

The Navy wanted them as Artificers, and this carried the immediate promotion to the rank of PO (Petty Officer). First they all had to do a trade test, which involved making a perfect one inch brass cube. The six faces had to pass through a one inch steel hole, without any gaps. They all helped each other because two of them were on the tools while the other two were working as draughtsmen at ICI, but they all passed because they shared their skills.

While they were taking their trade test there was one old chief PO, and he warned them to sober up a bit because they used to go out drinking at night. This trade test was very important, because if you became a PO you had a privileged life, in an enclosed mess and ate separately, whereas if you failed the trade test you became a stoker on the mess decks, a rough job. However, another ICI lad, a loner, six months younger who came up later, went down by himself without support, and failed. He did not have the same advice, and he ended up as a stoker. A non-smoker, one of his duties was to clean out the ships' funnels, a filthy task, and he contracted lung cancer later on in life.

The others were posted to HMS *Illustrious,* a cruiser-mine layer, which was sent to Korean waters, and they all dispersed to their respective ships. Lawrence was posted first to HMS *Implacable* aircraft carrier, and then HMS *Vanguard,* followed by submarine depot ships in Portland, on HMS *Sleuth.* They were used as targets, going down to around 150 feet, and lay quietly, smoking, and the frigates used to come out from Portsmouth, and it was their job to find them. The frigates located them by sending echoes down and they could hear a clear 'ping.' This sound echoed inside the submarine, and they knew they had been found. Lawrence was then sent to HMS *Vanguard* for nine months, one of around 100 National Servicemen, out of a crew of 1,500. It was intended that Vanguard was going to take King George VI to South Africa, and the crew had to be given three jabs because they were going through African waters. Between the two funnels they had built special cabin accommodation for the King, being Admiral of the Fleet. He died two weeks before the ship sailed, so they joined the Mediterranean Fleet at Malta doing manoeuvres, instead.

Previously they had done a lot of electrical training at Plymouth on three boats made of wood and iron, built in 1870, and used in the Opium wars against China. They were collectively known as HMS *Defiance*, a training establishment.

Lawrence finished his National Service in Gibraltar, swimming in the warm sea in late February, but coming home soon after on demob, he looked out at the snow falling outside the railway carriage window.

Enjoying every minute of his National Service, Lawrence is of the opinion that conscription could not work nowadays, because the young men just wouldn't do it. In the Fifties only about 1% rebelled against it, and the police rounded them up. If the government brought National Service back he reckons only 50% would do it, leaving the authorities to round up the many thousands refusing to go – an impossible task.

Not wishing to do any more work for ICI, just looking at engineering instruments all day, Lawrence became a Customs and Excise officer for 20 years until 1970. He then went to University to train as an English teacher, but left to do another degree in psychology at the age of 57, and worked as a psychologist privately. Nowadays, at the age of 81, Lawrence does a voluntary job visiting police detainees in the cells to see that they are being treated well.

(See also, Last Thoughts).

EDDIE CHARLTON

Royal Army Ordnance Corps, 1946-48

Based at the Bridge of Don Barracks, Aberdeen, for his basic training in 1946, Eddie followed this with an ammunition examiners' course at Bramley. He was then posted to No. 23 ASD West Tanfield, near Masham, Yorkshire, where he took charge of the returned ammunition group and demolition, with the rank of sergeant.

The Regulars at the Bridge of Don were Gordons, Black Watch and Cameronians, and wore the kilt proudly when going into Aberdeen. The new recruits soon learned the answer to that age-old mystery of what a Scot wore underneath the kilt. Before leaving camp all kilt wearers had to reveal all by straddling a mirror on the floor of the gatehouse; and they were not allowed to use the upper deck on buses or trams!

The Gordon Barracks camp had a new intake of 300 new recruits every fortnight. To assist these raw recruits with the basics of boot polishing, blancoing and brasses were a few old regulars, whose first 'scam' was the Gold Watch raffle. This was attractively presented, but couldn't be inspected. Tickets were a shilling each, and carried a guarantee that if the winner wasn't satisfied, they would receive 30 shillings instead. As a week's Army pay was just 28 shillings, almost everyone parted with a shilling. The raffle was drawn and the lucky winner was presented with his gold watch – but its movement had been removed. However, the winner was quite content with his 30 bob, the old soldiers turned in a very nice profit, and the gold watch awaited the next intake.

During their final week of training they were marched six miles north to the Black Dog firing range, where they fired rifles and bren guns in the morning, with the afternoon left for hand grenade training. Each man went with an officer into a sandbagged pit and threw two grenades, and quite a number of them didn't explode. At the end they were instructed to go forward and locate and mark the unexploded grenades with a small flag. After ten minutes a whistle was blown to call them back, and the last man had a big smile on his face that indicated: '*Aren't I a clever boy then*,' for there cradled in his arms were half a dozen unexploded grenades. He very soon found himself alone!

Bleanau Ffestiniog in North Wales was known as the Welsh town of women. All able-bodied men were either in the Forces or working in the coal mines in South Wales. One Thursday evening in March 1947 two troop carriers left the remote camp at Trawsfynydd for the weekly outing to Bleanau, arriving there about 6 p.m. Only one shop was still open, the chemists, and provided an amusing spectacle, seeing the queue of Army personnel arming themselves with condoms in anticipation of the forthcoming evening's entertainment!

The Education officer called in once a week to hold informal discussions, and was a welcome pleasant change to their otherwise rigorous training routines. During the Second World War he had been involved with top intelligence, and had some interesting stories to relate. One of them Eddie remembers vividly concerned the disappearance of Glenn Miller, the world famous dance band leader, and an officer in the American Army at the time, and his disappearance over the Atlantic has been the subject of much speculation over the years. According to this officer Glenn Miller was of German parentage, and his family name was 'Mueller,' and he had (allegedly) been sending military information to Germany in code, via his Forces music broadcasts on the radio.

According to one of those conspiracy theories his plane was purposely destroyed over the English Channel with the intention of producing an insoluble mystery, which it did. Had he been charged with spying it could have caused a collapse of the music industry based on his world fame, and hence it was thought the most expedient way of removing him.

Quite a lot of sensitive ammunition was stored in a densely wooded area of lower Wensleydale, Yorkshire, in 1948. They were informed that a quantity of mustard gas had been buried in a pit some years previously, and it was time to destroy it. On opening the pit the strong stench of garlic indicated it was leaking, and they found the stuff in large steel boxes, which they covered in lime and transported by lorry to the railway station, to be taken from there for disposal. Despite taking precautions by wearing protective clothing and gas masks, a couple of Ordnance staff sustained small burns, which took a very long time to heal. However, during the operation one of the Pioneer labourers was discovered to have a serious mustard gas burn. The injury resembled a fried egg, with a golden yellow yolk, about an inch or so in diameter, surrounded by a bubbling transparent white blister. It looked as though it had fallen fresh out of the frying pan onto his leg, and he was rushed to hospital immediately.

Eddie did not see or hear of this man again, but having seen the effects of mustard gas he wonders how anyone could possibly contemplate using this vile chemical, as of course they did in vast amounts in the First World War. The local citizens would have been horrified had they known that leaking canisters of mustard gas were being transported through their village and from their railway station.

ALAN BERRY

Royal Navy, 1948-50

Because his uncle had been on a battleship working as a stoker in the First World War, and he had told Alan what a great life it was, Alan wanted to join the Navy for his National Service in 1948. So he realised his ambition and joined the Navy, without being in the Sea Cadets, or having anything to do with sailing previously, which was highly unusual.

Alan did his basic training at Royal Arthur in Wiltshire, which mostly consisted of marching up and down. When he arrived there he was asked what he would like to do, and he replied that he would like to be a telegraphist, but he was told that he could not be a telegraphist because he was only there for two years. When Alan asked what he could do in two years he was told he could be an ordinary seaman, or a stoker.

Those jobs did not appeal to Alan and he asked to be a writer, which he was put down for, but when he got back to the billet he was advised by his mates not to be that, and go for a *Jack Dusty* instead, a nickname for a Stores Assistant. On top of that he was told to be on the catering side of things, to have control over his own supply of food. So Alan did that and he found out almost straight away that the Navy did not really want him at all, because he was National Service, and the number of those in the Navy was very low indeed.

After about six weeks Alan was posted to HMS *Ceres* in Wetherby, as far away from the sea as you can imagine, for the next three months. His final posting was to the Royal Naval Barracks at Portsmouth to await posting, but because Alan was National Service they told him he was going to HMS *Resource*, a supply ship in Portsmouth Harbour, a big old, rusty hulk of a ship, which had not been to sea for many years

Alan's main job was to go aboard those destroyers that were being mothballed in case World War Three broke out, but were ready to go to sea within 24-hours notice. All they had to do was to put provisions on and send them to sea. For example, he had to see that the thermometers were working properly, so that the temperature in the gun room did not reach danger point, etc. For anything that was short he had to put in an application to the Royal Naval Stores in Portsmouth for those items, and they used to make an almost daily journey to the stores at the Royal Naval Barracks, and load up and take them back to the particular ship.

Alan enjoyed being in the Navy, and if he had not had an established job to go back to he would have given serious thought to signing on for a longer period, and would perhaps have seen the world. He did go to sea, in the English Channel once. They used to tow target ships up and down the Channel, with trainees shooting at the ships. If the crew of the ship that towed the target ship were short of men for whatever reason, they used to come to HMS *Resource*, and one day Alan was put in the firing line. He was told he was going to HMS *Trafalgar* to replenish their hardware supplies, such as gunsights, etc.

In those days of course everyone in the Navy smoked heavily because they got them cheap. The civilians working with them used to benefit from that by being offered cigarettes by the rest of the group. This particular day they were all smoking and then came the end of the shift, say 4 p.m., and one of the lads who had been smoking said it was time to knock off for the day. He threw his cigarette down on the deck, and then kicked it and tried to put it out, and thought that he had done so, but instead of that it had skidded along the floor, and fallen down through the mesh hatch cover.

The sailors knocked off and the civilians still had another hour to work, so they just had a game of cards. Suddenly, one of them smelt smoke, looked over towards the hatchway where the grid was and saw smoke coming up through it. Panic stations – one of them tried to put the fire out, while the other civilian got hold of a motor launch and came racing over to where Alan and the rest of the group were, and told them that: *'Trafalgar was ON FIRE!'* They all raced back and managed to put the fire out, but they spent the rest of the night on *Trafalgar* just anxiously watching that hatchway. Amazingly, there was no comeback about the fire, because the smoke had not been noticed on shore, and therefore there was no one to report it.

Incredible as it may seem, despite having such a prestigious name, and an illustrious career, HMS *Trafalgar* finished up in a naval scrapyard, along with so many others, waiting to be broken up, just a few years later.

RON JEROME

Grenadier Guards, 1955-57

Ron started his National Service at the Guards Depot, Caterham in January 1955, and he joined the 3rd Battalion Grenadier Guards in June. This was followed by three months in a demonstration platoon at Pickering, before going back to Windsor, where he served in the Regimental Police for the rest of his service.

Ron had just joined the battalion at Victoria Barracks, Windsor, and it was only a few days before he found himself on guard duty for the first time at Windsor Castle. Being a raw recruit he was put with a trained guardsman, so that he could keep an eye on Ron, or so he thought. The Queen was in residence, so most of the posts were double sentry, and the senior soldier was always on the right. They were on the main gate about 2 a.m., and Steve tapped his rifle butt on the cobbles to signal to Ron that they were going to patrol. They came to attention, shouldered arms and started marching. Ron thought it was 27 paces, and they would turn and return to the sentry box, and keep going until the guardsman on the right decided that they had done enough. On this occasion Steve kept going forward, and Ron came back to the box, and went out a further 27 paces, turned, and he could see Steve marching on over Pescott Street, and he kept on going until he reached what was a cinema in those days. Ron could clearly hear him making his about turn, and then start on his way back up to the gate, where he signalled to Ron that they were going to halt.

When they were relieved from that stag they got back into the guardroom, and Ron said to Steve: 'I thought the post called for 27 paces, why didn't you tell me what the regulation paces were? and he calmly said: 'I was bored, so I just went for a little stroll.' Being as it was Ron's first guard, he was terrified that he was doing it all wrong.

The Suez conflict started in August 1956, and Ron was drafted out for that, stopping at Malta, awaiting the move to Egypt, which never came. The Suez problem calmed down, and they were waiting to see what was going to happen next. The Reservists that were called up in the Emergency were all itching to get back home to their wives and families, (having already served their two years National Service), but the powers that be kept them guessing. They were getting very impatient, and they had a Reservist in the police with them, and he told Ron that all the Reservists were going to mutiny if no positive news was forthcoming. That evening they were going to march on the officers' mess, and demand to be given a date when they could expect to return to civvy street. He wanted Ron to join them, and since it was getting close to when he was due to come out, he did. They got an audience with the CO, received some answers and went back to camp. Next morning Ron reported to the guardroom (tent) and the provost sergeant was there to greet him. He was not in a good mood, and wanted to know where Ron had been the previous night, because: 'Those bloody part-timers had a mutiny, and Ron should have been there to stop them.'

Ron thought his time in the Regiment doing National Service was the best thing that ever happened to him, and it was a great pity that we didn't have something similar in place today.

BOB TESTER
Royal Air Force, 1946-48

Reckoning that he had more excitement in a few minutes as a 16-year-old Boy Scout than in the whole of his two year's National Service, Bob, up on the hills near Ingleby, and his fellow Scouts became involved in watching an aerial dogfight between an English Spitfire and a German Junkers 88, a whole two years before he was called up. The Junkers was no match for the Spitfire, being shot up, riddled with bullets, and it spiralled down out of the sky near to where Bob and his pals were standing. They all made a dash for the scout hut, and were shocked by the noise and the huge size of the crater it gouged out of the earth as it crashed, but also by the smell, which he later realised must have been burning human flesh, mixed with oil and cordite, etc. Bob remembers taking some souvenirs out of the wreckage, but his dad made him take them to the police station.

Came the day of the National Service medical in early 1946, and Bob turned up with several others he knew, at the Wesley Hall in Middlesbrough, and they were told that one in ten of them were needed as 'Bevin Boys' to go down the mines, while the rest of them would go into the RAF, Navy or the Army. Bob, luckily for him, was put in the RAF.

Unlike 90% of National Service recruits, Bob actually got placed in the job that he did normally in civilian life, working as a hairdresser. He found himself working for an Air Ministry Unit at South Kensington, London, in what Bob irreverently calls the Royal 'Hair' Force. As Bob cut away at the RAF Officer's hair, he often reflected upon just how lucky he had been not to have suffered the same fate as the Bevin

Boys, who at that moment were at the coalface working deep down underground, in atrocious, hazardous and unhealthy conditions.

Bob went to a dance alone one night to the nearby Hammersmith Palais, because his friend Harry had to work late. Now Harry had a tremendous crush on a singer called Lita Roza, the resident singer at the Palais, and a very popular broadcaster in those days, so Bob asked her in the interval if she would give Harry a ring at work, because he was on night duty that night. She agreed to do that, and Bob told him that his girl friend wanted a word with him. When Bob returned to the building he could see his little head working away high above him, so decided to give him a surprise. He climbed up two outside stories to his office in the Air Ministry building and knocked on the window, and Harry let him in. After talking for a while about Harry's conversation with Lita, Bob realised that he hadn't signed in, so he had to climb down again, so that he could walk into the main doors and sign in properly!

Bob saw National Service as a waste of time then, because he couldn't help his father in the family hairdressing business, stuck in South Kensington for two years. All Bob was doing was cutting one or perhaps two officer's hair a day at most, then spending long periods in the NAAFI. However, looking back, he realises it was one of the happiest times of his life, with the friendship and camaraderie he found.

DEREK RIGBY

Royal Air Force, 1960-62

After his basic training at RAF Bridgenorth, Derek was posted to RAF Syerston, near Newark, for his National Service in RAF Flying Training Command, No. 2 Flying Training School, as a servicing recorder, a kind of technical clerk. This job entailed going round collecting information every day, regarding repairs that were being carried out on aircraft.

It was 1960, and mainframe computers were just coming in, and they were starting to put everything technical on this computer. Before every flight a Form 700 had to be filled in, recording everything done to it, and the pilot would not fly the plane until he had seen a Form 700. Derek collected data out of this log and then a group of people in an office translated it into a digital code and fed it into the computer. Each defect was recorded on one of the cards and then analysed by the computer. His other job was being with an officer in a control cabin that was advising an aircraft's captain when he could or could not take off. They had to plot a graph of what every aeroplane had done each day – how many hours grounded and how many actually flying, with how many hours under repair. Plotting the graphs could show what was happening to every aircraft, and all this information went off to be fed into the computer.

Derek was in at the birth of the new age of computing, and they were told that if anyone wanted to sign on they could be a sergeant within six months, instead of waiting years as was usual; they were so short of new Regular recruits at that time. They could make a career of it because the RAF desperately needed technical people.

One day when Derek was in the Technical wing HQ the phone rang, and the warrant officer who he was working with told him that one of the aircraft had crashed, and he was to go 'at the double' to the main control tower with the aircraft's documents, which would be impounded for the investigation. He set off at the double, only to come face to face with a flight lieutenant as he turned round the hangar corner. Derek threw him a salute, but a loud voice shouted: '*Airman, come here,*' and he was told the correct way to salute an officer at the double. The officer made him do it correctly twice before sending him on his way – not remotely interested in the fact that there had been a crash right there on the airfield!

In his opinion, National Service in general, was a complete waste of time. Even though Derek enjoyed parts of it, for him it was a waste, because he lost a lot of money on what he would have been earning at home, and he spent a lot of time doing nothing, because there were too many of them, and not enough work to go around. The RAF just did not know what to do with them all! *(See also, Last Thoughts).*

BRIAN THURM

Royal Electrical and Mechanical Engineers, 1957-59

Going for his REME basic training at Honiton, Devon in 1957, Brian really landed on his feet, because his best friend in civvy street, Jack Renton turned out to be his platoon training corporal. After being posted to Taunton for trade training, Brian met up with Jack at his sister's house in London for a weekend. She had arranged to have two seats in the front circle at the Prince of Wales Theatre spotlighted, as Shirley Bassey sang a song especially for them.

On guard duty at his final posting to Longtown, Carlisle, Brian was disturbed at the amount of coughing he heard during his guard. He later discovered that *sheep* have a very similar cough to that of humans.

One of Brian's jobs at camp was to set up a device for diffusing tank mines. One day one of the mine's screw-to-fuse became cross-threaded, so he climbed over the sandbags, unscrewed it, took out the live fuse, put in a blank and screwed it up again. The captain in charge took Brian to see a film of an RAF hangar roof being suddenly blown off. The officer told him that was what the mine was capable of doing, and if he ever did that again, he would be put on a charge.

Another night on guard duty, a chap came into the guard room and asked if someone could help him with his car, as it had got stuck in the mud in the woods. The next morning police arrived and asked for guards to look after the car, and they were told that it contained a body in the boot. Apparently the chap who had asked for help was from Scotland, stationed at Longtown. He had killed a man and had tried to hide his body in the woods, but had got his car stuck.

They used to have demob. parties at Brampton village, and one night when they were all particularly merry, their warrant officer challenged them all to a fight in the nearby field. All eight of them onto him – it was very strange being at work the following day.

GORDON DIXON

Royal Air Force, 1956-58

Starting his National Service the day after his 21st birthday, in 1956, Gordon went to Cardington for his kit, and then Padgate for his basic training. From there he was posted to Abingdon Transport Command, training as a Clerk Air Movements, to load the aircraft so that the weight bearing was equal in all compartments, and the aircraft could fly level. Within six months he was an LAC, leading aircraftsman, then SAC in nine months, and squad leader.

The majority of the work involved loading Blackburn Beverley aircraft with supplies for overseas RAF bases, but there were emergencies when round-the-clock working was necessary, such as the Hungarian Revolution of 1956, sending out emergency relief food, tents and blankets. Gordon was involved with one particular aircraft, and became one of the crew, flying with a Blackburn Beverley to Marseilles, El Adam in Libya, Malta, and then on to Cyprus, Habanya in Iraq, then Bahrein, Sharjah, Muscat, and Aden; also Karachi and Wadi Halfi in the Sudan, then back to the UK again. It was like a tour every month, picking up supplies and dropping them off at these places.

The airbase at Abingdon was used for the making of two films while Gordon was there. The first was *Babbette Goes To War,* starring Brigitte Bardot, where she was supposed to parachute behind enemy lines, but only jumped from a three-step platform. The second film was *Carve Her Name With Pride,* starring Virginia McKenna, where she pretended to prepare to jump out of a Dakota. The airmen watched both of these, and a few were used as extras.

Princess Alexandra visited the base to inspect the troops one day, and Gordon had been given the task a few days before of painting the steps used as her exit from the plane, from RAF blue to white. The Princess stepped out of the Dakota and a gust of wind blew her skirt up, as Gordon looked up and said: *'Whoops!'* He was overheard, and received five days detention for this, and the job of repainting the steps back to RAF blue.

The MOD at Howarden in Cheshire were trying to find a way of transporting helicopters out to Malta and Cyprus, instead of making individual flights, and Gordon was there to see that the weights were distributed evenly. He came up with the idea of putting one in frontwards, and the other in backwards, thereby keeping the weight level at the front and back. Gordon got full credit for this and was promoted to corporal, and was asked to stay on for another six months, which he did. The director of Beverley Aeros told him just before he was demobbed that when he got out of the RAF there was a job waiting for him as a personnel officer at Beverley, but Gordon did not bother, as he had other things on his mind, such as getting married in 1959. He is now National Treasurer of the Fellowship of the Services, an ex-servicemen's association. *(See also, Bahrain, Cyprus).*

ALBERT LOMAS

Royal Air Force, 1947-48

Sent to Padgate for his RAF basic training in 1947, Albert found it hard, but not as hard as those 18-year-olds who were away from home for the first time, because he had been to Teachers' Training College for two years previously. Being older than the majority of his intake, and looked upon as a father figure, Albert was called upon to write letters home and to girl friends, and read the subsequent replies. He was later posted to Grantham railway station for a few more weeks, this being the staging post for all the airfields of Lincolnshire.

Albert was then posted to No. 3 MU, Liverpool, situated in the Liver building, where he was responsible for shipping men and supplies to and from foreign postings. After that he went on and passed an education course at Wellesbourne Mountford, but when four of them were asked questions by an officer later, they all told him that conscription was a total waste of time and resources. Their feet didn't touch the ground, and they were all returned to their units. He was subsequently sent on a course to gain promotion in movement control at Chigwell. He returned to Liverpool as an LAC, then corporal, running an education section, to be joined later by two sergeants. There they were, three qualified teachers, with nothing to do all day, except crosswords and unnecessary paperwork.

Albert was just about ready for demob. when National Service was extended by six months to two years, which it stayed at until the end in 1963.

The one thing that makes Albert stand out from 99% of the other two-and-a-quarter million National Servicemen between 1945 and 1963 was that he did not live in a crowded barrack room for over two years of his service, or queue up at the cookhouse for his meals. Because of his job in Movement Control, he had to live in private accommodation to be near the job for most of his National Service, and the only questions he was asked were how he liked his bacon, and did he like his eggs sunny side up, or not?

In Albert's opinion National Service overall was a complete waste of time, because he lost two years of his professional life, lost out financially, and had great difficulty in finding a post after his demob. The only things he got out of National Service were that he learned to type with two fingers, and how to cope with authority and adversity.

(See also, Last Thoughts).

DENNIS THIRKELL

Royal Air Force, 1947-50

The notoriously bad winter of 1947 started, and Dennis had only been in the RAF doing his National Service for about three weeks. With no fuel they had to burn all the fencing, then the wood off the huts, to try to keep warm at RAF Padgate, where he was sent for his basic training. After this Dennis was posted to RAF Fairford, 47th Air Support Squadron, working as a technical librarian.

One day they were doing a demonstration for all the top brass, showing what they could do, such as dropping jeeps by parachute from aeroplanes. It took three parachutes to hold a jeep, and this one was painted a bright yellow so that it showed up. The Halifax they were using as a carrier took off and flew around the airfield, and the announcer told everyone it was approaching, and would release the jeep and the three parachutes. Unfortunately, none of the parachutes opened, and the jeep dropped like a stone, and gouged out a huge hole in the runway, with the jeep reduced to a small crumpled yellow piece of wreckage! The watching VIPs were not impressed.

There was a murder across the road from where Dennis was billeted. Irish Katy as she was known, used to frequent this pub around the corner, but was found dead by the canal bank one night. The fire alarm was sounded in the early hours, but eventually everyone then went back to bed, except Dennis, who had to work for the next 36 hours non-stop, typing out list after list, giving the police the strength returns, ration returns etc. of everyone who was permanently there, or who had passed through in the previous few days.

The order went out that no-one was to be demobbed until the murder was solved, and this concerned Dennis, because he had already done six months over his two years, and it took him a while to convince the authorities that he was not one of the suspects, and be allowed to go home.

Looking back on his National Service, Dennis reckons that he enjoyed it. Towards the end he was asked to go on a short term officers' course but refused, because he was all set for going home. Later he regretted this decision, because back home there was nothing much doing in the Town Hall, and the Town Clerk's Office where he worked. The three who worked there had all done their National Service and had been taken back, but two of them had to go after that, and Dennis was one of them.

ALAN BIRCH

Royal Signals, 1947-49

A signalman in the Royal Signals from 1947 to 1949, Alan was given no choice in the matter because he was a Post Office telephone engineer at home. After basic training with the Royal West Kents he was sent to Catterick on a telegraph mechanics course, followed by secret courses on electronic cipher machine maintenance. During World War Two the Germans developed the Enigma cipher machine, thinking it impregnable, but a captured machine enabled British experts to break the codes at Bletchley Park. Britain later developed its own variation of Enigma called Type X, which Alan was trained to maintain.

Alan had great comradeship and many amusing episodes during his time at Catterick. During training one task was to take a teleprinter 7b to pieces and reassemble it. They laid out all the parts in neat rows so they could remember where they came from. However, they were shocked when the instructor shuffled all the pieces up, telling them to now put it together again. Alan found it amazing how a teleprinter could work with so many of its bits missing!

(See also, Egypt).

GORDON DUCK

Green Howards, 1952-54

Being at Richmond for his six weeks Green Howards basic training in 1952, Gordon then had ten weeks continuation training at York, followed by an unforgettable time at Barnard Castle for ten months. While he was there, Gordon and another 15 or so soldiers were excused from all duties for eight of their ten months posting. These were all good club footballers, but Gordon and another Leeds lad were the only professionals. Gordon was a professional footballer with Middlesbrough Juniors, and did not do any military duties –

he just wore a pullover and a towel, and it was football all the way in England, after the basic training had finished.

(See also, Egypt).

KEN COAN
General Service Corps, 1946-48

National Service for Ken began on April 18 1946, at Hyderabad Barracks, Colchester. When the personnel selection officer heard that Ken worked in a photographer's shop he said: *'Good, the Army is crying out loud for photographers,'* so naturally Ken finished up in the Army Dental Corps at Aldershot! This turned out to be quite a cushy number, being billeted in the Dental Centre there, with no Army boots to wear, and no guard duties or drills to do. He got a Red Cross armband instead, because he was then attached to the Royal Army Medical Corps., a non-combatant unit.

While at Aldershot he received a letter from his good friend Bob Tester, also doing his National Service in the RAF at that time, which contained a request to meet him in London on the following Saturday at King's Cross railway station for the 2.30 train. 'Don't let me down', it went on, 'If you haven't got any money, don't worry I have plenty.' There was no phone number or address on the letter so Ken bought a ticket and went there. He decided to have a walk around as he was had arrived early, and was just outside the station when a voice over the road shouted: *'Hey soldier,'* and Ken was amazed to see it was another of his pals, Roy Gaten, who had also joined the RAF. Roy had received a similar letter from

Bob, but it did not mention that Ken Coan would be there, and of course likewise with Ken's letter. They had no money left between them at all so they just waited for the 2.30 train, and the next and the next, but there was no sign of Bob Tester on any of them.

They spent the rest of the afternoon travelling together on the underground and escalators, because of course they didn't have any money to spare to do anything else, and they eventually returned to their respective camps. But not before vowing what they were going to do with Bob next time they saw him, as he was a renowned practical joker, and they realised they had just fallen for his latest trick!

(*See also, Egypt*).

THE BEVIN BOYS

WARWICK TAYLOR
Bevin Boy, 1943-45

Having served as a Bevin Boy in Oakdale Colliery, South Wales, Warwick Taylor MBE has never lost his respect for the miner, but is determined that the role of the Bevin Boy will not be excluded from the history of the nation. These men could well be described as having served in the secret underground movement, but not in the sense that most of us imagine, for the majority of people today have never even heard of the term 'Bevin Boy', even though famous personalities such as Jimmy Saville and Eric Morecambe had been ones.

In 1943, at the height of World War Two, the British government realised it had conscripted too many of its miners into the armed forces, as the coal mines had lost some 36,000 men in this way, and appealed for some of them to come back, but very few responded. From December 1943 until 1946, 47,859 Bevin Boys, so named after Ernest Bevin, the wartime Minister of Labour and National Service, were directed to work underground in the coal mines. This was necessary because of an extreme shortage of coal for the war effort, so an extra 50,000 men would have to be conscripted to meet the demand. The system used was that of a ballot scheme, whereby young men of call-up age, upon registering, would be selected according to the last digit of their registration number, the draws being made every fortnight. Pre-service training in a cadet force was not even considered for exemption. Not all Bevin Boys were ballotees, as unballoted young men were given the opportunity at the time of call-up to choose this employment in lieu of service in the Armed Forces, and were classified as optants or volunteers. They were not Conscientious Objectors.

After a medical examination, travel warrants and instructions followed to report to one of 13 government training centre collieries in Britain. Upon arrival a Ministry of Labour official would allocate accommodation at either a miners' hostel, similar to an Army camp, or in private billets, where the cost of 25 shillings a week would be deducted from an average wage of three pounds and ten shillings. Training would be for four weeks, and involve physical training, with classroom, surface and underground work. Bevin Boys were supplied with a safety helmet, a pair of overalls and steel capped boots, and carried a safety lamp, a snap tin containing sandwiches and a water bottle.

Following the training period allocation would be made to work at a colliery within the same area as the training took place, with accommodation again either in a hostel or in private billets. All Bevin Boys worked underground and were usually employed on conveyor belts, or the loading and haulage of tubs using machinery or pit ponies. (*See Pic. No. 38*). The work was hard, often in appalling conditions, working in cramped spaces, and in pitch darkness, except for the light from their helmet. The young Bevin Boys had to walk long distances from the pit bottom over uneven surfaces in areas that were either hot, cold, wet, draughty, dirty, dusty or smelly. The constant noise of machinery was deafening, with the ever-present risk of explosion and fire, caused by 'firedamp' or methane gas, or rock falls, and there were no toilet facilities.

Going down the mine shaft in the cage lift was an unnerving and terrifying experience for the young Bevin Boys at first, until they became used to the speed of the cage as it plummeted down to the mine hundreds of feet below the surface. (*See Pic. No. 37*).

Some of the larger collieries had pit-head baths to shower and change into clean clothes, but where these were not provided it meant going back to the hostel or billet. The Bevin Boys did not have a uniform, and therefore wore civilian clothes when off duty. This attracted public attention and adverse remarks as to why they were not in Forces uniform. Being of military age invited challenges by local police on suspicion of being a draft dodger, deserter or even an enemy agent. (*See Pic. No. 39*).

With the ending of the war in Europe a release scheme was introduced similar to that of the Forces, and most of them were released by the end of 1948. However, Bevin Boys received no other form of recognition for their services to the war effort in which they played a most vital part.

In 2007 after a campaign led by Labour MP Gordon Banks, and after more than 60 years, the 'forgotten conscripts' were informed that they were going to be given a commemorative badge in recognition of their contribution to the war effort.

FRANCE

SHAPE

(Supreme Headquarters Allied Powers Europe)

Fourteen months after the Allies signed the North Atlantic Treaty the Korean war erupted in June 1950, increasing fears of a Soviet attack on Western Europe.

The Alliance possessed an extremely limited structure. No NATO military commanders had been appointed, NATO military Headquarters or commands established and all the Allies' military forces remained under national control.

In Autumn 1950, the United States Secretary of State proposed to the NATO Allies establishing a large integrated military force, consisting of units contributed by individual nations, including West Germany, controlled by a centralised military organisation which would administer and train those forces under a single NATO commander.

It was agreed to appoint a Supreme Commander Allied Powers Europe (SACEUR) supported by an international staff. He would be delegated limited authority to ensure that national units assigned to his command were organised and trained into an effective force.

General Eisenhower established SHAPE on April 2 1951. It comprised 183 officers from 9 nations of the 12 NATO Allies; Portugal and Luxembourg sent staff to SHAPE later.

Buildings were quickly constructed and the new HQ was handed over to SHAPE on July 23 1951. In 1952 Greece and Turkey, followed by West Germany in 1955 joined NATO and all three nations sent officers to SHAPE, bringing the number of nations represented at SHAPE in the mid-1950's to 12.

One of Eisenhower's major lasting influences on SHAPE was his insistence that SHAPE staff's loyalty was not to their nation, but NATO and SHAPE.

PETER BIRD

Royal Military Police, 1960-62

In the very last National Service intake, on November 17, 1960, Peter was placed at first into the Royal Engineers, but on his first day went in front of an interviewing officer, who told him he was ideal for the Military Police. So he was sent to Inkerman Barracks, Woking, along with a few from every other Corps and Regiment. Although he had already done two weeks in the RE he had to do another eight weeks basic training in his RE uniform. After this he sat an examination for police laws, etc., passed, and was issued with an RMP's uniform and given another eight weeks square bashing! All in all he did 18 weeks of this before his Passing Out parade.

Peter's first posting was to SHAPE (Supreme Headquarters, Allied Powers, Europe), Paris, serving a year there, responsible for all the security at the North Atlantic Treaty Organisation (NATO) Headquarters, and he never had to salute anyone below the rank of Brigadier General, due to the number of high ranking officers there.

There were 13 nations at the time in NATO, and it was the responsibility of the military police to ensure no security regulations were broken, and no-one got in or out without the right pass. At night they had to check that no-one had left any confidential documents. If a security lapse was found and was really bad, the person responsible was sent back to his own country, irregardless of rank.

Peter was at SHAPE when President Kennedy visited the HQ and was about ten yards from him, while carrying out security duties. The biggest gathering of Generals in the West, was known as SHAPEX, when they used to discuss the NATO exercises for the coming year. He looked after Lord Mountbatten, and stood guard outside Lord Home's bedroom when he was Foreign Secretary, before becoming Prime Minister.

He was chosen for the NATO International football team in France, but he had to play every country's sport; basketball, cricket, etc, as every country at NATO had its own national sport. As a result of that he was chosen for a two-week tour of Germany to the Green Howards' base at Iserlohn, and the weekend they were there Sunderland had just been relegated, and they were playing Middlesbrough in Division Two. You would have thought that you were in the Cleveland pub on

Linthorpe Road, with all the banter from the North- East lads there.

While he was at Iserlohn it was announced that those National Service soldiers stationed in Germany would have to serve an extra six months, due to the lack of recruitment of Regulars. Fortunately, Peter was only touring, so it did not apply to him. That night all the big French windows at one end of the mess were broken, as the lads were just throwing their empty bottles of beer at them, so before long there were no windows left! Up on Jankers on the Monday morning the CO told them he knew how they felt, and he would feel exactly the same in the circumstances, but pointed out forcefully that *they* had to live there after the National Servicemen had gone, and any more misdemeanours like that and they would be in big trouble.

After his year at SHAPE Peter was posted to Catterick for his last six months of National Service. During that period he went down to police the Bisley Shoot in Surrey, and policed the Edinburgh Tattoo for a month, carrying out police duties at Edinburgh Castle for 43 performances.

When Peter first arrived at Catterick there were 80 Military Police lance corporals stationed there, but when the National Service intake stopped in November 1960 there was still a demobilisation every fortnight. Consequently, when Peter left in November 1962 there were only three Regular lance corporal MPs at Catterick.

Peter is now Chairman of the Cleveland Branch of the Combined Services Association. *(See also, Last Thoughts).*

GERMANY

Germany for the average National Serviceman depended on when you were there. Between 1950 and 1953 when the Korean War was waged; 1956, when Russian tanks rolled into Hungary, and the latter part of the 1950s, when the United States and Russia were talking and threatening war, Germany was the most likely place for conflict between the two superpowers to break out. During the 1950s Britain had nearly 100,000 men stationed there, the majority of them National Servicemen. In between those flashpoint periods Germany was regarded as a safe but sometimes boring 'home' posting, with superb centrally heated barracks, much better food than at home, unlimited sport, and an opportunity to travel the country.

GEORGE GAMBLE
Royal Air Force Regiment, 1951-53

Basic training for George was at Bridgenorth, Shropshire for eight weeks, and was brutal as was usual, followed by RAF Catterick for a further 12 weeks, which was even worse, with one bully in particular, Cpl. Jones. George answered him back one day and had to go up and down a 12 ft. telegraph pole in plimsolls, but kept on doing it because he was super fit. They were made to go across the River Swale in winter, which was very cold, and when reaching the other side which was banked one-in-three, the NCOs threw thunder flashes at them. If you lost your grip you were back in the water again. (*See Pic. No. 27*). This RAF Regiment training was very hard, and if you failed you were out and put into the RAF. But

George wanted to travel a lot, as you did in the Regiment, and so he passed out. Doing drills in a hangar all day, George was at the slope, but his rifle moved down slightly. Cpl. Jones rapped him with his paystick at the rifle top, and George finished up in a heap on the floor.

George and a few of his friends, nine of them altogether, were dropped off a lorry one night in total darkness, not knowing where they were going, or where they were, and they had so many hours to find their way back to camp. When they woke up in the morning they were out in the open on the lookout for food, and came across a small farm. George being the thinnest, got through the bobhole, took what there was in the nest box, got back out again, and had the stove going. However, George had taken five POT eggs, put there by the farmer to encourage the hens to lay. Needless to say this did nothing for George's credibility with the rest of the lads for quite a while!

Next stop for George was Lytham St. Anne's where he wrote his will out, because he was going to Aden, and had to have all the jabs for it. Then they were told that they were going to Germany instead, on the *Empire Wansbeck*, arriving at Gutersloe, where the CO was mad Johnnie Johnson, fresh from his Spitfire exploits in World War Two. Every Wednesday, on sports day, they played football in the middle of the airfield, and Johnson would fly a Vampire aircraft straight at the footballers, making them dive for the floor.

One night George and his pals got drunk, someone called the guard out, but they threw him into the pool. A Flying Officer and a guard came out on pushbikes, and they threw them into the open air swimming pool as well! They were all up before Johnnie Johnson and got between 14 and 28 days punishment.

A local German businessman had a big trout farm, so they went out there one night and fired a .303 into the water, and lots of fish came to the top stunned – so they all lived on trout for a while. Later on George was transferred to Todenoff, but had to go through Hamburg, and he was struck by the people there scrounging about in the rubble for something to eat. This was terrible, six years after the war had finished, and the buildings there were still absolutely flattened. At Kiel on the Baltic, he found there was a very strong anti-British feeling there, because of the incessant British bombings on their shipyard and submarine bases, etc., during the Second World War.

George spent ten days with his pals on leave around the Moehner Dam lake, famous for the Guy Gibson 'bouncing bomb' exploits, and one afternoon they were joined by a few young German girls, who proceeded to strip off to become completely naked. None of the lads had experienced anything like this before, and were stunned.

There was a listening post at Gatow, situated about 100m from the Russian sector, which required a 24-hour guard. They also looked after the Germans who were coming across to the West each night. Every morning two airmen and an officer picked the briefcase up from the listening post containing whatever information they had picked up during the night, and walked one in front and one behind, both with sten guns, accompanying the officer to the jeep. They then sped off to Templehof, the main Berlin airfield, a few miles away, taking a different route every day. More officers sealed the leather briefcase with sealing wax, and it was then transported to an awaiting plane, which took it straight back to London.

Apart from Belsen Concentration Camp, the Russian Garden of Remembrance impressed George the most, going through the Brandenburg Gate to East Berlin. There were many massive marble blocks on either side, each representing 20,000 fallen Russians, amounting to an estimated quarter of a million deaths. In their haste to be the first to take the Reichstag in Berlin, Russians were killing Russians by shelling their own positions instead of the German ones, which partly accounted for their enormous losses. Up massive steps, it was like a big lighthouse, with all the different Russian creeds engraved on the mosaics on the walls. A stained glass ceiling depicted Mother Russia with a baby in her arms, and a hammer and sickle underneath.

MICHAEL KAYLEY

Northumberland Fusiliers, 1957-59

The Queen sent Michael a letter on his birthday, August 14, 1957, asking him to help look after the country for the next two years. So he reported to Fenham Barracks later for basic training in the Northumberland Fusiliers. In early December Michael's detachment was posted to Munster in Germany, and on the first Sunday there he went to church, at which the padre asked for help to decorate the church for Christmas. The padre's last clerk had just been demobbed, so he asked Michael if he would like the job, and when he agreed, the padre wrote out a letter to give to his RSM.

Came the day of giving jobs out; like a miner from down the pits becoming the company clerk, and a cook being made a driver, etc., it was Michael's turn, so he handed the RSM the letter from the padre. He read it slowly, looked at Michael, and told him to: '*Get out of here – I don't want puffs in my Company!*'

So Michael reported to his place of work, the Garrison Church, Munster, with his daily duties for the vicar being clerk, messenger and verger. He also had to answer the phone, polish the brasses, trim the candles and do some general duties. No wonder he said yes to the job!

Monday was the padre's day off, so Michael had to open the church, put any hymn books away, send the surplices to the laundry, and listen for the phone ringing. So he put it on a ledge outside and laid out on the grass.

Tuesday was Michael's day off, so he changed into civvies and went into town, walked along the canal in the morning, watched a film on the afternoon, and spent the evening in the NAAFI.

Wednesday he was given a few general duties from the padre in the morning, and given the afternoon off for the battalion cross country run.

Thursday and Friday were very quiet, with a few jobs the padre wanted doing, and choir practice on a Thursday night, when Michael had to give out the choir hymn books, and collect them in afterwards.

Saturday was the battalion's day off – but Sunday was the big day, with services at 08.00 and 09.00, when a few turned up; 10.30, when the families attended; 14.00-15.00 Sunday School, where officers' and other ranks' children came, and 18.30 Evening service.

When the battalion went on manoeuvres in Germany Michael could not go, as he had duties to do back at the church. But the padre and his clerk were required to give a mid-week service for the troops on manoeuvres, so Michael had to take the hymn books. When they got there a tent had already been put up, and all his 'mates' were sitting there, up to their eyes in mud, (and were in the tent just to get out of the cold). Michael went in giving out the hymn books in his best uniform, and couldn't resist saying to each one something like: '*Bless you my son,*' or '*Say a little prayer for me,*' or '*Having a nice time?*' Michael refuses to reveal what his 'mates' did to him when they returned from their little trip!

Michael returned to Fenham Barracks with his detachment for their last six weeks and they were told to attend the TA fortnight in Sennybridge, Breconshire, South Wales. Marching down to the station to catch the train they saw the TA lads – some in civilian jackets and army trousers, some the reverse, some in shoes, others in boots, and some even had bottles of beer in their pockets. But it was when they all got to the barracks that Michael got into trouble, when the TA lads were halted and ordered to slope arms. Michael started laughing, and he couldn't stop, even when the RSM shouted and his mates whispered for him to stop. He was marched off under escort, and was still laughing when the cell door was slammed shut.

He was later 'interviewed' by the RSM, who saw the funny side of it when Michael told him that he was laughing at the state of the TA men and the fact that the TA sergeant had sloped his rifle DOWNWARDS, just like the Americans do. The RSM told him to stay out of trouble, but asked him if he would be his batman while they were there. So Michael did, and really came up laughing in the end. He completed his National Service in August 1959, and admitted – *it had been rough*!

GEORGE PARRY

Royal Air Force, 1954-56

While George was doing his trade training at St. Athans in 1954, his section was called on to do the Retreat on Battle of Britain Day. They were issued with white webbing belts and white rifle slings. So George and his mates thought they would get these new recruits in the next billet. Two of them dressed up as SPs (RAF military police), got some white cloths and put them into their caps, and one of the other lads turned his number back to front on his sweater and put his battle dress on, and he finished up looking like the padre.

So they both went in to see these new lads and into their billet, as they had just finished their square bashing. They lined them up and informed them that the padre was coming to see them, and in walked this lad – he had them kneeling and praying, and this went on for some time, until the rookies noticed all the lads at the windows laughing at them.

A fortnight later on a Friday night it was the Servicemen's Dance, and the girls were being bussed in from all over South Wales. They were all getting ready in various stages of undress, when two chaps came in, saying they were from a local church, and they would like to have a few words with them. At this point a big lad from the Midlands said: 'You can just *f... off,* because we've just given it to you!' But as the two men made their exit they dropped religious leaflets on George's bed, and left quietly. They really _were_ from the local church!

George was sent to the 2nd Tactical Airforce at Wunstoft, near Hanover, Germany, doing second line servicing of Venom aircraft as part of a team of four, for 19 months, not on squadrons, but on the station strength. The Venoms needed special modifications to the undercarriage, and they finished up doing these modifications to all three squadrons that were on this station.

He had two friends that he went around with; all of them having joined up on the same day, did the same basic and trade training together, and even worked in the same hangar servicing Venoms, but in different teams. They got on very well with the Regulars, because they recognised that they could all handle tools as well as they could.

George reckons that his National Service was not a waste of time, and being away from home did not bother him, because with his job back in England he had travelled the country mending organs. He enjoyed the camaraderie, and made a lot of friends. *(See also, Last Thoughts)*.

GEORGE HUTCHINSON

Royal Army Ordnance Corps, 1946-48

Starting his basic training with the Green Howards at Richmond in 1946, George remembers practising with all sorts of weapons, including live hand grenades. One nervous young recruit pulled the pin from a hand grenade, lifted it above his head and dropped it. Luckily the training sergeant saw what had happened, shouted a warning, and jumped over the row of sandbags, pulling the recruit with him. The recruit had a small slice taken out of his bottom, otherwise there was no damage done.

George's overseas posting was to Oldenburg, in Germany. Twenty miles away, scattered around in some woods were the remains of some V2 rocket launchers, which had a very basic design, but they had wreaked havoc on southern England as late on in World War Two as March 1945. There were also piles of German, American and English planes, which had been shot down, and were all mixed up together.

In Oldenburg there was the Café Central which would be open for a week or two, and then closed down by the British military police because of fights. George only went in twice, and there were some soldiers from the British Army, as well as Polish airborne troops, Yugoslav guards and Danish troops. The second time he went in a fight broke out. Two MPs came in, and one of the Poles, who was drunk, pulled out a gun and shot them both. George did not go in there any more.

The Germans were stealing wheels from lorries in George's camp to sell or put on their own lorries – that was the only way they could get them. The Yugoslavs guarding the camp were trigger-happy. You did not dare go too far on a night, because they shot first and asked questions afterwards. Several Germans, desperate to get their hands on tyres and wheels were shot and killed by these Yugoslavs.

George was then moved to Hamburg Wald for about the last three months of his National Service. The most interesting event that happened there was a Short Arms Inspection. For this the men all had to line up inside, and were told this was to check for any infections. They had to drop their trousers and underpants and lift up their shirt fronts. They were expecting the Army doctor to come in to do the inspection, but in came a rather glamorous young woman armed with a pencil. She went along the line lifting each one of them up with the pencil, looking very serious all the time. When she had finished she just nodded to the warrant officer and went out.

They all found it very amusing, and George is still not convinced as to whether she was a doctor or not.

Occasionally, George and a German driver were sent off for spares, and they once went into the American Zone and into one of their Forces' canteens. They were both served large T-bone steaks, with more meat on them than an English family would have had for a week on their rations.

The National Servicemen were given Baff currency which was especially made for the Forces in Germany, and could only really be used in English run canteens. They were also issued with 50 cigarettes each week, and this was the currency used to exchange things with the Germans.

GEORGE CAIRNS

Green Howards, 1946-48

Called up in 1946, George was sent to Newark and did six weeks training with the Guards, before joining the Green Howards at Richmond Barracks. George did his basic training there and found it easy, because he had done it all with the Guards beforehand. They were told they were going to India, with the 2nd Battalion, and given tropical gear to go with, and they all realised that they would not get back home for months from there, so they all went off on an unofficial 48-hour leave.

When they went back they were all confined to barracks. The Indian campaign was cancelled, because we were about to be ejected from there. They had to hand all their gear in and were sent to Berlin, where George spent most of his remaining time looking after Rudolph Hess, at one time Adolf

Hitler's No. 2, at Spandau. They could spend their spare time in Berlin, but were told not to fraternise with the Russians, because those who did had a tendency to disappear!

One boring hot Sunday, not allowed out of camp without a special pass, a friend of his called Alec suggested that they go through the wire near the fence at the back of the camp and they could go and have a walk in the woods. This camp was right on the Russian border, and their territory was just after the woods, but they knew nothing of this. So they wandered about through the woods and George wanted to get back, but they could hear music in the distance. They continued their walk through the woods and came to a plateau, high up, where they could look down, and saw that a restaurant was visible, with people sat at tables, laughing and talking loudly.

As they got closer George realised that there were a lot of Russians in there. As they half turned to make their way back there were shouts of '*Comerade, Comerade,*' coming from officers mostly, waving their hands and motioning for them to come and join them for a drink. George and Alec did not know what to do, but agreed to have just the one drink, then beat a hasty retreat. As they sat down at the table the head waiter who spoke Russian and English, explained that they just wanted them to sit down and have a drink. So they had two or three drinks of vodka, and they started to feel a bit woozy, at which point the waiter came along and warned them that it was time to make a move, or else they wouldn't get out of there. Next moment a tray of food came out, and they were invited to '*eat, eat,*' and they decided to do that. They did not realise that the food was in fact raw fish, and it made them baulk.

Alec whispered to George that he was going to the toilet, and said to join him after a few minutes, as an excuse to get out of there. George asked the waiter to inform their hosts that his friend was just going to the toilet, which he did. After a short while George motioned to the waiter that his friend was a long time coming back, and he was just going to find him, which was relayed to the Russians. At first George couldn't find his friend anywhere, but just then heard: '*I'm over here,*' and Alec motioned him over to where he was hiding amongst the corn. He joined him, and they quickly made their way back to camp, full of booze and hardly able to walk. They found the hole in the fence again, and made their way back to barracks. Later they realised just how dangerous a situation they had been in – once they had gone along with the Russians they would have been classed as deserters. Back in camp they hadn't even been missed …

George was disturbed by the fact that Berlin was absolutely wrecked, with not a building left standing. They were welcomed into the American sector and went to a club where Mickey Rooney used to perform. They wandered about Berlin, avoiding the Russians. Walking along the streets, say two or three of them, they would come across a bunch of Russians swaggering and laughing, and always drunk; you had to move to one side to let them past.

Three of them were in Berlin, with nothing to do one Sunday, and down by the river they saw a notice 'boat for hire,' so they hired it for five cigarettes. Off they went for two or three miles down the river, before trying to turn round and go back. This proved tiring, so they turned into a slipway and tied the boat up and got a lift back to Berlin, and then camp. Later, talking to their transport sergeant they told him about the boat, so he commandeered a wagon and six men, drove to the boat, pulled it up onto the wagon and brought it back to camp.

The boat was duly painted khaki green and taken to the Lido, a local sailing club, where they could now mix in with the posh boats. Sailing at the Lido became a daily occurrence, for so long – then one day they had been out sailing, brought the boat back, and fastened it up by the jetty. Just then a large motor launch was spotted coming up the river towards them, with a few Redcaps and the German boat owner. George and his pal turned to go away but they were warned not to move. The owner identified the boat as his, but did not like the idea of it being coloured khaki.

When they got back to camp they were locked up, and George had to share a cell with two hard cases, who immediately grabbed him, and searched him for cigarettes. He was in there for two nights before being summoned to appear before the CO, Lt. Col. Eden, brother of Anthony Eden, a future Prime Minister. It was suggested to them both that they must have been drunk at the time, but George insisted they were not. Somehow, in spite of this they both got off, and the case was dismissed – lucky again!

In George's opinion National Service was good, and he would not have missed it for the world – being one of the best things he has done in his life. *(See also, Last Thoughts).*

BARRIE SHEPHERDSON

Barrie was posted from Libya to Wuppertal, Germany for his final six months in 1962. When they stopped National Service the battalions were down to the bare minimum. Just up the road the Loyals were down to about 100 men out of a thousand, during the height of the Cold War, when the East Germans were building the Berlin Wall, so the draft after Barrie's had to do an extra six months service while they got their numbers back up to strength.

Speculating on their chances if the Russians did attack, it was rumoured that they were expected to hold out for three days, to give the Allies a chance to get their nuclear weapons operational. Approaching demobilisation time Barrie was asked to sign on, but he had a good job as a photo lithographer at home, so declined the offer.

STAN HARRISON
Royal Electrical & Mechanical Engineers, 1954-56

For his basic REME training in 1954 Stan was at Blandford. He then went to Arborfield to train as a telecommunications mechanic, repairing and maintaining communications links, with radios. This was the time of the birth of computers, but they had big valves in them, and were not yet reliable or efficient, and Stan just worked on radio communications. He was still in the Arborfield area when he found out that he had been posted to Germany, and finished up at Dortmund for the full 18 months.

On guard duty for two hours on and four off, 6 p.m. to 6 a.m., they used to stay in the guardroom with just a bunk bed, but no mattress. One snowy night in January, during his 12-2 a.m. shift, Stan was walking around the perimeter of the camp with his rifle over his shoulder, and had to circle in on the parade ground, and a German was walking around. Stan called out: *'guten abend'* and the German answered: *'guten abend.'* Stan asked the sergeant of the guard if any German civilians were working that night. The sergeant asked around and no one knew of any work being done. When Stan mentioned that the German had got as far as the manhole cover, taken it up and gone down it, the sergeant went spare, because that led to the armoury, and he called out the guard and the officer of the watch to surround the manhole cover and point their rifles down it. The officer shouted: *'kom, hieraus.'* The German replied: *'nicht schiesen, don't shoot, don't shoot.'* They only had two rounds each and two in the guard room, so with a serious incursion, the result could have been catastrophic.

They all had a cigarette allowance of 200 per week, and most lads could not smoke that many, so Stan used to buy tickets off the squaddies who didn't smoke, go down the town into a local pub with a carrier bag full of packets of cigarettes, put them on the table and charge the locals a mark for 20, making 8p profit for every 20 packet he sold. The Germans were paying a lot more than that for their cigarettes, so Stan was able to sell about 500 at a time in just half an hour. Stan would then have to wait another week to get some more coupons to exchange for cigarettes, and go back again. However, if you were caught you went straight into the glasshouse!

He sold 120 cigarettes to a German cleaning lady in the camp, and she got caught going out of the front gate, and they held an identity parade to find out who had sold her these cigarettes. She pulled Stan and another four out of the parade, and Stan denied all knowledge of it, while the other four all admitted it and received about three months each for the offence. Stan was called in front of the CSM who told him he was not bothered whether he had sold them to her or not. As long as he stuck to his story with the MPs he would get away with it – and he did!

Stan's impression of National Service in the beginning was not good, a waste of time he thought, except for the discipline, but training for a trade was interesting. It was thanks to the Army that Stan received electronics training, so that when he got home he went straight into television engineering. After a while he noticed that the sets were getting bigger and heavier and realised that he could not be doing that when he got older, so he decided to go into teaching, and finished up lecturing at a local college.

ROGER RAMSDALE
Royal Engineers, 1957-59

In the first three weeks of his National Service in the Royal Engineers Roger was at Malvern, where he found that 21-year-olds were picked on by the 18-year-old-boy soldiers, etc. – a few nasty pieces of work. Then followed 11 weeks field training at Farnborough, where one lad had all sticking plasters, TCP, etc. in his cupboard, but could not even polish his own boots, iron, blanco or do anything, and had to be helped by Roger for all those things, while he just sat on his bed and cried! Amazingly, he went off for officer training soon afterwards!

From there Roger was posted to Alanbrooke Barracks, Paderborn, Germany, driving his new scout car with two radios – ground to ground and ground to air. Roger's job was to drive a lieutenant around while he talked to his brigadier when he was airborne – which was possible with this equipment; cutting edge technology at the time.

However, later on one morning when he was informed his father had been killed and his brother was in hospital, the Army moved very fast indeed, and he was driven to the nearest airport and put on a plane at Dusseldorf in a matter of minutes after arriving, and flown back in a few hours, and was back in Darlington by late afternoon.

Roger kept busy updating his driving and wireless courses, etc., and nearly did his cadre course, but the weekend it was due to take place a sergeant kept them in camp bulling up for an OC's inspection, and the OC was so impressed with the result he gave the whole camp a 48-hour pass.

However, a vigilant sergeant found that the equipment on camp did not tally with the inventory, so two trucks were loaded up with the surplus and told to come back later, but they arrived back too early, and an enthusiastic lance corporal ordered Roger and his mates to unload them – just as they were going out of the gates. They refused and carried on regardless, much to his fury. All four were put on a charge when they arrived back and locked up for 21 days without pay, and so Roger did two years and 21 days as a result.

During his time there Roger's unit built Bailey bridges and light assault floating bridges meant for training only, but a few are still there today, in the River Vaser area. Belsen was his most disturbing experience, where no birds sang and nothing moved, with the thousands of bodies buried there, and it stayed in his mind long afterwards. Just down the road was a British war grave with hundreds of graves of 18 and 19–year-olds – some of them sergeants at that age, with most of them paratroopers in that particular one, and that too affected him.

Many years later, on a courtesy visit from Sedgefield Town Council to Rheinehausen, Roger and one of the councillors went to Paderborn camp while the rest went shopping. The 1st Rifles were in command at this time, and Roger wanted photos, He approached the guard and asked to take some photos of the camp, but was refused and put under arrest, as this was in the middle of the IRA troubles. Roger told them about being on guard duty in that same guardroom 40 years previously, but to no effect. Meanwhile, the German Mayor with his party and the Sedgefield party were waiting for him at the other side of the road. Forty five minutes later he was told he could go. The following year Roger and his wife went on a private visit to a host family in Rheinehausen, and were taken on a surprise trip back to Paderborn camp. They pulled up at the guardroom again, and a rifleman came over and asked for Mr. Ramsdale, saying he was expected. He was told to follow an Army vehicle to the officers' mess and greeted by a captain, who asked to be introduced to Roger's wife, and Roger was told to take as many photos as he liked!

(See also, Last Thoughts).

COLIN RUTHERFORD

Northumberland Fusiliers, 1956-58

On his first day of National Service Colin reported to Fenham Barracks, Newcastle-on-Tyne, home of the Royal Northumberland Fusiliers, an infantry regiment with a proud military record and, of course, quite local. Passing through his barrack room during the two-year period were lads from Shildon, Berwick-on-Tweed, Tynemouth, Amble and Byker, not far from his home town of Bishop Auckland.

Most of his basic training was spent on the barrack square learning to march in step and salute, or to the range at Whitburn to learn how to fire a rifle and a bren gun. There were occasional route marches out of town, and a one-night exercise to Otterburn camp. After that, a short leave and then they were off to join the 1st Battalion based at Palace Barracks at Hollywood, just outside Belfast, Northern Ireland. After being there for about nine months, the battalion was transferred to Western Germany and he spent the remaining year of his National Service in Buller Barracks, just outside the city of Münster in Westphalia.

The good times were of course the leave you were given - two weeks from Northern Ireland and two weeks from Germany. The nights-out with the lads on Saturday in Münster, with plenty of Dortmunder Union beer, and getting involved with the MPs: 'His speech was slurred, his gait was unsteady, his breath smelled strongly of alcohol, HE WAS DRUNK' - how often had he seen those words on charge sheets passed in the Orderly Room on Monday mornings.

There was an attempt to introduce them to interesting places around Münster by having bus trips on Saturday afternoons, which got them to visit the Mohne Dam, famous for the 'Dambusters' raids in World War Two. But on the way back to barracks they would always call in at a Gasthaus for a drinking session, resulting in mayhem on the last stage of the journey back to barracks. Result: - an end to those 'cultural' trips.

Colin learned two things during his two years service - to drive and to type. A friend in the Motor Transport Section would take him out in his Champ., and all he did was take over the wheel and drive. At last he was 'ready' for the test – and the MT Captain took him. At the end of the test he signed a scruffy piece of paper, which to his amazement he was able to exchange in 'civvy street' for a driving licence – but not before he had learned to drive properly!

GEOFF BARWICK

Royal Signals, 1960-63

When Geoff. and the other Signals lads with him first arrived in Germany they were addressed by the CO, and he finished by asking for any questions. This prompted Geoff. to ask him if there was any Christmas leave, at which he laughed arrogantly and said that it had been sorted out two years ago. Back at the barracks Geoff. asked the other five lads with him if they would support him in carrying it further. One of them agreed, so they asked to see the OC at 8 am on OC's Orders. Eventually the men were told that four of them could go on Christmas leave, two of whom would be Geoff. and his mate. To which Geoff. declined, saying that was not what it was about, and requested that all the men's names went into a hat, and then draw four names out of it. Ironically, neither Geoff. nor his mate drew leave, but he was satisfied that justice had been finally done.

There was a bully in the ranks, and he often picked on one lad, a gentle giant, who did not want any trouble. This particular day in the mess, the bully had been badgering, and was going to have a go at him. The lad had two drinks in his hand, and asked the bully to hold them for him, which he did. He then punched him so hard in the face that he pole-axed him, and he never had any trouble at all after that day.

IAN MALLOWS

Royal Air Force, 1949-51

Ian was stationed at RAF Wunsdorf while doing his National Service in Germany in 1949. One day there the Signals Officer, an ex-air gunner, went into the control tower and asked the corporal there had he painted around the accumulators with anti-acid paint? The corporal said no, and was asked why not? Because, the corporal said patiently, they are alkali, and the remarkable reply was: 'Same bloody thing, aren't they?'

'Sleepy' Pearce was a regular airman, so called because he had been known to fall asleep on kit inspections; a bit of an oddball, and he was on parade with Ian one day. They had to have their full pack on, containing overcoat etc, and the warrant officer came along and tapped 'Sleepy's' pack with his cane, and it flew up and hit the next man on the head. It had nothing in it, just a bit of cardboard!

Shortly after this he defected to the Russians, and it was all over the national newspapers for quite a while – especially as he was described as a radar expert, which would have been of use to them. This he most certainly was not, because he was never allowed anywhere near electronic equipment of any kind. 'Sleepy' wanted to marry a German girl and the authorities wouldn't give him permission, and maybe that had a bearing on it. The rest of the lads were all quizzed by the

Special Investigation Branch as to what he had said beforehand, etc., but nothing came of it.

The consensus of opinion was that he would do more for this country by being over there with the Russians than he could ever do remaining in this country!

Determined to keep up his level of fitness, Ian still does ballroom sequence dancing at least three times a week, at the age of 82!

LEN DILNOT

Yorkshire Light Infantry, 1953-55

After his basic training at Strensall in 1953, in the Yorkshire Light Infantry, Len was posted straight to Berlin. He decided to have a haircut before he went in, at Leeds City Station barbers, and he thought he would be all right, with a really close haircut. As they all lined up at Strensall on that first day the sergeant came round to Len and asked whether he was hurting him or not. Len replied: 'No,' and the sergeant replied that he should be, because he was pulling his hair – *'get a haircut!'*

The western part of Berlin where Hess was being guarded in Spandau, was all lit up at night, with plenty of goods in the shops, whereas in the eastern part of Berlin it was the opposite, dark and forbidding, with very little in the shops. They were not allowed to go into the eastern sector without being escorted, and had to be in by midnight. They got on well with the Americans and the French, operating their sectors of Berlin – but not the surly Russians. Len at times guarded the likes of Rudolph Hess and Admirals Doenitz and

Raeder, amongst others. He was at Wavell Barracks, and found the local Germans mostly well disposed towards them, especially as the Russians were nearby.

Len's strength was basketball, and he went all over Germany playing for the Army, when not guarding Hess, etc. He remembers going through the Russian sector when going on leave, with their sullen faces and grey greatcoats – a very hostile people.

There were four turrets around Spandau prison, and he used to look down on the four gardens, from where he was stationed, 40 feet above Hess. The prisoners had one apiece. He remembers watching Hess come into his garden and pick leaves up, hold them up in the air and let them blow away – a very strange fellow he thought. Later on, Hess was supposed to have committed suicide, by hanging himself, but Len heard that he had been strangled – a more likely scenario, as by that time Hess was very weak, and he could not physically have committed suicide, which was the verdict given at the time. Hess was the only reason that the Russians were allowed into the west of Berlin.

Every half hour Len had to turn a key which registered in the guard room – to prove that they were still awake. Spandau was the only place that he did guard duty with live ammunition. There was about 40 feet of barbed wire, then electrified barbed wire, and beyond the wall there were police with Rottweiler dogs.

Len enjoyed his National Service, the German beer and the German women, where he saw plenty of action – but with one in particular. Her name was Reta, and Len called round many times at her home, which was very near to Wavell Barracks, where he was based, and courted her for 22 months while he was there. *(See also, Last Thoughts)*.

MALCOLM SCRATCHERD

Royal Air Force, 1947-49

During 1948 Malcolm was sent out to Germany, where his squadron used to practise firing against the sandbanks in the Baltic, and much practise work was done over there at this time, with lots of low flying.

The full squadron was massed at RAF Lubeck, with the ground crew going over first, and this was the time of the Berlin Blockade, and the squadron had to stand by there in case they were needed. The runway at Lubeck ran right up to the Russian border. At that time the squadron were using Mark VI Meteors, the fastest fighter in the world at this time, and with all these jets massed right on the Russian sector of Berlin this was creating a problem, as the Russians thought they were massing to retaliate for their blockade.

Madame Butterfly was being performed locally in Germany the following month, and tickets were hard to come by, and as Malcolm loved the music of that opera he wanted two tickets. He offered a local fraulein some money for two tickets, but she refused, wanting two cigarettes instead, and she asked what she had to do with the change ...for two Woodbines!

After three weeks the squadron was recalled to England as soon as possible so as not to upset the Russians any further, and Malcolm never did see his *Madame Butterfly*.

FRED SIMPSON

Royal Signals, 1947-48

Being a boilermaker by trade, Fred was not called up until he was nearly 22, because this was an important reserved occupation. When he was asked what he wanted to serve in at the recruiting office, he put down Royal Engineers, but he was told that he was going into the Royal Signals. The recruiting officer then asked him if would like to be a switchboard operator, but as Fred was used to working outside he replied: '*Definitely not, sir,*' but that he wouldn't mind being a lineman, so Fred at least got his fresh air.

He did his basic training at Richmond with the Green Howards, and was then posted to Catterick, which he did not mind too much. From there he was sent to Celle in Germany, only a couple of miles from Belsen Concentration Camp, but when Fred went round it had all been cleared up, and at that time there was nothing to see, or suggest that it had been a concentration camp of the very worst kind.

Fred spent about 18 months of his service in Celle, rather a quiet place, but an important Displaced Person's camp, before being posted to Celle airfield for nine months as a lineman. This entailed putting the lines up, and the telephones in, etc., a hard job sometimes, and having to work at great heights also on occasions; but working outdoors all the time suited Fred and his fitness.

Later on, Fred was posted to Wuhn, where he and his mates experienced some resentment from the local German youths, and they had to go about with their belts around their hands, but as they were ready for any bother it never materialised, but relations remained a bit strained.

Fred visited Cologne and was shocked by all the devastation the Allied bombing had caused to that once great city, and was amazed by the fact that while the main target, the marshalling railway yard had been flattened, the beautiful Cologne Cathedral was left almost unscathed, as promised by the Allies during their bombing raids, although only a very short distance away. Another place that Fred visited was Dusseldorf, and that was flattened too.

Being so soon after the Second World War, Fred thought the attitude of the German people towards them was not too bad. In fact they had quite a few working for them in the camp doing various jobs, including ex-German Army officers, one of them being a master on teleprinters, so they used his expertise working on those.

Incredibly, considering the utter devastation wreaked upon that country, the Germans were using mechanical diggers, and other advanced mechanical tools to clear away the rubble and get on with the rebuilding process, while the English soldiers were using spades!

Items bought from the NAAFI, such as soap, sweets, cigarettes, etc. could be bartered outside the camp to the German people, starved of these 'luxuries.' The soldiers in the camp were issued with Baff bakelite money, which could only be used in the camp's NAAFI, to encourage the troops to stay in the camp, and in any case the German pubs outside the camp were out of bounds to the British troops.

Fred thought at first that National Service was a waste of time, and as he was on a decent wage at home, he lost a lot of money during his service, but later he realised that he did get something out of it after all.

ROY STURGEON

Royal Engineers, 1952-54

Starting off at No. 9 Training Regiment, at Cove, Hampshire, for six weeks basic training in 1952, Roy actually enjoyed it. After that he went to nearby Longmoor as a fireman loco, which would have been for two years, with a fireman's course, then on a steam driver's course, and a diesel driver's course. However, in the first lesson in the classroom the subject was coloured light – and Roy was colour blind, so after a medical he was off the course, much to Roy's relief. After that he was posted to Hamel in Germany, got on Motor Transport as a DI, motorbike, and finished his time there.

One day several of the lads were touring around with nothing to do and no money to spend, as usual. There was a guest house at the side of a village on a red hot summer's day, and they were watching the landlord bringing the beer up from a well. The lads decided there and then they were going to get some of that beer. So late at night when the guest house was closed they went back and opened the well up, grabbed some bottles and made off quickly. When they got back to the vehicles, knocked the tops off and drank them they found it was not beer but German lemonade, which is just like spa water, vile tasting, so after one mouthful they threw them away. The landlord must have known that it was the Army lads, but nothing was ever done about it, because they were still occupying troops at the time.

Out on an exercise in a farmyard orchard, some of them were wrapping thunderflashes and throwing them into a river at the back of the orchard, to see if they could kill some fish. There was a little gully running down from this cow byre, and it was full of slurry, running down to the river. There was a deep hole in it and someone dropped a thunderflash in that, and it blew up all over the German farmer's wife's washing, covering it, and them, in slurry. Next morning everyone involved was up before the CO.

The German's attitude to the British soldier was OK, far better in their eyes than Russians. They carried their rifles with them on exercise and as Roy was riding a motorbike it was a sten gun. In a guest house one night with some ex-German soldiers, they were stripping their weapons, and there was no animosity at all. Roy and his mates pulled the weapons to bits and let them have a look and put them together again. In their unit they had two German workers, Gustaf and Johann and they used to kid them that the Russkies were coming, but they hated the very mention of them.

On one occasion outside Hamel they were swimming, and the wagons had arrived to pick them all up to go back to the barracks. All of a sudden on this very hot day, and the water warm, Roy got severe cramp in his legs, but he knew to make for a hump in the middle of the lake, so he did. But he couldn't stand up, he could just shout for help to his mates. They all rushed over to get him out as Roy's legs had locked solid, and he was very close to drowning, barely keeping afloat with his hands.

Roy started his National Service at the age of 18, and felt that he went in as a boy, but came out grown up, and does not regret doing it at all.

JOHN THOMPSON

Queen's Dragoon Guards, 1960-62

Serving two months less than most other National Servicemen, because he had signed on earlier for sentimental reasons, John cancelled this when his engagement to a German girl fell through. He did his training for the Queen's Dragoon Guards at Deerbolt Camp in Barnard Castle for 13 weeks in 1960, which included basic and trade training, as a radio operator on Saracen armoured cars.

There were five of them from the same town, none of them enjoyed the training but it had to be done. However, one lad absolutely hated it, and was always in trouble fighting with the trained soldiers down town. When he was transferred to his posting which was the tank regiment, life was different, he signed on, and went right through the ranks to become a colonel of the regiment.

One day the RSM gave a demonstration of battery care, and lined all the batteries up to show that they had to be properly lined up or they would explode. When they <u>did</u> explode they all laughed, but not for long, as he had them running round the square with a sub-machine gun above their heads, which was exhausting after a while.

They were on the range one day with fully loaded machine guns, and the sergeant in charge warned them to keep their weapons in front of them at all times, and never to turn round with it. A Taffy lad next to John jammed his fully loaded weapon, and trying to free it, turned round pointing it towards John, and the sergeant came along, took the weapon off him and hit him one. The young lad was warned never to do that again, and was told that he could have killed John. This was witnessed by the full squad, and it had a sobering effect on all of them.

After the six weeks training it was time for the Passing Out Parade, and there was quite a good attendance from the families, with the proud parents, brothers, sisters, aunts and uncles, all there to watch the parade. They had a bit of a rehearsal first, and the sergeant was shouting the orders out and the language was blue, and could be clearly heard by the onlookers. Anyway, the band of the 15/19th Hussars started up and they marched around the square as proud as peacocks. When the parade was over John's father approached the sergeant and asked him why he had to use all the bad language, not just to me but to everyone? He was very relieved that none of the lads heard that conversation, otherwise his life would have been hell off the parade ground.

From there John was posted to Wuffenbuttel in Germany, near Brunswick and he enjoyed it. He used to go on trips all over Germany to get the most out of his stay there. One day the sergeant major asked for volunteers to baby-sit for the officer second in command's young children. Quick as a shot John put his hand up, and so he had found a way of financing his coach and train trips around Germany at five shillings a time for a night's babysitting.

John met his girl friend in Berlin and she took him to see the Berlin Wall, No-man's land and the Friedrichstrasse, etc. The Wall had just recently been built, and he saw it under construction, being built very quickly with pre-cast slabs. He also witnessed distressed Berliners, east and west, waving white handkerchieves at each other as their only means of communication. Previously of course they could travel between East and West, but the East German Government had to stop the ever-increasing wave of East Germans from flocking over to the West somehow, and the Wall did that efficiently.

For John National Service was definitely not a waste of time, because you got to know yourself, became disciplined, improved your social skills and learned to respect other people and their property, and also the value of camaraderie.

BILL CAMPBELL
Royal Air Force, 1947-49

After his RAF training in 1947 Bill was based at Wunnsdorf in Germany, arriving from Duisburg at night, and next morning was told by an officer that they were taking over as loadmasters to oversee that all the cargoes were lashed down properly. If they did not do that properly they would be charged with manslaughter in the event of a crash.

What became known as the Berlin Airlift meant that every three minutes cargoes of food, fuel and supplies were taking off from Gatow, Tiegel and Wunnsdorf airports. Wheat grown in Germany was milled and then shipped to Berlin to make flour for bread, rather than transport bread, because it contained water. This went on for nine months and saved Berliners from having many thousands of deaths.

Russia wanted Berlin to become a Russian enclave, and then eventually take over the whole of Germany, because the theory was that anyone who runs Berlin runs Europe. The winter of 1948 was extremely cold, and conditions for older people were very bad, with rations not enough to keep them alive, and they had no heating, so coal had to be carried by air.

The main tonnage was coal, not only for heating, but to run generating plants, etc., and the next was wet fuel.

The Russians had helped themselves to a lot of the equipment and taken it back to Russia, etc. So, not only was there no coal, but there was no equipment either. Bill and his crew worked 12 hours on and 12 hours off. His job as loadmaster was to look after these planes, and they employed Germans and displaced persons to carry stuff onto the plane, and lash it down. Bill's main task was to see that the stuff was distributed evenly, so as not to move around the aircraft when in flight, and thus possibly cause a crash.

There were lots of Regulars being demobbed at that time, so they were short of men to relieve them after the Second World War had ended. On one occasion Bill was given side arms to protect the cargo when loading up, but never used them. This food was for starving people, and he never encountered any trouble. Another time he had six cases of oranges on board, one over the top. He told the pilot he had one extra case on board, and chained it on, but it was not where cargo should have been, and it made the aircraft slightly heavier, and he was reprimanded for that.

Bill was up very early loading planes one morning when he was told to load an Avro York full of sides of beef, and they were easy to deal with, so he completed the job, signed off, and went to bed. Two hours later he was awakened to be told that there was a problem at the airfield, so he went back the two miles to find that all the planes were still there. This plane should have gone at 6.30 a.m. to Berlin, but a US. Boeing had landed at Gatow, burst its tyres, carrying 20 tonnes, and dug up the pierced steel plate (PSP) runway surface. Nothing could land on it so they couldn't take off for

Berlin either, until emergency repairs were carried out, which took valuable time.

MICHAEL KEENAN

Royal Army Education Corps, 1954-56

Basic training for Michael was for 13 weeks with the Sherwood Foresters at Derby in 1954, before going to Beaconsfield, the Army's School of Education. His next posting was to Hohne in Germany, where all the Education people were sent to. While at Hohne Michael was very near to Belsen concentration camp, so he went along one day, along with several of his mates, and saw the many mounds depicting in several languages how many people were buried there. After visiting Belsen they were taken on a trip to Fallingbostel, and they did not like the look of the place, and they all agreed that they did not want to get posted there! As luck would have it Michael _was_ posted there later on, but being attached to the 47th Royal Dragoon Guards he reckoned that he could not have been anywhere better. At Fallingbostel, he was attached to the Education Centre, up on the Luneberg Heath, with two regiments of tanks, and a REME workshop etc. Hitler had cleared away 14 German villages before the war for his tank crews to practise on this huge open area.

Michael spent about 15 months there, and during this time his father died. They flew him home on a 14 day compassionate leave, and he was supposed to get a letter to say not to go back, but he did not receive it, and so went back to Fallingbostel. His CO said that the letter had been sent to him, and he gave him the choice to stay or go home, and Michael decided to stay.

Michael had applied for a compassionate discharge when his father was ill earlier, during his time in Germany, but he was then sent off on a scheme playing soldiers. He came back from that, and the lad he was sharing the bunk with, a sergeant with the 47th, had been with the SAS, and he told Michael that they had a fire while he was away, and all his gear, including his mail had been destroyed in the fire. In amongst that mail there might well have been a letter from the War Office telling him he was getting out early, but he will never know.

National Service was not a waste of time for Michael, because he had been very lucky. Not many National Servicemen achieved three stripes in under four months, particularly when they were only 18 years old! He reckoned that he was lucky because there was a shortage of personnel to do his job at that time.

BRYAN HIRST

Towards the end of his National Service Bryan was sent to Lubeck in Germany on exercises, but his stay there was lengthened by the onset of the Berlin Air Lift, and all National Service at this time was extended from two years to two years and three months, because of the emergency operation and Cold War international tension at this time. Round-the-clock flying operations to deliver food into Berlin meant that flight crews were working from early morning into the evening to keep the aircraft flying, but he enjoyed every minute of it.

Because of the tension between Russia and the West, Bryan could not fly home, but had to return to England overland, and was sent to Thorney Island to look after a brand new squadron of Meteor 7 aircraft, all painted in peace-time silver, showing the Squadron markings. (*See Pic. No. 35*). But very soon after he was sent to Wheaton, near Blackpool, where he was demobbed just before Christmas, 1948. Bryan then returned to the firm of accountants he had left to do his National Service.

FRED WILLIAMS
Durham Light Infantry, 1951-53

Fred did his basic and battle training for the Durham Light Infantry at Strensall in 1951, before the battalion was sent to Berlin at Spandau Barracks, to guard convicted German war criminals, such as Rudolph Hess, etc. At Spandau it was all bull and training for ten weeks before two weeks final training at Senelager, a huge training centre where the German General Rommel had trained his troops during World War Two. Fred remembers going on an organised trip to the Brandenburg Gate, and having to pull the window blinds across as soon as the train crossed over into the Russian sector, because the Russians did not want them to see how poor it was over there. *(See also, Korea)*.

JOHN SCOTT
Durham Light Infantry, 1951-53

After his Durham Light Infantry basic training at Brancepeth in 1951, John found himself on his way by train through the Russian sector to Spandau in Germany. John and his mates were told to hide their weapons under their seats, or they would be taken from them. He spent a year in Spandau

Barracks, Germany, but it was bull all the time he was there, taking it in turns between the Russians, Americans and French, to guard Rudolph Hess, Doenitz and Speer, and other German war criminals from World War Two. (*See Pic. No. 19*). One day a DLI soldier demanded that a Russian party repeat the password, but the officer couldn't understand English, so the DLI lad opened fire over their heads, and he finished up on a charge – for upsetting the Russians, while only doing his duty!

Coming out of the NAAFI one night with his pal Barry, they had just missed the last transport back, and they would have been picked up by the RMPs. John decided there was only one thing to do, so they climbed up the ladder to the top of the last tram to Spandau, and arrived back in camp with only a few minutes to spare. Another night they came to Spandau railway station, and walking along the platform were two Russians on the other side, the Russian sector, and John and his mate were on the British sector. Knowing that the Russians liked to open fire in such instances, thinking that they were 'spying,' John and Barry wisely decided to 'run like hell.'

The battalion football team had gone slightly astray one day and the Russians had fired on them. John was very keen on his football while in Berlin, and made the most of his opportunities to play as often as possible. (*See Pic. No. 18 and Pic. No. 20*). John's platoon were training another time in Spandau forest, half being in the British sector and the other half in the Russian sector. They were expecting supplies from a 3-tonner, but the new driver took the wrong turning in the forest, towards the Russian sector, and the 3-tonner, supplies and driver were never seen or heard of ever again!

In Berlin there was a detachment for Wilhelmsdorf, and when on that they had to fill in a next of kin form because they were going to be the listening post for Berlin, in case the Russians were to attack. This was for them to give a few minutes warning back to base, and they would have been the first to be killed.

(See Front Page, also, Korea, and Last Thoughts).

HARRY WILSON

Green Howards, 1955-57

Before being posted to Minden in Germany, Harry was at Richmond for his Green Howards basic training for 13 weeks in 1955. *(See Pic. No. 44)*. They found that the barracks at Minden were immaculate, being ex-German SS, and far superior to what they had been used to in England.

The cross-country run was a sacred weekly ritual for the battalion there. The colonel had a rule that if anyone finished behind him they were put on a charge. There was keen competition between the good runners to win, and keen competition by some NCOs to finish as near to the colonel as possible, without being put on a charge. The rest just ran the race. *(See also, Hong Kong).*

KENNETH COY

18th Hussars, 1959-61

After serving in Malaya for 12 months Kenneth was posted to Germany in 1961, and one night in the officers' mess the officers were entertaining some American officers of the 7th Cavalry, all in their No. 1 dress, and were waiting for their Chinese meal to be cooked. It was being prepared by a National Service cook who had just arrived from England, and in those days Chinese take-aways were unheard of. 20 minutes away from service the officers and their guests were having their pre-drinks, so Ken called into the kitchen to see how the new cook was getting on. He had cooked the rice with milk, and of course ended up with five big trays of rice pudding! Ken wasn't a cook but he knew the difference, after being in Malaya and having had boiled rice at least once a week there.

The meal with the newly prepared boiled rice was the first formal dinner for the new and old officers, plus guests in Germany, and of course they wanted to impress. Due to Ken it turned out all right in the end with only a few minutes delay.

AUSTRIA

Regarded as one of the best postings in the world, British troops were stationed in Austria, along with American, French and Russian troops, similar to the situation in Berlin, until an international agreement could be reached about what to do with Austria. Food and drink were cheap and plentiful, with an agreeably warm climate, and duties were few and mainly ceremonial. However, the granting of Austrian independence in 1955 brought this idyllic posting to an end.

TERRY OLIVER

Royal Army Medical Corps, 1952-54

Terry's RAMC National Service career began in 1952 at Crookham Barracks for 12 weeks basic training, and then after trade training he was sent to the Army School of Health for a further 12 weeks. From there he was posted to Austria, which at that time was divided into four zones, occupied by Britain, US, France and Russia. The British HQ was at Klagenfurt, now a picturesque tourist destination, where Terry went to work in the hygiene section, medical branch, RAMC.

On his first day there the corporal issued the squad with their International Red Cross Identity Certificate, and said: 'If an enemy soldier points a gun at you … you get the card out of your pocket and show it to him.' They weren't very impressed, particularly with the minute half-inch square size of the Red Cross, which could only be seen from less than two feet away. They didn't think 'an enemy soldier' would take too much notice of it anyway.

Among the hygiene stores Terry took over when he arrived in Klagenfurt were several thousand sterilising outfits, for use with water bottles. These were small tins about two inches square, containing two small bottles of tablets to use to make a bottle of water safe to drink. Just one of these tins would now fetch about £25 at a militaria fair. An investment opportunity missed.

On detachment with the Middlesex Regiment in December 1953, Terry took a phone call to go to barrack block 7, where someone had a bullet wound. So Terry grabbed a first aid kit and tore round in the ambulance to find a trail of blood leading to the victim lying on his bed in the barrack room.

Sure enough, there was a bullet wound – an entry and exit hole in his calf, but there was an in and out hole in his other calf as well. His white faced mates stood around, and one of them told Terry what had happened. They had found some German 9mm wartime ammunition in a disused hangar at the base. One of them had been asked to clean his officer's revolver, and they found that the bullet fitted it. They inserted the bullet into the revolving chamber and started playing 'Russian Roulette.' The gun was pointed at the victim's head, the trigger pressed, and nothing happened. This was repeated four times, the gun being aimed progressively lower, finally being aimed at the legs, which was when the gun went off. Fortunately, the bullet missed the vital parts of the leg, and the victim made a good recovery, but Terry has never forgotten this incident, and just how lucky that young soldier was!

The most memorable experience of Terry's 730 days National Service was the journey from Aldershot to his 'jammy' posting to Klagenfurt. He remembers the wonderful classic 36-hour train journey, passing the windmills and canals of Holland, the vineyards of the Rhine, and the snow covered Salzburg mountains, which at 18, was his first experience of foreign travel.

Terry's two years as a hygiene assistant, with some other medical duties, provided a very good basis for his remaining three years of PHI qualification as an environmental health officer, which he did for the next 40 years, after he finished his National Service. For once the Army had managed to place one conscript in the right occupation!

CHAPTER FOUR

South America

BERMUDA

The Bermudan military garrison existed primarily to defend the Royal Naval dockyard, located on Ireland Island. It was announced in 1950 that the dockyard would be closed, and the military garrison was to be withdrawn along with it. The British Regular Army was eventually withdrawn on April 25, 1953, but detachments would be posted to the Island until 1955, when a company of the Duke of Cornwall's Light Infantry (DCLI) was withdrawn.

TONY WILLS
Royal Army Ordnance Corps, 1948-50

On a cold wintry day in January 1949, on a barrack square in an RAOC depot at Aldershot, Tony Wills had spent the morning scraping urinals with a bayonet, and awaited posting to a unit after completing his basic training. A sergeant came and asked for two volunteers for an overseas posting, which turned out to be Bermuda for him and friend Taffy.

It was so expensive sending replacements to Bermuda, that they wanted troops with over a year to serve. Previously, replacements had been sent on the *Queen Elizabeth* to New York, and then flown out to the colony. After the War Office queried the cost of all this, Alan and Taffy sailed on the *Empire Bure*, an old coal burning troopship, bound for West Africa with over one thousand married families and servicemen. The War Office decided to divert this ship two thousand miles across the Atlantic, and another three thousand miles back to West Africa, just to drop the pair of them off in Bermuda!

The RSM asked Alan if he would like to become his batman on board ship, so he was excused all parades and fatigues for the whole journey. His only duties were to collect a mug of tea for him at 7 a.m. each morning, fold his blankets and tidy the cabin. They landed in a sunny Bermuda to be greeted by a smiling corporal. 'Call me Bert,' he said. After Aldershot this was like being on another planet, driving through flower decked lanes to Prospect Camp, their base for the next nine months. They had truly been posted to Paradise! Down the road was the Ordnance depot where they worked from 8 a.m. to 2 p.m. each day, after which it was siesta time at Navy Wells, a small shingle bay with a diving board into the sparkling coral blue sea.

The whole set-up of the military base at Bermuda was pure farce, consisting of 22 soldiers, some warrant officers, a few NCOs, plus the Company Commander and adjutant, who they rarely saw. Their only function was to send off orders for requisitioned stores to the Royal Signals for transmission to the UK, and also supply stores and goods to the other support groups. In 1948 someone in the WO queried the expense of the establishment, and two audit officers were sent out to investigate. Realising this was going to be a very long and complicated job they requisitioned two houses overlooking the bay, and sent for their families. Four years later in 1952, a team was sent out to Bermuda to find out what had happened to the previous investigation team, and the following year the military base on Bermuda was closed down.

Meanwhile, Tony was making the most of the situation. All you had to do was to walk around purposefully with a piece of paper in your hand, and no one would ever query what you were doing – difficult if you also had your towel and bathing trunks under your arm as well. They only had one formal drill parade a week – to see if anyone had gone AWOL.

Social life there was restricted only by a lack of money. Bermuda was expensive, with most of the bars catering just for rich American tourists. They usually went out on a Saturday to the dance at the Army and Navy Club, but if they had more than a couple of drinks they had to walk back to camp. Looking back, Tony remembers all those golden afternoons and evenings they spent down at Navy Wells bathing areas. Also when they had a trip around the islands, seeing more beautiful beaches and rocky bays, and the camp out at Warwick, with more of the same.

There was the significant moment when Tony was asked by his sergeant to take over as an assistant in the married families' library, which involved spending a couple of evenings a week sorting out the book stock and checking new books in and out. There was a highly efficient filing system used which meant that each book took about ten minutes to be checked in and out, and he was paid an extra £2 a week for this, which paid for all his drinks in the NAAFI club. As well as getting to know the stock Tony got to know the families as well. His pals were all jealous of the fact that when someone was leaving and parties were held, he could dance with the officers' daughters who knew him from the library, while they just stood around the bar.

All good things have to come to an end, and he and Taffy sailed for home on the *Empress of Australia* in November, calling at Kingston, Jamaica, Belize and Trinidad on the way. Back in England he found he was posted to Chilwell, only a few miles from his home, so he was able to renew old acquaintances and plan for his future after demob.

Tony was sent to Aldershot to be demobbed, and waiting at the station for the train back to London was John Tarrant, who had been on the same WOSBE course as him, only he had been successful, and became an officer. 'What happened to you?' he asked, so Tony told him about Bermuda. 'How about you?,' Tony asked. 'I became officer in charge of stores at Didcot,' he replied, sadly. There *were*, after all, some things to be thankful for! *(See also, Last Thoughts).*

DEREK LOVEMORE

Devon and Cornwall Light Infantry, 1953-55

Shortly after arriving at Prospect Garrison, Bermuda in March 1954 and being despatched to 3 Platoon under Lt. Frank Drake, Derek Lovemore, DCLI, was detailed to act as 3 Platoon weapons storeman, which entailed managing the entire platoon armoury and locking himself in the storeroom at night. While still a private soldier at this time, the main benefit for him was some peace and quiet away from the main billets and the challenging smells of 20 blokes living together in the tropics; although the alternative smells of oil and spent cordite took some getting used to initially. Derek also assumed exclusion from rostered billet duties, bed, sheet and blanket bull, and simply made up his bed each morning. He was never ever challenged by Lt. Drake at morning inspections he thought, because he appreciated Derek's negative approach to most military matters, and was sure of a perfect pass on CO's inspection on Saturday mornings.

This task continued whenever they were shipped out to Warwick Camp for manoeuvres. The downside of course meant that not only was Derek locked up at night in the Warwick Camp armoury, but also kept company with thousands of rounds of .303, .38s, rockets, energa bombs, and all the spread of 2 inch mortar ammunition, including HE, that could only be stored under, and alongside his cot. What a fireworks display that would have been, knowing that much of the ammunition was unstable and probably out of date. However, Derek was comforted by the words of Ken Young, their acting platoon sergeant, and a Malayan vet to boot, that it was unlikely there would be problems, so who was Derek to question. To prove the point Ken would often join Derek at break times, kip on the spare bunk, and smoke away as if there was no tomorrow.

Don Puckey, Phil Taylor and Derek were good mates, and most times shared platoon and section roles, and, being unaware that they were being groomed for promotion, still played up and looked for a good time whenever they could. Their mischievous appetites were amplified by Derek's suggestion that a 2 inch mortar and parachute flares fired over the range area at night would no doubt disturb the lucky natives who trespassed the area after dark, to enjoy the balmy nights and romantic beckoning of the warm Atlantic.

Warwick was off limits to civilians while military exercises were being undertaken. The ever-present voyeur was rampant in those young soldiers, and without another thought they chose the high ground, and with infantry precision put several flares in the air in rapid succession. What they never bargained for was the fact that the flares were World War Two issue, and only one in four actually ignited, which of course resulted in several 1lb. incendiary objects plummeting down from the sky, unsighted and unmarked for future demolition.

In later times, when some remorse set in, Derek often pondered on their dangerous and careless actions that night, and while they had some fun, and generally achieved their mission in sighting scores of naked people diving for cover in the dunes, he shudders to think what might have happened if a rogue flare had landed on a human body from a 300-400' trajectory.

The irony was that Don Puckey, Phil Taylor and Derek were the first soldiers to earn NCO stripes after the initial Bermuda posting, which entailed lecturing among other things, on: *The safety of live weapons firing.* They frequently played soldiers on the Warwick ranges, and while they dug weapons pits and trenches, and ran for miles up and down the dunes, they never found a single dud 2 inch mortar flare.

Their times at Warwick camp were always a welcome relief from the Garrison, and they made full use of the wonderful location next to Horse Shoe Beach. *(See Pic. No's. 40, 41, 42 & 43).* Derek reckons that Frank Drake must have been a very tolerant officer to overlook their boyish pranks. While nothing was ever said over these incidents, and other night-time expeditions to pinch water melons, and absences from the camp into the local off-limits bars, he must have had his suspicions. *(See also, Last Thoughts)*.

NEIL SWANSON

Devon and Cornwall Light Infantry, 1953-55

Neil was conscripted into the DCLI in September 1953, doing his basic training at Bodmin, before being posted to Bermuda.

Whilst carrying out his duties one day as a DCLI Pioneer, Neil was doing some work in the cookhouse area when a shout came out from a Sgt. Tug Wilson, who he hadn't previously had any contact with, as the sergeant had only recently arrived in Bermuda. He shouted at him again in his loud Yorkshire accent, but Neil still couldn't understand what he was saying, and the next thing that he knew was that he was being marched into the guardroom cells.

Shortly after this happened the Company Commander was told about it and Neil was released to appear on orders the next morning, when he was marched in before Major 'Toots' Williams, and the CSM Jan Passmore. When asked what this was all about, Neil replied that he didn't understand a thing that the sergeant said. When Sergeant Wilson told him why he had been charged in his strong Yorkshire accent, he repeated that he still didn't understand him. Apparently the sergeant had asked him, had his rifle been BLR'd?, and Neil had said again that he still couldn't understand.

On hearing Sgt. Wilson's strong accent, Major Williams said that there was no wonder that Neil couldn't understand him. The major told Sgt. Wilson that he was not surprised that Neil could not comprehend what he was saying to him, being a Cornishman, because with that accent he sounded just like a German – case dismissed! Neil reckons that they were biased in the DCLI as the County Regiment, and that their Cornish NCO's and officers would always look after their own first.

JAMAICA

After World War Two the Commonwealth Caribbean colonies temporarily looked to Britain for defence and security. Although they held no strategic importance for Britain, they remained interested in the region, owing to economic obligations. Britain gave its Caribbean colonies increasingly more self-government, but retained an unlimited obligation for their defence against external aggression, which at that period in time was coming from Guatemala. Full independence from the UK was achieved on August 6, 1962.

BARRY UNETT
Royal Hampshire Regiment, 1959-61

Belonging to the 1st Royal Hampshire Regiment, and doing his basic training in England in 1959, Barry was coming back from manoeuvres one day, and they were told that there was to be no talking in the ranks, but of course Barry did, and he was sent to the guard house every hour, for a change of different kit inspection every time. After their Passing Out Parade they all had their pay docked by a few pounds each, because they had been using their barrack room door as a dart board – with their bayonets!

As part of a stand-by company stationed in Jamaica in 1959, Barry Unett used to go all over the island sorting out problems. He had only been out there a month, and the sergeant was looking for a working party to bury a horse. They all hid, but eventually a working party was found and they had to dig a hole to put it in, but the ground was very hard, and the horse would not fit into it, so they had to chop off its legs to make it fit into the grave.

Also very early in Barry's National Service career was the day of the CO's inspection, and when he came round he saw that a light bulb was missing, and Barry was told by the sergeant to replace the bulb. So off he went to get a replacement light bulb from the quartermaster's stores, but he found on his return that he had been put down as being absent without leave on parade. He got back to see them going out on parade! 'I didn't mean NOW, *straight away*, I meant LATER! bawled the sergeant, afterwards.

They did not get on very well with their sergeant. Because of the heat there were open billets in Jamaica, and the floors had to be washed every day. There were ten soldiers to a room, and one day the sergeant told them that they didn't have to wash them every day – he suggested that they just paint them with floor paint. This seemed a great idea at the time, but the surface of the floors did not last long in the heat, and very soon it began to flake off. They had to scrape it off every night in their spare time with their knives – it took three months to do it. Then they had to go back to washing the floors again!

On one occasion they wanted volunteers to hold the pass against a threatened Guatemalan invasion, and most of the people who volunteered were National Servicemen, with only a few Regulars interested. They saw an American frigate while they were on their way by Navy frigate HMS *Ulster*, and they were told to hide on deck because the US had a treaty with Guatemala, and they didn't want the Americans to see them. In the event nothing happened; Guatemala threatened to attack British Honduras on her border, but never did. The Guatemalan situation was resolved eventually, and they went no further, always threatening to attack but never did. When the English soldiers went there the Guatemalans always pulled back.

On Barry's 21st birthday some insurgents were reported to be in the hills near Kingston, and were armed. So with the West Indian Regiment they were told to surround the top of the hill and lay an ambush, and the West Indian Regiment would drive the insurgents towards them. However, the rebels were behind them, killing two and wounding three of their lads from 5 platoon. They had to reorganise and search for them, and found their camp and set fire to it, but the insurgents had escaped. For the next week they set up ambushes to catch the insurgents, but eventually it was the West Indian Regiment and police who caught them after another week.

Besides his Jamaican service Barry went to Nassau for three months, and while he was there they were told that some Cuban rebels in the Caribbean were using the small bays to stash arms catchments, ready for their 'Bay of Pigs' invasion of Cuba. So about a dozen of them with an officer were chosen to search for the rebels, in a small fishing boat with two local fishermen, and after a couple of days they found an anti-tank gun and some other military gear. They then tried to radio the fishing boats to pick them up, but the fishermen could not receive their signal, so they set fire to the scrub on the beach for smoke, and signalled with their mess tins by reflection from the sun, to pick them up that night. This worked, and they went back to Nassau very pleased with themselves.

Was National Service a waste of time for Barry? No, he loved every minute of it. Back home he had been a Teddy Boy, a rebel, who always answered back, but he became more mature then, because of his service.

Despite being in the Caribbean, what most people might see as an ideal posting, there were no volunteers among Barry's intake to sign on for Regular service. He might have thought about it, but he was engaged to be married, and he did not get back to see his fiance for 21 months.

1—Cunard White Star SS Scythia

2—156 Transit camp at Port Fouad, 1949.

3— Alan Birch, left, with the rest of the Signals team at 156 Transit Camp.

4— 'Brassed Off' Alan Birch, left and Tim .

5— Sgt. Peter Fowle, right, Intelligence Section 1st Btn. DCLI, Palestine 1946

6—Royal Warwickshire Regiment, new intake, 1958. John Prentice is sitting left, front row.

7— John Prentice and his little helper, Ali

8—Above. 'This is the life for me,' says John Prentice!

9—Left, John Prentice stands proudly in front of his beloved water bowsers.

10—Donnington Railway Station— Pre-Beeching.

11—Left, Malcolm MacGregor and his pet fox, sitting next to the soldier with 'no swallow.'

*12—Tent area and parade ground, Prim Barracks, Tripoli, Libya.
Albert Wilson's tent is in the foreground.*

*13—View from the gunsite on Stonecutter Island, looking
towards the New Territories.*

14—Tung Chung village, Lan Tau Island. Arthur Watson is on the left.

15—Stan Hawthorne standing by an RB19 earthmoving vehicle, Kuala Lumpur, 1948.

16—'Home Sweet Home' for Stan Hawthorne, for four months at Batu Caves, near Kuala Lumpur.

17—The new training squad at Hilsea Barracks, Southsea, 1958. Bill Hubbard is fourth left, middle row.

*18—'A' Company five-a-side football champions.
John Scott, is second left, front row.*

*19—'A' Company DLI, outside Spandau Barracks, in Berlin,
previously used by German SS troops. John Scott is in the second
row, sixth from the left. Corporal Moore MC, is second left,
second row up.*

20—'A' Company football team, Spandau Barracks, Berlin.
John Scott is fourth from left, back row, .

21—John Scott, back row middle, on his last day awaiting
transport home from Kure, Japan.

22—'Dukes' filling sandbags and doing repair work, after
another night's enemy shelling.

23—Ron Shaw, on right, inspecting damaged bren guns and rifles after the third Battle of the Hook.

24—The Hook.

Ken Coan, 2010

25— 'Speechless' - Field Marshall Montgomery of Alamein,
inspecting the Passing Out Parade of the Royal Warwickshire
Regiment MT section (and especially John Prentice), at
Worcester Barracks, in 1958.

26—Nee Soon Garrison Rugby Fifteen . Alan Newman is fourth left, back.

27—'The Dirty Dozen,' RAF Regiment 'H' intake, RAF Catterick, 1951.
George Gamble is far left, middle row.

*28— P.E. with limited equipment—National Service style.
Bill Hubbard centre, with his War Office pals.*

29— From left, Jim, Steve, Mick, author centre, John, Alex and Dennis, 1959, Donnington Garrison.

30— Jim Shipley, Bill Hubbard and the author, right, in a 9 Btn. RAOC barrack room, Donnington, 1960.

31— War Office Auditions for Mr Universe title, with Slim, centre front, Taffy, middle and Bill Hubbard, right.

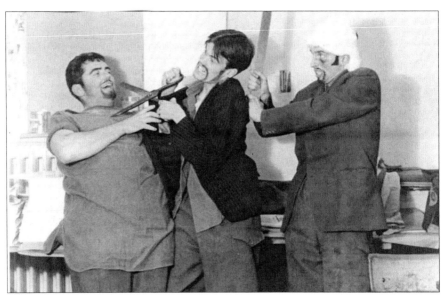

32— Playtime at the War Office, with Taffy, left, Slim, centre and Bill Hubbard, right.

33—Casualties being stretchered from a MASH helicopter to the Surgical Unit. (From 'Korea the Forgotten War.' Courtesy of F.W.).

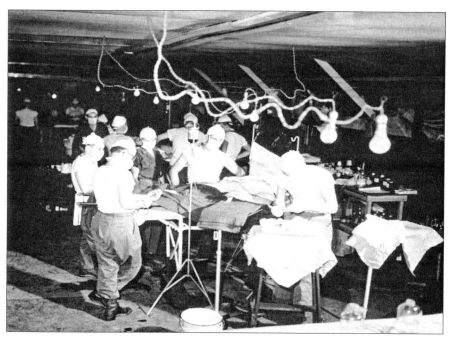

34—Surgeons tending casualties in a MASH unit in Korea, 1952.

35—Meteor 7 Jet at Duxford Air Museum.

36—Ron Shaw right, with Bill Speakman VC.

37—Above Bevin Boys emerging from the lift.

*38—
Bevin
Boys
tending
a pit
pony.*

39—Bevin Boys leaving a Durham pit in 1944 after a hard shift.
(All three pit photos courtesy of Middlesbrough Evening Gazette,
Remember When, Sept, 2010).

40—Platoon members on manoeuvres, Warwick camp, Bermuda.
Derek Lovemore, far right.

*41 & 42— Derek Lovemore, above right, on Horse Shoe Beach,
Bermuda, with fellow squaddies.*

*43—
Derek
Lovemore,
front, with
Gordon on
Horse
Shoe
Beach,
Bermuda.*

44— Green Howards' Passing Out Parade, platoon photograph, at Richmond, August 1955. Harry Wilson is front left.

45— Colombo, Ceylon — 'D' Company, 1Btn. Green Howards stopped near here for a game of cricket and high tea.

46— 1st Btn. Green Howards leaving the Empire Fowey, at Kowloon, May 1956.

47— Queen's Birthday Parade, 1956, being reviewed by the Governor of Hong Kong. Harry Wilson is fifth from the left.

48— 1st Btn. Green Howards, Trooping The Colour, New Territories, Hong Kong, 1956.

49— Troopship Empire Fowey, taking the Green Howards back home again to England.

50— NCO Cadre Course at York. John Robinson is far left, front row.

51— Green Howards Passing Out Parade, August 1954. John Robinson is second left, front row.

52— Green Howards 6th Platoon Cross Country Team. John Robinson is third left, back row.

53— On their way home! Leaving Famagusta, November 1955, on the Empire Clyde.

55— *Ireneous, now a Bishop in the Greek Orthodox Church.*

54— *Left to right, Abbot Ireneous, Cliff Baker, two EOKA activists, a real monk.*

56— *Greek Orthodox Monastery, Panaia Tou Machera.*

*57— The Balloon Unit from Cardington landing at Adelaide,
fresh from a holiday in Hawaii, before going to Maralinga test
site, (Courtesy of Adelaide Advertiser).*

*58— Hydrogen gas
cylinders being
unloaded, used to
inflate balloons
later.*

*59— Four balloons
needed to lift the atomic
bomb and box up to 800
feet before detonation.*

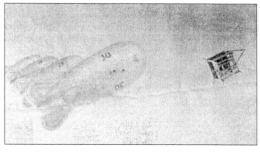

CHAPTER FIVE

Middle East

ADEN

The Indian Empire had to be supplied by sea, until becoming independent in 1947. This led to a series of Company bases along the route to the Far East. Aden, at the southern tip of Arabia was a fuelling point for steam ships passing from Suez, and a naval base for patrolling the Red Sea and Indian Ocean. To protect British interests in Aden a Protectorate was declared over the surrounding area, which became known as the Aden Protectorate.

JOHN PRENTICE
Royal Warwickshire Regiment, 1958-60

Celebrating his 21st birthday in Darla, Aden, in the mountains, John was in the NAAFI having a beer with his mates and was very drunk, and looking out saw the 'B' Company flagpole, so he climbed to the top of the flagpole, and just as he was about to lean over to get the flag he felt it breaking at the bottom. John fell on his back outside the medical tent, but somehow survived.

At his first camp John's nickname was 'Blanco,' because the blanco board was higher than him, so he was always covered in the stuff. When he arrived in Aden his nickname changed to 'Chuffnut,' because he was always so happy. John's best mate in Aden was Stan, who was also a driver like himself, and they had many good times and laughs together.

This officer came into the stores one morning, checking everything was all right, and he asked Dave who worked in the stores: 'Who was this Private Chuffnut?' Dave replied that he must know him, because he was that little fellow, like. The officer replied: 'That's not Private Chuffnut, that's Private Prentice!' Dave saw John later and told him that he honestly thought his name really was Chuffnut, and that's why he put it into the book.

From John arriving there at Novat Dkeila to leaving, he only did one guard duty, because the officers needed their gardens watering. (*See Pic. No. 8*). Previously, John had been put on a water bowser's course at Aldershot, and all it entailed was to mix some chemicals and put a couple of tablets into each tankful. He used to put two scoops of powder into the bowser, and a tablet, and that was it. (*See Pic. No. 9*).

As part of his job fetching water to the desert from wells, John came into contact with people from villages on his route, and everywhere he went his little helper Ali accompanied him. *(See Pic. No. 7)*. The head of one of the tribes told him that no soldiers except him were ever allowed in a certain village, but as he bought cold fizzy drinks called 'Skim' off them and gave some to the children, that made it all right.

John used to go around wearing just a little pair of shorts, a beret and flip-flops, every day. He got away with this because the officers had their little gardens needing watering. They used to approach him and say: 'Prentice, drop of water on the old garden, if you are passing.' 'Yes sir,' replied John, and that's how he got away with murder for those 10 months, which included writing off three vehicles going down the mountain pass during his time in Aden. He really enjoyed his time there because he reckoned that he had the best job in the whole British Army.

John reckons that National Service was the best thing that happened to him in his entire life. It taught him a lot of things; how to stand up for himself, and also useful things like ironing and sewing. But the main thing was the friendship, which he loved, and he knows that he will never get friendship like that again.

CAPTAIN BILL GOLDTHORP

Royal Army Medical Corps, 1958-60

Starting his six weeks basic training for the RAMC at Crookham, Salisbury Plain, in 1958, Bill Goldthorp recalls that only two of them involved drills. After the fortnight he had forgotten the lot, and all he could remember was to stand to attention, stand easy, and salute after a fashion. In fact a future CO was to tell him not to salute at all because it made him cringe. *'Just smile, nod your head, say hello or good morning – but for Christ's sake don't salute!'*

Bill was posted first to Aden and spent a couple of months there before he was told that he was being transferred to

Dahla, 80 miles away on the Yemeni border. Bill's first job two days after he arrived at Dahla, on the Jebel Akhdar in the Oman, was to climb the Jebel Jihaff, a further 2,500 feet above the 3,500 feet they were already at. He had been warned that it was a dangerous place to be going to, so he carried his .303 rifle with a bandolier of 200 rounds of ammunition up the mountain. This was in addition to his doctor's bag and kit for inoculating a company of men. That was the first and last time he carried a rifle with him, and his team drove and walked everywhere unarmed, but no harm ever came to any of them.

When Bill left Somaliland and returned to Aden he was attached to 10 Brigade Group Medical Company, and moved his things into an hotel at Steamer Point. His dislike of playing at soldiers was only surpassed by his dislike of the RAMC Colonel in charge, whom he describes as *'Colonel Pillock, all brasso, blanco and bullshit.'*

Bill spent his last ten weeks at Little Aden with the Royal Dragoons, and enjoyed their company, before saying his goodbyes to them and his CO. A very pleasant way to finish his National Service. (*See also, Somaliland*).

MICK HAMMOND
Prince of Wales' Own, 1957-59

Mick was given a detail one day to transport a 3 inch mortar platoon on a live firing exercise whilst serving in Aden/South Yemen with the 1st Prince of Wales' Own as a driver. The journey took them from Kormaksar transit camp to Elephant's Bay, where they turned off a main road on to a track leading up the lower slopes of Mount Sham Shan, a mountain commanding an imposing position on the Aden southern peninsula. After a while the track petered out and the going became hard for the old Bedford truck, so the officer in charge decided to walk to the firing area, leaving Mick to guard the truck. He managed to turn it around with a struggle, ready for the return journey.

The views from Mick's position on Sham Shan were magnificent, and he could see the smoke haze rising from Crater City, Steamer Point, the harbour, Kormaksar airfield, round to Little Aden, and below him was their 'B' company's tented camp at Elephant's Bay. At this point he noticed a platoon of infantry struggling up the track towards him, and as the lead man, a corporal, approached, he asked if Mick had any water. Mick recognised him along with others from 'B' Company. 'Yes, corporal, there's a jerry can full round the other side of the truck, help yourself,' Mick replied. 'Don't tell the officer and sergeant you've given us water,' he added. It was then that Mick noticed two others moving up towards him, and after filling their water bottles the platoon moved off. Mick moved to the front of the truck and watched the officer and sergeant approach, standing to attention and saluting the officer, a captain in the RAMC. 'Good morning, driver,' he said: *'Is it warm enough for you?'* *'Yes sir,'* Mick replied. The sergeant said nothing and they moved off without stopping.

A few days later Mick was attached to 'B' Company in readiness for a tour of duty up country. He arrived in the afternoon, and the night was spent in the NAAFI, where he met again the lads from Mount Sham Shan. They explained about the water, and it turned out that the officer was none other than Roger Bannister (now Sir Roger Bannister CBE), the first man to run a mile in less than four minutes, on May 6, 1954, with a time of 3min. 59.4. He was also doing his National Service as an officer in the RAMC, and was at the time on the mountain, testing the troops on their ability to perform with limited fluid intake. Mick hoped that he didn't spoil his test results too much that day ...!

JOHN MacGREGOR
Royal Air Force, 1956-58

After his square bashing at Padgate in 1956, John was then sent to a maintenance unit at Marston Moor near York, dismantling RAF equipment from airfields etc. At the end of World War Two this equipment was no longer needed, so there they were in 1956 still mopping up thousands of pieces of military equipment from all over the world. Our airfields were closing down, and this stuff needed disposing of. At Marston Moor unit no. 5, a former bomber station, there were miles and miles of equipment, packed solid everywhere, including the runways.

From there John was sent to Hereford on a course, and then to Burton Woods transit camp, where his posting came for Aden, which was a Protectorate, only a small perimeter being protected, the rest relied on goodwill, and he ended up at Thorn, Kormatse. A native police force, ACL, with only an armband to show his authority, got on the wagon to the airfield. It took John a whole day to get his gear and find a department to work in. The following day he found that he had to work on Wellington metal and wood aeroplanes, but he could repair anything, including fighter planes, etc. The temperature in Aden was 140 degrees f, very hot every day, and they could only work from 8 a.m. to 12 a.m.

John flew to Sudan, etc., where they were paying local tribesmen to protect the airfield, who relied on this as co-operation to them in the form of a bonus payment, etc. Anything to stop attacks on the airfield. Britain had many advance airfield bases in different countries, with just skeleton staffs operating them. He was told one day to collect a parachute and a mae west, a formal procedure they had when a flight in the air was granted for ground staff occasionally. This was John's first experience of a flight over beaches and water, going to different countries, and he remembers a few trips later, to Egypt, Libya, Sudan, etc.

John and his pals used to like to go to Steamer Point for relaxation. There were different facilities there, with good clubs and pubs, also an RAF hospital. They also liked to go to the NAAFI building for a quiet drink or two on a night, but there was not a lot to do around the camp, and it was too hot for football at 140 degrees f.

One of the natives on the airbase was carrying a knife. A plane had crashed in Aden, outside the Protectorate and this person tried to rescue a few of them, and managed to save two or three, and was granted permission to carry a knife around with him, as a reward. Not too far away was Crater City, built inside an extinct crater. You could go there, but it was dangerous, because it was outside the Protectorate.

In his spare time John liked getting into a taxi to the open-air swimming pool, where the puffer fish could inflate themselves like balloons. If you followed the perimeter of the camp you would come across this open air swimming pool. When the tide came in it would fill the pool up, but when it went out it would leave in the pool whatever had been left in the pool.

John was on the second floor of a block of flats, and he awoke one morning to find himself covered in bites off sandbugs, after sleeping on a wooden frame with palliasses. The bed went out of the window and the palliasses with it, and he got some natives to set fire to them. He got a new bed, put the legs of the bed in tins of petrol, but the sandbugs then climbed up the wall and dropped onto the beds.

In John's opinion National Service was a waste of time, even though it brought him into contact with many people, and he appreciated their friendship, but he just wanted to get it over and done with.

TREVOR SHIELD

15th/19th Royal Hussars, 1960-62

One of the last to be conscripted in 1960, Trevor was posted to the Royal Armoured Corps, and was then placed with the 15$^{th/19th}$ Hussars, at Deerbolt Camp, Barnard Castle. He served there the normal few weeks, followed by a course for three months as a gunner on armoured fighting vehicles. After the course he was posted to the 1st Royal Dragoons, the oldest Cavalry Regiment in Britain, now called the Household Cavalry.

Trevor's first overseas posting was to Aden, sailing on the *Oxfordshire*, and going through the Bay of Biscay he was the only one on board not to suffer sickness. He arrived at Steamer Point, on his 21st birthday, and celebrated it on board ship, because they were not allowed to disembark until the following morning. He stayed in Aden for only six months, because the Regiment was moving to Malaya.

On one occasion they were on patrol around the BP oil refinery at a camp called Little Aden about 10 miles from Steamer Point. They used to do guard duty around it because there was a lot of unrest in the Middle East at the time, as there is now. They went out during the day and stayed overnight with the armoured vehicles, and the Arabs in the distance were shooting at them. Ironically, Trevor and his mates only had two rounds each, so they wondered afterwards what would have happened if the Arabs had really come for them... *(See also, Malaya).*

STAN CROOK
1ST Btn. Royal Warwickshire Regt, 58-60

Stan did his basic training for the Royal Warwickshire Regiment at Budbrooke Barracks for 13 weeks, before being posted to Aden for 13 months.

While he was in Aden he used to drive regularly to a place in the middle of the desert called Nobat-Dakim, Little Aden, a tented camp halfway to Dhala where the Warwicks were based. One day Stan was sent to Dhala to be the OC's driver, a two-day journey, stopping off at Nobat-Dakim. He was on the last truck of the convoy with a mate of his, Ron Heard, a platoon commander. Being a driver, Stan's weapon was a sterling small hand weapon, and on the way up he had put his sterling and webbing in the toolbox of the truck. They stayed outside the camp and all the wagons formed a ring like the old Western cowboys and Indians. The next morning they all set off for Dhala, but Ron Heard and his platoon changed from the back truck to the front truck, so Stan went with him.

Stan had left his weapon and webbing in the last truck, but as luck would have it the convoy came under rebel fire in the mountains. When this happened the procedure was for everyone to jump off the wagons and hit the ground with weapons at the ready. Stan was without his, because it was still in the last truck. He was far more worried about being found out by the convoy commander, Captain Keen than he was about the rebels, so he ran from the front of the convoy to the back to retrieve his weapon and webbing. When Stan reached the last truck he found that it had been hit and the bullets had gone through the panel of the truck, through the water bottle on one of the lad's webbing and into his right side. He stayed with him until the rebels had been beaten off, and then Captain Keen went into the truck and radio'd for a plane to come up to Nobat-Dakim to pick the injured lad up and take him to hospital. The convoy then carried on to Dhala, and they found out later that the injured soldier was in a stable condition. Stan realised that he had had a lucky escape in moving from that truck, as the injured man could well have been him.

While in Dhala, Stan had to take the CO to the ruler of Dhala's palace for a meeting with Sir William Loose, the Commanding Chief of Armed Forces and other high ranking officers and their aides. Stan drove to the palace with the CO and parked up after he went in, but half an hour later two of the Emir's men came for Stan and insisted that he went with them into the palace. He tried to tell them that he should not go in, but they took his weapon and led him in. Stan washed his hands in a small bowl they held out for him and he had to take his boots off, and was then taken to a small room where his CO was. Stan explained to him what had happened and he told him it was OK, so they all sat on the floor and were served some food. When they had finished they were led into a smoking room where Sir William was presented with a dagger by the Emir. Afterwards Stan drove the CO back to camp, and reflected on what a strange experience he had been part of, in a totally different culture to that of his own.

A little later Stan was sent back to Little Aden and was told that he was going on a posting to stay in Aden and drive a Brigadier General of the Education Corps, and that he would be made up to full corporal. Stan said that he did not want to go, but was told that he had to obey orders. He was upset because he would have to leave all his mates behind, and he knew that the Regiment was going to Hong Kong, and after being in Aden for 13 months that would be like paradise.

BAHRAIN

Bahrain was a British stronghold, a strategic point for the three Services. From there Britain administered the foreign and defence affairs of the Trucial States, Oman, Qatar and Kuwait, as well as Bahrain. British rule was more wide ranging than in any other Gulf state, partly because of their control of foreign oil workers in the oilfields, and the military stayed on until 1971 when Bahrain became totally independent on December 16.

GORDON DIXON
Royal Air Force, 1956-58

In 1957 Gordon flew from Malta to take supplies to Bahrain, during the Arabian War, and stayed for ten weeks. This was a war most countries denied knowledge of, yet the Cameronians were fighting alongside Trucial Oman Scouts, aligned to the Sultan of Muscat against Nasser's rebels, who were trying to take over the Arabian peninsula.

On one occasion, while on a supply run to Sharjah they dropped the jeeps and ammunition, but shortly afterwards one engine stopped, and the pilot said he would have to come down in the middle of the Arabian desert, so they landed on a landing strip used by an American oil drilling group. Two jeeps appeared and the American crew took them to the oil drilling camp at Fahud. When they arrived there was an old English type pub on the site, called '*The Swinging Tit,*' and inside they had a beautiful chicken salad and ice cream, followed by Watney's Red Barrel beer. It was going to be a while before a new engine came, and on his second night there two Land Rovers arrived. One of the drivers walked in, and George recognised him as living in the same street as he did back home, and they celebrated for the rest of the night. (*See also, England, Cyprus*).

CYPRUS

In 1954 the British Government decided to make Cyprus their new British Middle East Forces Military Headquarters, leaving their previous HQ in Egypt because of severe disruptive actions by the Egyptians. Cyprus had been in Britain's possession since 1878, but this decision angered the Greek Cypriots who were against British Colonial rule, and were aiming at self-determination and union with Greece, known as *Enosis*, or union with the Greek mainland.

British soldiers soon found themselves fighting terrorists, known as the Greek Cypriot Freedom Fighters (EOKA), under the leadership of Bishop Makarios, the Orthodox Bishop of Cyprus and Col. Grivas, an officer in the Greek Army. In April 1955 the first shots were fired by EOKA against the British Army, and this continued until 1959. Over 350 British Servicemen were killed between 1955 and 1959, many of them young National Servicemen.

CLIFF BAKER

Grenadier Guards, 1957-60

After his basic training for the Grenadier Guards for 13 weeks at Caterham, Cliff did another eight weeks field training at Pirbright before being posted to the 3rd Battalion near to Nicosia in Cyprus. The main duties there were patrolling in Nicosia, searching nearby villages for EOKA activists, and doing static guard duties at the central prison, various police stations, and most importantly as it turned out, at a Greek Orthodox Monastery named Panaia Tou Machera, near the village of Lzania. (*See Pic. No. 56*).

The monastery played a vital role during the armed struggle by EOKA (The national organisation of Cypriot fighters), and it was near there that the second-in-command of EOKA, Gregoris Pieris Afxientiou was killed by British soldiers. The

Grenadiers did many guards at the monastery, and Cliff remembers doing quite a few himself, and it was there that he got to know the Abbot Ireneos Vassilou, and began to take a lot of photographs of the monastery and the monks who lived there.

After Cliff left the Army in 1959 he became friendly with a Greek Cypriot who had left Cyprus to come to England when the EOKA trouble started. He knew about Cliff's time in Cyprus, and suggested that he should visit the Island again, and Cliff agreed to go with him and his wife, on condition that they visited the old monastery. Armed with lots of photographs that he had taken on his previous time there, but not expecting to know anyone in the monastery after 20 years or so, Cliff was pleasantly surprised to see one of the monks still living there. The monk told him that Abbot Ireneos Vassilou was now a Bishop based in Birmingham. (*See Pic. No. 55*).

The next day Cliff and his friend went to see his friend's uncle who lived in Nicosia. They told him about their visit to the monastery, and showed him some of the old photographs, to which he responded by saying that some of the monks in the photographs were actually EOKA, dressed as monks. (*See Pic. No. 54*). In fact he said that one of them posing as a monk in the photographs, now actually worked for the British Consulate as a chauffeur, and he arranged for Cliff to meet him the next day, and he verified that he was on the photographs.

When Cliff arrived back in England from his Cyprus visit he decided to look up Bishop Ireneos Vassilou, and arranged to meet him at his home in Birmingham, and they had a long chat. He saw the photos, and confirmed that some EOKA were dressed as monks, and he also told Cliff that he had given permission for British soldiers to use rooms in the monastery, instead of sleeping outside in tents. The British authorities had been suspicious of EOKA activity inside the monastery for some time, as the area around the monastery was known to be a hotbed of EOKA activity, but had no actual proof of this. By having soldiers inside the monastery it was seen as a way of keeping the EOKA out, and the monks were under virtual house arrest. Unfortunately, as was confirmed later, this also meant that all military radio messages both to and from the monastery were monitored by EOKA, and this must have had a negative effect on any future house-to-house searches for EOKA terrorists in the nearby villages, as they would have been given advance warning.

RAY MILES

Devon and Cornwall Light Infantry, 1947-49

For his National Service Ray started off in Greece in 1947 with the 1st Battalion Devon and Cornwall Light Infantry, being just outside Athens, fighting the Communist guerrillas, who were out to destroy the Greek monarchy. Ray remembers being on duty one day in Greece, and had arranged with a mate of his to have a kip. He went into this little place and found what he thought were some packing cases, but he discovered later that he was having a kip in a morgue, lying on someone's coffin!

When both battalions of the DCLI amalgamated they met up in Cyprus, at Dhekelia, where they were guarding between 14,000 and 20,000 Jews, impatiently awaiting their turn to be transported to Israel. They used to dig tunnels from inside the camp to the outside, to try to escape, and on one occasion Ray was on sentry duty on top of the sentry boxes. The Cypriots used to get paid by the Israelis there to sabotage the electrics, so that when the lights went out they had to come down from the sentry box and patrol the perimeter.

On one occasion Ray heard a rustle in the bushes, so he let four rounds go, just say ten feet away from those bushes – and Ray was a marksman! Two of them stood up and screamed: '*No shoot, no shoot.*' Somehow, marksman or not, Ray had missed them. Then out of another bush close by another two stood up with their hands up. Out of the 26 that had escaped there were only four that were caught, all by Ray. The others were later captured at Famagusta. When there was an incident like that they used to turn out from the battalion in Dhekelia and come up in trucks to investigate.

From Cyprus Ray Miles was posted to Argeisha, Somaliland, and then to Mandeira, up in the mountains, on peacekeeping duties. They occasionally went out lion shooting. The lions came down from the mountains to attack the camels, so it was protection for the villagers to take a shooting party. They used to go out in a truck to the foot of the mountains, near Mandeira prison. On one occasion when they shot a lion the officers presented it to the governor of the prison.

In Ray's opinion National Service should never have been done away with, because young men of today really need it.

REX STRAWSON

Devon and Cornwall Light Infantry, 1947-49

Choosing the King's Own Rifle Corps for his National Service in 1947, (because his brother was in that regiment),

Rex did his basic training in Northern Ireland at Hollywood Barracks, Belfast, and volunteered for paratrooper training. He embarked on the troopship *Otranto* and set sail for Athens, Greece, a civil war zone where the Greek Nationalists were fighting the Greek Communists, and joined his new regiment, the 2nd Battalion of the Duke of Cornwall's Light Infantry. Rex wanted to be a regimental policeman, but he was made company runner in the HQ office instead.

He was then sent to the 1st Battalion of the DCLI at Famagusta in Cyprus, where he became company clerk. In 1948 Israel was being formed, and only so many Jewish immigrants were allowed to settle in Israel each month. Anything in excess of that number were shipped over to Cyprus and put into camps at Xylotimbu, holding some 20,000 people at any one time, and were known as illegal Jewish immigrants. Their feeding and medical welfare was the responsibility of the British, and that is why they were there, but not for long, because they were soon to be on their way to Somaliland.

(See also, Somaliland, Kenya and Last Thoughts).

JACK TURNER

Devon and Cornwall Light Infantry, 1946-48

Responding to a command to 'Come and Join Us' for two years, with no way of getting out of it, except as a conscientious objector, Jack saw his National Service in the Devon and Cornwall Light Infantry (DCLI) between 1946-48. He shared good and bad times with lots of lads in the same predicament, and made many good friends along the way. For that reason he prefers just to remember the daft things they did, hoping not to get caught out.

There was one camp in training, where ATS girls (Auxiliary Territorial Service) were also in, but separated by a road and a high fence, and covered in camouflage netting to give them privacy, and strictly out of bounds to squaddies. One morning at RSM's parade when the Light Infantry flag was to be put up, it was seen that two pairs of 'passion killers' (large ladies' khaki bloomers), had been hoisted at the top of the flagpole. This caused a hell of a stink and lots of extra drills, but at least it showed that PK's would stay up anywhere!

Jack was off duty one night in Cyprus when he was told to escort an ambulance taking four expectant Jewish women to hospital in Nicosia. After leaving Xylotimbu one woman was getting upset as her baby was starting. The driver pulled up alongside a house and Jack was told to go and ask for hot water. A Cypriot old man answered the door with a gun in his hand, and he was glad to get away with the hot water. The nurse was telling him to hurry up, so he did, just in time to see a baby's head popping out. Jack had to stand with a pail in his hands, while she delivered and washed the baby and mother. Told to return the pail, Jack left it near the door and ran over to a bush to leave his stomach contents behind. On his way back to the ambulance he saw the driver laughing his head off, as he had known what was coming, being an old soldier, having driven many women to hospital.

In the early 1990s a request was made through a national newspaper for help in finding three soldiers who had served in the Xylotimbu camps in Cyprus in 1948 from a Jewish lady, who had been a little red-haired seven-year-old girl at the time, called Mirium. She used to stand at the main gate, and was seen by a corporal who delivered post to the camp, who told two others, one a camp driver, and the other a cook (Jack Turner). They devised a plan to give the little girl fruit, sweets, and chocolate every day when the post corporal arrived. But in the middle of 1949 the DCLI were moving to East Africa, so they had a photo taken of the three of them and gave it to the young girl before they left. Many years later the girl, now a married lady, decided she wanted to find her three soldiers and thank them, and appealed through the English media. This was seen by Jack, who eventually found the other two, and was instrumental in re-uniting them all together at a DCLI re-union night in Cornwall. *(See also, Somaliland and Last Thoughts)*.

JOHN ROBINSON

Green Howards, 1954-56

After completing his basic training in the Green Howards in 1954, *(See Pic. No. 51)* John went on an NCO's cadre course for six weeks at York and qualified as a lance corporal, *(See Pic. No. 50)* but the lads he trained with went on leave and then to Cyprus. He was still sent to Cyprus, but by then the next platoon had trained. John was given two stripes to transfer these new lads by train from Darlington to a transit camp at Goole Street, centre of London. On the way to King's Cross a young officer passed down the corridor and noticed John sitting with the others, and reprimanded him for it. He told John that it was not right to travel with ordinary soldiers, he had to sit somewhere else.

John eventually arrived in Cyprus and was based at Alma Barracks in Famagusta, a tented camp with a concrete floor.

The previous tenants had served in Suez first and then Cyprus, and that is how the camp had come to be there. To start with John noticed the Turkish flag in one part of the area, and the Greek flag in another, and that is how it started. One night a Greek was found with his throat cut, the next a Turk, the same. The Howards were fully stretched to try to keep them apart.

Six Green Howards were taken by Greek police to a police station in the mountains, to live there for 48 hours on iron rations, where a jeep would visit on a night to see if they were all right. They were told one particular night to sound the alarm and they turned out, but the Greek police did not bother, saying later that they knew it was just a practice - but the Howards were there for their benefit.

They had a detachment in Larnaca police station on another occasion, and were turned out to find youths throwing large rocks. An officer gave the order to fire tear gas into the crowd and advance, but he gave the order too soon, and the remnants of tear gas made them all cry, and they could not see anything.

Being good at any sport could make life a lot easier in the Army, as John soon found out. He enjoyed being part of 6 Platoon's Cross Country team whenever they competed – and all the perks that went with it! (*See Pic. No. 52*).

One day top Commissioner Sir William Slim was coming to their camp, so they were up at three in the morning to do lots of bulling, and lined up on the parade ground for his arrival by helicopter. Clouds of dust were caused, which wiped out all those hours of bull in just one minute. Slim left from Famagusta and all the battalion turned out with five rounds each, because they were expecting trouble.

On a training course in Cyprus in the armoury, a corporal was messing about with a small millimetre mortar bomb mechanism, which exploded, and John got a piece in his arm, and a sergeant called Tom Heron got a piece in his leg. They were rushed in an ambulance from Larnaca to the military hospital in Nicosia, where they were told the pieces would work themselves out, so no operations were needed. John went out drinking with this sergeant before the ambulance came for them to go back to camp.

The Howards came home by troopship, (*See Pic. No. 53*) and the troubles had really started in Cyprus by then, with Bishop Makarios and Colonel Grivas, leader of the guerrillas, stirring up most of the disturbances. Fortunately, none of their 800 men were killed during their tour of duty.

In 2006 John and nine other Green Howards went to London for the annual Remembrance weekend, with tickets for the British Legion Show at the Albert Hall. They bumped into some Guisborough Green Howards, who put them in touch with the secretary of the London branch of the Green Howards. He advised John to get in touch with the Newcastle secretary of the Green Howards' Association, who turned out to be Tom Heron – who he had not seen for over 50 years!

GEOFF BARWICK
Royal Signals, 1960-63

Geoff reckons that the fitness he gained during his Royal Signals basic training at Catterick has lasted him for the rest of his life. He was prevented from going home on leave one

Friday night, because of having dirty boots, and was told to go and see the sergeant major, but he told Geoff. to get himself home.

His overseas posting was to Episkopi, in Cyprus, where there was a good set of lads with good officers, and it was a quiet time for that country, but even so there had been snipers taking pot shots as the lads played football at Happy Valley. Because the Government were running National Service down, and were short of Regulars, Geoff and his pals had to serve another six months, making two-and- a-half years in total.

On the aircraft going out to Cyprus, in the days when Jack Spot was a leading gangster in London, and this lad's uncle was part of that scene. The 19-year-old had accidentally bumped into Jack Spot in a London street by accident, and Jack Spot put out a contract on him. So there he was sat in the aircraft, and the pilot came along to go into the toilet. The young lad inquired who that was, and when told that it was the pilot, the blood drained from his face, and he went absolutely white. Geoff asked what was the matter, and the lad asked: '*Who's flying the aeroplane?*' Geoff gently explained that the pilot had either put it on to automatic pilot, or the co-pilot was flying it. This brought a huge sigh of relief, but he didn't quite believe him. Not until he saw the pilot get back into the cockpit.

One of the lads had been a Teddy Boy back home, and one of the corporals was on his back all of the time. So eventually he told the corporal straight: 'You have another go at me, and they will find you outside the billet one dark night, and you will be in a mess.' The corporal persisted in the bullying, and it happened exactly as the bullied victim had forecast. The young lad was up before the RSM the next day, and when he was asked later how on earth he had got off the charge, he replied that he had written down ten very good excuses, whittled them down to three, then used the best of the three.

Geoff experienced great camaraderie during his National Service, not equalled since. He knew that if ever he was in a critical situation then his mates would be there for him.

(See also, Germany).

MIKE FOSTER

Royal Military Police

Mike served with 6 Dog Company, Cyprus. Their unit consisted of an HQ at Dhekelia, and several small sections spread across the Island.

Prior to the annual inspection by the CO to outlying sections, their sergeant (Big Nick) Nicholls decided to spruce up the compound area at Episkopi, which consisted of five RMP dog handlers and 12 Cypriot auxiliary handlers. One of his ideas was to create a garden area around the flagpole base. They toiled under the hot sun building a dry stone wall from broken paving slabs, and it was then filled with soil. There was only one thing missing - plants, until a couple of their Turkish police auxiliaries said they could provide plants. They arrived, were put in, watered and grew well, putting on plenty of foliage, and Sgt. Nicholls was very pleased.

The week of the CO's visit they were all very busy, painting anything that did not move white; the compound area was raked over, and the duct boards scrubbed. Then they practised their drill, but the auxiliaries did not get it right, so Sgt. Nicholls did his 'Grand Old Duke of York' act until they did. They all thought this highly amusing so he made them join in. It was then pointed out by an auxiliary NCO that the plants were hashish (cannabis). The foul language could be heard in Nicosia, as plants and Turkish Cypriots were scattered to the four winds. They all fell about laughing, and their lives were made hell for days after. But, as Mike says: 'It was worth it.'

Another tale took place at the Cambria Camp, Dhekelia, HQ 6 Dog Co. RMP, where the CO, Major Tapply was taking his Saturday morning inspection of the tent lines.

CO: *'Why is this tent looking like a Chinese laundry?'*

Tent spokesman: *'We are drying clothing and kit that got wet on duty last night, Sir.'*

CO: *'Why don't you hang it up outside to dry?'*

Tent spokesman: *'Because it's raining outside, Sir'*

CO to CSM Lowther: *'Take that man's name.'*

GORDON DIXON

While in Cyprus the Suez campaign started up in 1956, and Gordon was involved in getting supplies of transport, ammunition and rations to the troops on the ground, ensuring the pallets were dropped onto the dropping zone. On another occasion in Cyprus, during the civil war involving Archbishop Makarios and Col. Grivas, he was nearly killed there because they were all staying at a transit camp outside Nicosia airport and a liberty wagon used to take them to the NAAFI. Gordon's truck left at 21.45 and they had just cleared the perimeter when terrorists blew the NAAFI up killing dozens inside. (*See also, England, Bahrain*).

JOHN FAWCETT

Royal Air Force, 1955-57

Just before the Habbanyia base in Iraq was closed down in 1956 the Suez crisis blew up, and John and a few others from the RAF Signals unit were sent to Cyprus to man the radar units there, at El Greco, just south of Ayia Napa, for around eight months.

There was plenty of trouble with the locals there, because the EOKA uprising was at full strength, and a lot of National Service lads were killed during that period, including one from South Bank, killed in the NAAFI at Nicosia. The civilians employed there had been smuggling bombs into the camp before the explosion. They had to bring all the supplies and water up from Ayia Napa in tankers, and the lads had to run the gauntlet from a number of attacks from the Cypriots.

When they had to move the radar installations, the Royal Artillery were needed to go before them in their armoured cars to ensure a safe journey. They would have to crawl forwards and knock a wall down to get round a tight corner sometimes, which did not go down too well with the Cypriots. Crawling down a very narrow street they would hear a rattle, and usually it would be large stones being thrown by the local youths, but they would fear the worst, because hand grenades had been thrown at them in the past.

(*See also, Iraq*).

GIBRALTAR

Gibraltar was captured from Spain in 1704, and was formally awarded to Britain in 1713 by the Treaty of Utrecht. Since then, Spain has laid claim to Gibraltar on numerous occasions. Gibraltar is well situated to observe shipping channels through the Straits and could dominate the western entrance to the Mediterranean in time of war. Its communication systems, runway facilities and harbour make it an important base for NATO.

In 1992 the last British Regular Infantry battalion left Gibraltar, and was replaced by the Royal Gibraltar Regiment. Despite this, the headquarter staff appointments are still filled by members of the British Armed Forces.

BARRIE SHEPHERDSON
Prince of Wales' Own, 1960-62

Barrie was a member of the boxing team, and on one occasion between boxing bouts a wrestling match between a Ted Fussey, in the Regimental Police, (but in the process of 'buying himself out' to become a professional wrestler) had washed his gear, because he had been asked to put on a demonstration wrestling match with a black belt judo chap, from HMS *Rook*, Gibraltar. At some stage of getting ready someone had stolen his leotard, and so he decided to do this bout in his swimming trunks. During the bout, after much rolling about on the canvas, his 'tackle' slipped out of his trunks, unnoticed by Ted, but definitely noticed by the Governor's wife, Lady Keightley, and all the WRACS from the Princess Royal block who were attending. From then on everything that he did attracted a big cheer from them and the boxing supporters watching, and Ted mistook this for encouragement. He went to every rope in turn and gave his growls and snarls, as per 'Haystacks,' and the whole place was hysterical, until the RSM decided enough was enough! Ted subsequently made a career in wrestling, and appeared on television on several occasions.

Another day, practising for a big parade, the Colours presentation for the amalgamation of the Regiments, and his friend Bob was in the front rank. As it was a practise they were all in shorts, puttees, etc., semi-tropical. During the course of this they were marking time, and Bob's underpants dropped down and formed two great loops around his knees, which as they were marking time in slow time, his marking time got shorter and shorter, until the RSM spotted him and said: *'Sarn't major, Gladys here is losing her knickers.'* The whole parade was called to a halt while Bob pulled his underpants up, and they all carried on.

One morning at muster parade the Company Commander approached Barrie and said that he had heard that he had been having good results with the Energa anti-tank grenade launcher which clipped onto a rifle on a discharger. He asked Barrie to try to break up a rock lying above their incinerator, which threatened to fall onto it and damage it. They had tried everything to dislodge this rock, even a rocket launcher, but all that did was to blow out all the office windows, so it was now up to Barrie. His first shot loosened it, and the second shot brought the 60-ton rock down, and did Barrie's reputation no harm at all.

While on leave at home in Hull, he had heard about an oil tanker that had blown in half in the Mediterranean – the *Esso*

Durham. They towed the two halves into Gibraltar on the mole out at sea. At the time Barrie and his pal were on an initiative test and their project was to go and interview the captain and ask him how he had managed to blow his ship in half. As luck would have it he had not been in charge at the time, that had been his relief, so he told them everything over the contents of his beer fridge.

As a bonus, two other people had been shown around the ship at a different time, and the only way they could all get back was by climbing down this ladder, and they would then be run ashore in the ship's lifeboat. While Barrie and his pal were sat in the lifeboat they were told to hang on because there were some more people to come, who turned out to be visiting dignitaries, a mother and daughter, in the days of suspenders and stockings, and Barrie and his mate had a ball! The climb down the ladder by the two ladies was most instructional!

One of the lads had been brought up by his uncle, a bookie. While shopping in Gibraltar he picked up a very good pair of binoculars for his uncle who had looked after him. They were moved into another barracks just outside the Princess Royal block, occupied by the WRACS, renowned for not drawing their curtains when undressing on an evening. So these pristine binoculars were then used extensively by 100 sex starved squaddies, and in no time at all they looked very worn indeed. *(See also, Libya, Germany).*

JACK HORNBY

Northumberland Fusiliers, 1947-49

Basic training for Jack was at Catterick Camp for about eight weeks in 1947, and was with the Duke of Wellington's

Regiment for two months. He then went to Pontefract Castle for four weeks with the Yorks. and Lancs., at the Regimental depot, as an orderly room runner. From there he was posted to Strensall, an open camp full of Polish soldiers waiting to go home.

While at Strensall, Jack was standing in the barrack room near a lad called Dimmock, who banged with his fist at the window, which promptly fell out on to Jack's head, causing injuries to his nose and ear. He was on a draft to Khartoum at the time with the Green Howards, but because of his injuries his name was taken off.

One day Jack had had enough, so he walked out on the Thursday and reported back on the following Tuesday to the guardroom, and somehow talked himself out of trouble, and from there he was posted to Gibraltar.

Jack's remaining 16 months National Service was spent in Gibraltar with the Northumberland Fusiliers. One Friday at 5 p.m. he went to La Innes Bay, the nearest place to the camp, and woke up on Monday morning at 9 a.m. in the guardroom at Gibraltar. Jack never found out just how he got back over the border, but he got seven days CB for his pains anyway.

While he was there the Company Adjutant shot himself, his wife and four children, rather than face the consequences of his actions, for allegedly dipping into the garrison funds, which would probably have been very great in those days.

Jack was supposed to be back home in the August of 1947, and they were marched down to the quayside on the given day, waiting for the troop ship to come alongside, but it never did. It came in, but sailed straight out again without picking anyone up. In the event this delayed Jack's demob., and meant that he had to do an extra five extra weeks National Service, with of course no reason at all being offered for the delay.

Eventually Jack was demobbed at Aldershot, but he then went straight to the Union Jack club in London, and spent all his money, around £50, a princely sum in those days. When Jack arrived home he had the paltry sum of three pence in his pocket!

LES DALE
Royal Air Force, 1954-56

When Les and a few other RAF National Service lads arrived at Gibraltar in 1954 they found they were based next to the runway, four to a room, and worked with the Navy on transmitters under the Rock. The Navy personnel were all petty officers and Regulars, who showed them how to work these massive machines. They used to look after the Gibraltar Beacon, which used to send messages out to all incoming aircraft, and which had to be working at all times. Gibraltar was in a strategic position in the Mediterranean, that was why they were there. Being in Signals they were the only ones allowed on top of the Rock, which was over 1000 feet high.

They had just got new CRDF (Cathode ray direction finding) radar, and they had to put a new cable from the bottom to the top of the rock, and every night the Spanish fishermen would be waiting offshore to steal the cable that had just been laid. They were quite poor people and they would sell it, and this went on for quite a while until it got too high for them to reach.

Being at sea level, when it rained hard the drains could not take the water away, and you could go to the pictures at six in the evening and come out at eight, and have to take your socks and shoes off, and be knee deep in water, just like a gigantic flash flood.

Every day the Spanish workers would come across, and every day they would be sent back over the border, after their day's work was done. Les and his pals used to watch them where the bus stations were; standing above them as they were putting all the stuff away they had bought, and could see the ladies pull their skirts up and tuck things down their knickers.

When Les went over into Spain he could see where the old German Messerschmits and Dorniers were just lying there going to rust, about 10 years after the war. Despite being officially neutral during the war, Spain had been a little bit more than just neutral, and they had not even bothered to clear up the evidence of being involved with the Germans, as a friendly base.

A corporal was employed full time to look after the monkeys on the Rock, because legend has it that when the last monkey left, so would the British! Winston Churchill had ordered that the dwindling population of monkeys on the Rock be greatly increased during the war, so their importance was symbolic.

If you went to a dance, or you wanted to take a local girl out, things were a little different from what went on in England. Les did go to a dance and met this girl and asked her out to the pictures, and they sat there together waiting for the film to start. Suddenly, he was conscious that they were not alone. Les turned round to see that sat behind them were mummy and daddy, and also her brother and sister, too. They were there to protect her honour, such was the power of the

Catholic Church at that time in such matters. Parents were very protective of their daughters. Les decided there and then that this was not an experience to be repeated!

Another time a Scottish Regiment of soldiers came in wearing their kilts, and some of the local lads started making fun of these soldiers in skirts. This inevitably started a fight going, because they could not be seen to get away with that. Apart from the odd incident relations between the locals and the servicemen were very good, so much so that the locals used to try and save up enough money to go over to England for a visit.

GREECE

The reason for the trouble in Greece after the Germans were defeated in 1945, was that the Communists who had also been fighting with the Allies against the Germans, wanted rid of the Greek Royalty, and that explained why British soldiers were still there, to prevent that happening. However, they had to be relieved, because they had been right through the war, and were more than ready for demobilisation, and that explains why National Servicemen were sent there to relieve them.

CHARLIE ROGERS
Royal Engineers, 1945-48

Charlie did his basic training at Bradford in 1945, and was then sent to the Royal Engineers driving school at Chesterfield, before being posted abroad to Piraeus, near

Athens, in Greece. On his first night in Greece Charlie and his new National Service Royal Engineers mates had a night out in Athens going round every bar they could find. They were all dives, and they drank themselves silly, with Charlie being unable to get up the next morning for reveille, but he managed to escape any punishment somehow.

From there he was posted to Salonika, in Northern Greece, which was a terrible place in winter, and they were billeted in an old town hall. Their job was to transport heavy vehicles and distribute equipment, but one day Charlie was stuck in the mountains with a corporal. They had picked a trailer up and had four mountain passes to ascend, but got stuck on the third pass in heavy snow, so they rolled it into a ditch to stop the Communists getting their hands on it. Luckily for them there was a transport café at the top of the pass, and they had to stay there for a week until they were relieved. It seemed a long week, because it was weird and deathly quiet up there, and the café did not have a toilet, which meant of course doing everything outside, and listening to the wolves as they did so.

(See also, Israel, Egypt).

IRAQ

Britain's principal concerns for the control of Iraq after World War Two were to maintain connections with India and to sustain the flow of oil in the region. As naval power was overtaken by air power, air bases were now required to link Britain to her most important Imperial possession, India. It was for this reason that the British tried to maintain complete control over the air bases when negotiating for the technical independence of Iraq. This strategic importance was only eclipsed in 1947 when India was granted independence. By this time, the value of oil had increased in importance, and so Iraq remained a vital strategic concern.

JOHN FAWCETT

From Egypt John was posted to Amman, in Jordan, but it only lasted three nights, because they were closing that down too. From there he went to Habbanyia in Iraq, but he stayed about nine months there, where 123 Signals Unit, had a little radar unit on a plateau above the camp. It was well established, being there since the 1930s, with a swimming pool, and lots of Indians helping, who washed and ironed their clothes for a few shillings. This was a very civilised garrison with big generators for the power supplies, which sometimes had to be operated by hand when they became affected by the great heat.

They were on guard duty there one night patrolling around the tents, but during the night the wily Iraqis had cut open the supply tent and stolen all the tyres, and all the spare wheels had gone from the vehicles. Every tyre and wheel had been stolen while the guards had been having a quiet cup of coffee and a sandwich! There were a lot of Iraqi drivers employed by the RAF coming in and out of camp, and the odd RAF or Army lorry would go trundling out of the gates, and never come back again; stolen by arrangement. Regular Iraqi drivers in an Army wagon were commonplace to the sentry at the gate, recognised, waved on, and driven off, etc.

Towards the end, King Faisal (later killed by the Iraqi rebels), used to drive in with his MG sports car to have a civilised conversation with the officers. (*See also, Egypt, Cyprus*).

ALAN EDNEY

Royal Air Force, 1952-54

Alan went straight from school to work at the Atomic Centre at Harwell with his company, and they were in the process of laying oil pipelines through Kuwait, and he wanted to go, but he was told that he had to do his National Service first. Alan did his square bashing at RAF Bridgenorth for eight weeks in 1952, and was then posted to RAF Upwood, near Peterborough, and stayed there just over a year, where Lincoln bombers were based, and the CO had his own personal wooden Mosquito aeroplane. His training at Upwood was as Clerk EA, but he never did that again when he left there. Alan clearly remembers taking part in the Coronation Parade in pouring rain in June 1953, in navy blue with white webbing. Very smart at first, but it was reduced to a soggy mess as the day went on.

Shortly after this Alan was posted to Iraq, at a place called Habbanya, 60 miles outside Baghdad, and spent nearly 18 very hot months there before being posted to Basra in 1954, travelling by train with wooden seats. While he was at Basra, Alan was given a very unusual job indeed. He went to work every day by boat at the Shapelarab river, where the Tigress and the Euphrates meet. He used to go to the dockside, go on to the dock and was in charge of the local labourers who unloaded the ships, tied everything up with wire and sent them on their way, back up to Baghdad, or up to Shaiba.

There were three of them doing this supervisory job, two SACs, and Alan, an LAC.

Even though he was in the RAF Alan never saw an aeroplane while he was at Basra, because he spent the whole time at the dockside. Alan had to guard the armoury at Habbanya, with 'one up the spout,' a dangerous place even in those days, always carrying live ammunition. It was so big they had to have a taxi service on site to take them from A to B.

He saw terrible things while he was over there, like bodies floating in the docks at Basra, because no-one knew who it was, and they were just left there. In peacetime, even in Baghdad, people just openly urinated in the street.

Alan got different things out of National Service, like finding out how other people live, being made aware of different cultures, etc., and being grateful for what we have in England.

ISRAEL

(See Palestine introduction)

CHARLIE ROGERS

Charlie's Royal Engineers unit was disbanded after their tour of duty in Greece, and he found himself posted to Mount Carmel in Haifa, a Paratrooper garrison. On his first day there the oil refinery was blown up, with clouds of smoke everywhere, and he found that while the Jews were trying to get into Palestine by boat, both the Jews and Arabs were targeting each other – and both factions were aiming at the British soldiers!

It was the time of the handover, and the British were trying to get out. They were in civilian billets in Haifa, and had to tie their guns to their beds at night, or they would be stolen. There was a curfew on the soldiers at night, and they all had to be in by eight. There were guards on every bank, and they used sandbags to stop them being raided, and if the lads wanted an afternoon out, they had to go around in fours. The Paras were on guard duty at night, and fired intermittently all the time, because the Jews and Arabs were always causing trouble.

Occasionally Charlie had to drive officers to Jerusalem and back in a day, which was quite a long distance. This entailed driving at high speed both there and back, but he enjoyed the 'buzz.'

JORDAN

In 1946 Trans Jordan became independent, but gave Britain rights to maintain bases there. Trans Jordan then absorbed parts of Palestine, and became known as Jordan in 1950, and was governed by King Hussein, with the assistance of British Army officers. Anti-British feeling became high, especially after the Suez invasion of 1956, and the 1948 Anglo-Jordanian Treaty was terminated soon after. British troops finally left Jordan in 1957.

DESMOND MOORE

Irish Guards, 1956-59

Desmond was a student in Dublin in 1956, going into banking, but ended up in Liverpool, and knowing he would have to do National Service, he went down to the recruiting office to sign on. There he met the biggest man he had ever seen called Sergeant O'Hagan. He took Des into a back room, put a bearskin on his head and told him that in six months time he would be standing outside Buckingham Palace where all the young ladies of Europe would slip their telephone numbers into his jacket, and he couldn't go wrong. Des thought he would like to have some of that, as a very impressionable young man, and sure enough six months later, that's exactly what happened! The Irish Guards were stationed at Wellington Barracks, and were on public duties, and coming through the park were all the young ladies, very keen to go out with a Guardsman.

After a while Des grew tired of all that, and he volunteered for the Guards Parachute Company, pathfinders for the whole of the Parachute Regiment. It was all Guardsmen who founded the SAS, and this was a sort of spin-off, and when they disbanded them they made up 'G' squadron, SAS.

He served in Cyprus and Jordan, going many times up into the Troodos mountains chasing Col. Grivas' terrorists. In 1958 when King Hussain's cousin King Faisal was murdered in Iraq, they sent the Parachute Brigade into Jordan. They were surrounded by the Tank Regiment, and they had the Jordanian Army by its side to act as a deterrent to further violence.

One funny thing happened in Jordan. They had been drinking with some RAF lads who had a squadron of Hawker Hunters and the Red Arrows who were their support in Jordan, based on the Amman airfield. The Guards were going out on an OP (Operations Posting), and when on a mission in the desert they took off all their wing mirrors. They were in a 3-ton Bedford, and this pilot who had been drinking with them the previous night decided to chase them up the runway for a bit of sport. They couldn't see what was happening because they were in the back, but the Captain in the front saw this aeroplane getting closer, so he ordered the driver to stop, and he did, hard. The Valletta plane cut the canopy right off the top of the Bedford, and also knocked the cab down into a ravine, and the pilot ended up being cashiered back in Cyprus. Des. was in charge of the MT at the time, and he had to fill in a graph before and after the event, and the guys back at the War Office must have had great fun sorting it all out.

All the Guards were at Caterham before it closed, and coming round from their Company there was a very sharp corner, and they had to look down to see they didn't slip, as they were wearing hobnailed boots, and a voice would say: 'It's no good looking down, the Scots Guards have been this way – you'll find nothing on the ground!'

MALTA

Even Malta, the small Mediterranean Island awarded the George Cross for its bravery in resisting the Germans during World War Two, wanted independence. Unlike most other countries however, they did not go down the path of out and out violence to achieve it. There were only minor scuffles involving the British military and the local inhabitants, and generally relations between the two were friendly. In fact Malta was regarded as a good posting by those who served there, with its fantastic warm climate, if sometimes regarded as a little boring. Malta achieved full independence on September 21, 1964, and there was a withdrawal of British troops in 1979.

RON JEROME

The Suez conflict started in August 1956 and Ron Jerome, Grenadier Guards, was drafted out for that, stopping at Malta, awaiting the move to Egypt, which never came. The Suez problem calmed down, and they were waiting to see what was going to happen next. The Reservists that were called up in the Emergency were all itching to get back home to their wives and families, (having already served their two years National Service), but the powers that be kept them guessing. They were getting very impatient, and they had a Reservist in the police with them, and he told Ron that all the Reservists were going to mutiny if no positive news was forthcoming.

That evening they were going to march on the officers' mess, and demand to be given a date when they could expect to return to civvy street. He wanted Ron to join them, and since it was getting close to when he was due to come out, he did. They got an audience with the CO, received some answers and went back to camp. Next morning Ron reported to the guardroom (tent) and the provost sergeant was there to greet him. He was not in a good mood, and wanted to know where Ron had been the previous night, because: 'Those bloody part-timers had a mutiny, and Ron should have been there to stop them.'

Ron thought his time in the Regiment doing National Service was the best thing that ever happened to him, and it was a great pity that we didn't have something similar in place today.

GORDON NOBLE

Royal Air Force, 1955-57

Gordon had his RAF National Service training at Middle Wallop in 1955, before being posted to Malta during the Suez crisis. He was stationed at RAF Takali, but used to work in Valletta, where all the radar and plotting equipment was in the cliff face, as it was during the Second World War, but is now a museum. Canberra bombers used to fly from Luqa airport and from Cyprus and they had to plot them. Gordon used to plot the signals from the radar stations around the Maltese coast when they came back, and also plot the fighters when they were doing exercises. They only used to work from early morning to mid-day, due to the heat, and had to be ready for night flying duties later in the day.

He went back on holiday a few years ago and found that the hut he used to work in was still there, as were the other five, all in a line, as they had been in 1955, only now they were being used as craft huts, as part of a craft village, doing glassblowing, leather goods, etc. The locals were very friendly to young National Servicemen in those days, being not too long after the war, and thought a lot of English people, and most of them spoke English.

Gordon woke up one particular night when the lads from the next billet invited him round to see all these signs they had collected. Three Shell signs normally sitting on the top of petrol pumps, SL Extra signs, Pepsi Cola signs, road signs, a huge Maltese flag in the background, and the local newspaper bulleting board. How they got all these through the guardhouse is anyone's guess, and they only borrowed them for a short time and took them all back again. That was the fun of it, without anyone noticing they had been taken in the first place.

In Gordon's billet they had a lad who suffered from terrible wind, and could make one to order. One night after lights out he was wandering about in his pyjamas, and a discussion broke out as to whether it was combustible or not, so the rest of the lads decided to conduct an experiment. This lad lay on the bed, while another made ready with a lighter, and the rest of them gathered round. He let fire and there was a great blue flame and a great cry of pain with scorch marks on his pyjamas, and everyone just fell about laughing. All except the victim of the experiment, who finished up in hospital with minor burns to his rear!

They used to go out on a night for a few beers, and hire a gary, an open horse drawn cart; two or three in a line, officially holding six, but they had eight to ten in at a time. They played Cowboys and Indians when they were full of beer and larking about in general, until they were dropped outside the main camp gate, in a sort of taxi service.

For Gordon National Service was not a waste of time, enjoying his plotting job and swimming in the harbour in his free time, and he saw all round the Island beaches, etc., and found the different museums all very interesting.

After his National Service was completed Gordon went back to the sheet metal working job he had done previously.

KEITH LIPTHORPE

Royal Air Force, 1951-53

After his RAF training in 1951 Keith was posted abroad, and had a wonderful time in Malta, playing in the band most of the time. Although trained as an accounts clerk, he only spent a couple of days a week at the most doing that, and after 18 months he was transferred to Air Movements, with the same arrangements there as well, playing mostly in the band. He played in various bands, Combined Services bands, brass bands, and then he had his own band, playing in the officers' and sergeants' messes, and altogether was playing about six days a week. He also found time to play in other bands, and played on the Maltese radio, and later joined the Tom Warner band.

One day while playing in the band he was approached by Lord Mountbatten, who remarked that his instrument was all blistered. Keith explained that it was the long journey in the hull of the ship from England that had damaged it, and that he could not get it treated there because it was too expensive to repair for a National Serviceman; it would have to wait until he got home to lacquer it. A year later Mountbatten approached him again, remarking that he still had not re-lacquered his trumpet, but Keith repeated his story.

Sometimes Keith was playing his trumpet until three in the morning, and he had to be at work by 7.30 a.m. doing cost accounts. He also had to give information to the pilots before they went on a flight. In his first year Keith had no time for drills or guard duties, but in his last year he did have to do some of them.

Keith continued to have a fantastic time, playing in the Maltese band in the main square in Luqa, in exactly the same place as crooner Frankie Vaughan had performed a few years previously. Also in the band was a wonderful saxophonist, and a full-time musician from the famous Manchester Co-op band, making three good musicians playing a trombone, a tenor horn and Keith on the trumpet.

During his stay in Malta seven aircraft crashed during that period; the first had Commandos on board, which crashed on landing and burst into flames, but 44 of the 45 Marines survived it. The second was a Lancaster which had engine trouble on take-off, and side-swiped into a local village, with all seven crew being killed. Keith volunteered to play the Last Post for this funeral, with Lord Mountbatten and all the air crews, and NATO chiefs from several nations being present as well. Unfortunately, he started on the wrong note, and it became too high and gibberish, and was the longest and most uncomfortable two minutes of his life, but as he was only an amateur nothing further was done about it. No more volunteering for Keith after that though!

Another crash concerned the American Naval Air Force, with their habit of 'buzzing' planes, using them as target practice without firing. This time it happened to be a Lancaster they were 'buzzing,' and all the crew were lost, as it crashed into the sea. The American pilot then ran out of fuel and came into refuel. One morning a Constellation was coming in to land, and it burst into flames upon landing, and it took seven hours to even go near it, because all the shells and bombs inside the aeroplane were exploding all the time.

Keith bought a car in Malta, and saved the duty on it because there was no duty payable in Malta. One afternoon Keith drove up to a Signals camp on the west side of the Island and parked on the rough ground outside. He climbed over the fence, and went into the NAAFI, bought a cup of tea, and was asked by another Serviceman how long he had been there. Keith replied that he was based at Luqa, and the chap was astonished when Keith told him how he had just gained entry, because there were people on guard at this camp, and there was sensitive equipment and information there, and he would not have been let in normally. Unperturbed, Keith went out the same way that he had got in!

Unusually, he was demobbed in Malta, and drove all the way home through Sicily, Italy, Switzerland and France with another Serviceman, stopping at Rome, to see La Scala, and the Coliseum, Milan, Monte Cassino, and eventually reaching Naples and Mount Vesuvius. They had a fantastic journey taking about 12 days to reach England.

All in all, Keith had a wonderful time in the RAF, made lots of new friends, and would not have missed the experience for anything.

PALESTINE

Britain had a League of Nations' mandate from 1918 to administer the country, and try to keep the peace between the many thousands of Jews who were trying to enter the country, with the intention of setting up a Jewish nation, and the Palestinians who already lived there in 1945. Well over 300 British soldiers were killed in the process, some of whom were young National Servicemen. In 1948 Britain withdrew from their mandate, and handed the problem over to the

United Nations, and the state of Israel was formed in that same year.

JOHN BARBER
Irish Guards, 1947-49

After John's basic training for the Irish Guards in 1947 he was posted overseas, and spent just under a year in Palestine, and also had a few weeks in Trans Jordan for training. One day he was a member of a firing party for one of his colleagues, killed by terrorists while on escort duty in the Jerusalem area. They were all standing there at the side of the grave, and a swarm of locusts came by. The sky went black, and the locusts were settling on them as they stood, most disturbing really, as they marched away, crunching on them in the dark.

There were restricted areas in Jerusalem with areas cordoned off, and they, a corporal and two guardsmen, had to escort a rabbi into a restricted area for him to perform a circumcision ceremony, and get him out again safely. He was not supposed to be in that dangerous area of Jerusalem which belonged to the Palestinians, so it was a risky operation for all of them.

John and his platoon had to conduct regular house searches, and one day they found a cache of small arms behind a sink. When they found anything like that they used to turf everyone out of bed, strip search the occupants, and blow the house up. It became a daily business in 1947.

At breakfast one morning at Khissa camp, they were all given an egg cut in half and a piece of bread, and they were all having a good moan. John was really letting off steam, saying: 'That bloody CSM, and the orderly sergeant, they wouldn't put up with this rubbish.' At this point a voice behind him shouted loudly: 'Who's that taking my name in vain'? and there was the company sergeant major. '*Fall in two men,*' and he was escorted to the guard room, where he was given a few punishment drills, but he reckons that he got away with it really.

FRANK JENNINGS
Lincolnshire Regiment, 1946-49

Frank started his National Service with the Royal Warwickshire Regiment in 1946, and was later with the Leicestershire Regiment at Strensall, before being posted to Palestine. Frank had worked on the railways and learned to drive during the war, and drove a lorry before he was called up. When he arrived in Palestine he was in 'D' Company, and they asked for drivers. Not many 18-year-olds could drive then at 18, but he and a Private Kenny volunteered and joined the MT section.

Three vehicles had to go out at a time because of the troubles, and that is why Frank was driving along to a road block where a lorry had been blown up by a roadside bomb, and little did he realise that his friend in training, 19-years-old Private Kenny was killed in it. His name is carved on the memorial at Alrewas.

This was the first conflict after World War Two, and they were on a peacekeeping mission, but all of a sudden it didn't feel like it, especially when hundreds of British soldiers were killed in Palestine during the three years 'peacekeeping,' along with 141 British and Palestine police. The Arabs, and

Jews, between them blew up nearly everything, such as oil depots and police stations, and the railways, etc. Later on there was a troop train blown up where another 29 soldiers lost their lives, plus 36 injured.

Frank says that if you helped the Jews the Palestinians didn't like you, and vice versa, so whatever happened you just couldn't win. The Jews wanted your rifle, and to prevent that you had to chain your rifle to the bed, while the Arabs would just steal from you.

It all seemed just a waste of time, being always on the move. Palestine was a place of no kipping and no sitting down, out on patrols all the time; if not on patrol then searching for hidden weapons and ammunition. They were sent to places where the terrorists had hidden them and they had to dig up those places to find them. They found weapons on both Jews and Palestinians. Frank's mates just could not understand why the Jews were killing British troops, because some of the men had been in the war, and were the ones that had liberated the Jews from the Germans.

Frank was also stationed at Jaffa and Tel Aviv, and they sometimes had to do rooftop guard duties, but he was uneasy because of the Jews and Arabs, alone in a vehicle on occasions, waiting for his mates to come back, with no room to escape. He also had to wait in the truck while they were on railway patrol to take them back to barracks.

Just before Mandate Day in May 1948 they were posted to the 1st Infantry Division at Trans Jordan to sort out the trouble they had There was only one battalion there at the time, the Lincolns, with a few Paras, a few Royal Engineers, and a battery of artillery. The Jordanians were frightened that the Jews were going to take Akaba, and if they got that they could capture Trans Jordan. But the National Service lads didn't know what was going on at the age of 18.

PETER FOWLE

DCLI School of Infantry, 1946-48

The 1st Battalion Duke of Cornwall's Light Infantry (DCLI), were stationed at Palestine in 1946, and Peter Fowle was the Intelligence sergeant in charge of ten National Servicemen in his section. He was given the task of training them up for two different roles when occupying an unfriendly country. The DCLI was the demonstration battalion at the Middle-East School of Infantry. As part of that establishment they were to demonstrate how a British infantry battalion operated in various kinds of warfare.

Peter's Intelligence section was concerned with supplying maps and compass bearings, start lines and sand models for the many exercises carried out by, and in some schemes, against, the officer cadets.

When the battalion eventually assumed internal security duties, the section had to be retrained to deal with a more realistic situation. This included many difficult and unpleasant operations to help keep the peace in a very troubled country. There was now an element of danger in the various tasks undertaken, but those young National Service lads behaved throughout in an exemplary manner, being a credit to their country and regiment. They were a great loss to the Army when they returned to civilian life, and Peter reckons that he couldn't have had ten more proficient and reliable men, as they were boys no longer. (*See Pic. No. 5*).

CHAPTER SIX

Africa

EGYPT

British military presence in Egypt after World War Two was very unpopular, and anti-British demonstrations at first very soon turned into vicious guerrilla warfare against the British Canal Zone Garrison. Even the families of servicemen were targeted, and there were 54 British fatalities altogether. The unrest lasted right up to the withdrawal of British troops in 1955.

DERRY RAWLINGS MM

When the Korean War ended Derry was posted to Egypt for over five months, and enjoyed his stay there, unlike the majority of conscripts. The reason was that he and 14 others had a great job in the officers' mess, eating officers' food; after an exercise in the desert one day when an NCO asked for volunteers to work in there. They did everything, from helping in the cookhouse to cleaning the officers' canteen, acting as batmen and drivers, and had a whale of a time. He was aware though that the Egyptians had thrown hand grenades through the windows of a picture house near Fayed, killing and wounding innocent people. As a result of the Egyptians' hatred of the British at that time, they had to go out of camp four at a time to avoid trouble. *(See also, Korea).*

KEITH DART

Royal and Electrical Mechanical Engineers, 1952-54

Keith was at Blandford Forum in Dorset, for a month, doing his basic training for the REME in 1952, and then moved to Barton Stacey for trade training, before being posted to Egypt by air. Instead of landing in the Canal Zone in the morning it was much later, due to technical problems, and they saw the Pyramids – which they would not otherwise have seen.

From the transit camp they were sent to their different posts in the Canal Zone. Keith was sent to 1 Infantry Division Workshops, Fayed, then to Cassino camp at Fanara, about two miles away, in an ex-POW camp. Relations between the local Egyptians and the troops were strained and it got worse as time went on. Canal Zone incidents were read out after pay parade every two weeks, to keep the soldiers alert and aware of what was going on. Between Fanara and Fayed there was an open-air cinema, and one night the lights went out, and by the time they had the emergency generator going and the lights put on again the Egyptians had stolen miles of copper wire.

One day they saw a Bedouin man riding a camel, with his wife walking 150 yards in front in case of mines exploding, because it was much cheaper to buy a new wife than a camel.

They had heard of this but were sceptical, until they actually saw it!

The Guards used to mount guard over a water filtration plant in that area. About a mile inland from the Suez Canal was the Sweetwater Canal, which was so contaminated that if you fell in there you had to have 14 injections to cover all illnesses. It was basically an open sewer, used for anything and everything, from washing clothes and themselves, calls of nature, a dumping ground and even for dead animals. The smell from it was quite obnoxious, and remarkably the water for the camp came from the Sweetwater, purified by going through the filtration plant. One night the Egyptians took a shot at one of the guards at the filtration plant. They called the Guards out and they went to the nearest village and found over 100 British rifles.

Another day at Suez Docks a wagon had come out and Egyptians jumped on the back and the Regimental Policemen (RPs) on the gate shot them. The local Egyptians waited until the two RPs were back on duty again, and there was a demonstration outside the gate, a distraction, and in the confusion both of the RPs were killed.

There was the canal road which the military were not supposed to use, and there was the military road further inland. The locals reckoned that the military vehicles used to destabilise the banks of the canal. When you came to the end of the military road there was the junction to the Suez-Cairo highway – and the Egyptians were there trying to lob grenades onto the petrol tanks. Also there were trucks with the tarpaulins folded up and some of the trucks had seats in for taking the children to school. The military had to resort to putting mesh front and back, to stop the Egyptians throwing grenades into the trucks.

There were two cinemas out there, one at Fayed and the other at Fanara, and both had ventilation windows at the top of the buildings, and the Egyptians used to try and lob grenades through the windows. So they had to build a 16ft fence so far from these walls, and form a cinema picket, which meant that there had to be military in all the corners of the building, and at the main gate for every performance. Four went in to see the first performance and when it finished there were eight around the building, the same for every performance. All this civil unrest was designed to drive the British out of Suez, and for them to get the Suez Canal back into Egyptian hands.

Keith learned a lot through his National Service, and it definitely was not a waste of time for him, because he was determined to get something out of it, and he did, but not as much as he would have liked.

CHARLIE ROGERS

After six months or so in Israel Charlie applied for a transfer to Egypt, near the Canal Zone in 1948, where a lot of his mates were at the huge depot there, and he was soon swimming in the Suez Canal, watching British ships making the return journey from the Far East. Sometimes they were taken on trips to town in the Canal Zone, or the small lakes for a swim – which was all to change in a few years time! The only entertainment in camp was in the canteen, where they could have a few drinks on an evening.

Now and again he used to take heavy equipment like bulldozers, cranes, etc. down the Suez Canal road to Port

Suez, because they were needed for the British Government's ill-fated Groundnuts Scheme in Kenya. While Charlie was there they regularly employed German POWs awaiting repatriation, as guards, and one even cut Charlie's hair every week.

When out with his mate delivering equipment one day, Charlie realised that some Egyptians had got onto the trailer they were towing and were stealing their equipment. But when he tried to stop them they began stoning him, and he made the decision to let them get on with it, and climbed back into the driver's cab. The Egyptians would steal absolutely anything given the chance, although in those early days a small number of them were employed in the units doing various kinds of work, while women were employed for washing and ironing.

Charlie does not regret doing his National Service one little bit, because it 'livened him up.' He met some great lads who you could trust with your life; his only regret being that he did not keep in touch with them for very long.

ALAN BIRCH

For his second year's Royal Signals National Service in Egypt by the Suez Canal in 1948, Alan sailed there not in an old freighter, but a Cunard liner, the SS *Scythia*, (*See Pic. No. 1*). The journey was like a cruise, with no fatigues, and a running commentary of the wonderful scenery and features they passed. After a couple of months at Suez, repairing radio sets from all over the Middle East, Alan was sent on detachment to 156 Transit camp, Port Said, as the radio station mechanic. (*See Pic. No. 2*). The 'detachment' part of this posting was great, because they were excused all fatigues, drills, guards, parades and inspections, but could 'attach' themselves for things they fancied, like the afternoon swimming, being taken there by truck.

Then Alan slipped up one day. Asked for new socks, the quartermaster said that he would give them out to Alan on parade that evening. The quartermaster nearly had a fit when he explained that he wouldn't be there, because the six lads in the Signals team didn't parade. *'I'll soon sort that out,'* he exploded, and he did! As you can imagine, Alan was not very popular with his mates when they were ordered to attend all parades in future. This meant lots of blancoing and polishing, and his name was *mud*! (*See Pic. No. 4*). All six of them attended parade, and the next day they heard that the colonel had gone berserk the previous evening, because there had been no telephone, teleprinter or radio communications at all, and the camp had been cut off from the rest of the world. From then on it was back to as it was, with no more parades, etc. (*See Pic. No. 3*).

The NAAFI club at Port Said was a fine old building, previously used as the Italian Embassy, and Alan remembers seeing Ivy Benson and her All Girls' Jazz Band there. On another occasion Alan and his mate were late leaving the club, and rushed to catch the last ferry, but it had just left. This was not good, because there had been incidents where British servicemen were robbed and left in their underpants, and at least one killed. They found their way to the quayside where there were some Egyptians with rowing boats, and one of them agreed to row Alan and his pal across the canal. They negotiated a price, and set off across the shipping lane, but halfway across he stopped and demanded about twice as much money, wailing about his starving children. There they were in the dark, in a rowing boat at 10.45 at night, halfway across a shipping route, having a heated argument in poor English versus poor Arabic. They threatened to take the oars, and he eventually relented. After paying off the boatman they ran like mad back to camp, arriving five minutes late, but were let in with a telling off.

EDNA (SANDY) HASTINGS

NAAFI worker, 1945-47

Working with around 20 other girls in the NAAFI at Ramleh, an RAF base in Palestine, Edna (Sandy) thoroughly enjoyed herself overall. She had to join the ATS (Auxiliary Territorial Service) to go overseas, but had nice billets and decent pay, although she had to wear a khaki uniform. The NAAFI was a civilian organisation, nevertheless they had to do Army training before being posted.

Sandy came across lots of National Service lads, saw some wonderful places and met many interesting people while she worked for the NAAFI from 1945 to 1947. She spent nine months in Egypt, at Camp 87, Fayed, an Army camp, went to the Pyramids and did all the tourist things there, and spent the rest of her time in Palestine. It was not so good there - too much terrorist trouble, with a terrorist gang going around, blowing up places. If they wanted to go out shopping they had to have four armed escorts to accompany them. She remembers the night a gang of youths there went berserk, blowing up a military installation and kidnapping two sergeants and hanging them in an orange grove. That same night they blew up the King David Hotel.

Sandy has one medal from an overall marvellous experience she had in those two years. Asked whether she had fallen for some of those young lads, Sandy sighed deeply and answered: 'Oh yes, ... *oh yes!*'

GORDON DUCK

The final posting for Gordon Duck after his Green Howards basic training was to Egypt in 1953, sailing from Liverpool through the Suez Canal. Gordon was based in the Sinai desert, and he never had a night out, because they were shot at by the Egyptians if they went outside the camp. To go for a drink it had to be in the NAAFI, as they were more or less locked up for ten months.

In Egypt football was very different from what he had been used to in England. They got a game every week, but if they went out of camp there had to be two escorts with them, because of the danger of being shot at. Football matches were played against other Army camps around the Suez area, but were not of the quality Gordon had been used to in England, and it was too hot, and the matches were always played on sand, instead of the usual grass back home.

Gordon's only respite in his time there was when he and a few others went on a fortnight's holiday to Cyprus, instead of England – and it was like getting out of jail! When it was over they had to go back to Egypt, and the normal boring activities after that, but Gordon still thinks he was lucky, because no one actually *invaded* the camp while he was there. While on guard duty he had to have a bullet 'up the spout' all the time; there was no question of being able to relax for a second, such was the anti-British attitude in Egypt in those days.

Gordon reckoned that his National Service was an experience never to be repeated, but without a doubt, his best times were at Barnard Castle.

REV. CANON ROLAND MEREDITH
Ox and Bucks, 1950-52

Joining the Army at Shorncliffe in September 1950, Roland was posted to the Middle East with the Ox. and Bucks 3rd Infantry Division, under Major General Templer in November 1951, sailing from Portsmouth on the *Illustrius* aircraft carrier to Famagusta in Cyprus. It took three days to unload the stores and motor transport after they arrived there, but two days later came the order to re-embark for Egypt, where they moved into a camp at Suez which was reasonable, but some nearby companies stationed in the water filtration plants saw some action.

Christmas was spent there, and he remembers playing the harmonium for the outdoor Midnight Eucharist, and playing the hymns for all the services, until the chaplain, the Rev. Worthington was injured in a skirmish, and was sent back to the UK.

After commemorating the death of King George VI and the accession of Queen Elizabeth II, they moved from their camp at Suez to the garrison at TEK, which was west of Ismailia, along the Sweetwater Canal. TEK was a large ordnance depot surrounded by barbed wire in the middle of the desert, and was miles from anywhere. There were reasonable facilities, including an open-air cinema, and a permanent garrison church, of All Saints, where Roland sang in the choir and read the lessons at morning service.

In September Roland's time was up, and he flew home via Malta to Bovington airfield. It was time to move on to Cambridge, where the green grass at Trinity was a welcome change from the sand at TEK!

Roland is now an Emeritus Canon of Blackburn Cathedral, and of Christ Church, Oxford, and also acts as Chaplain to the Regimental Chapel of the Ox. and Bucks. Light Infantry, also at Christ Church, Oxford, where he conducts a monthly service.

STAN CALVERT

Royal Engineers, 1952-54

National Service basic training with the Green Howards for Stan was at Richmond in 1952. However, prior to being called up he had worked as a railway fireman, so he was transferred to Longmoor in Hampshire, with the Royal Engineers, which was a railway unit. He stayed there for a while and after that he was posted overseas, and embarked on the *Empire Ken* to Egypt, docking at Port Said.

Stan then found himself repairing heavy plant earth moving JCBs at Quassasin, around 25 miles from Fayed. The depot was two miles from the camp and they used to go in Army trucks every morning to the workplace and work only until 1 p.m., because of the heat. They travelled in the back of open-sided trucks. On reaching the depot the truck sides were supposed to come down before they got off, but being young fit lads full of energy, they just vaulted over the side, and onto the ground. There was a metal strip running along the top of the side boards, held in place with metal rivets. On one occasion as they were jumping off, one of the lads got his ring caught on one of the rivets, and it severed his finger clean off, his finger landing on the ground ahead of him. He and his finger (both in ice), went straight to hospital.

They were fortunate to have a swimming pool and a cinema on the camp, bearing in mind they were right in the middle of the desert. Like every other unit in Egypt at this time they were not allowed out of camp, because of the hostility of the local Egyptians towards anyone or anything to do with Britain. Every night they had to take their turn for guard duty – 40 at a time – in sandbagged trenches, to prevent the Egyptians from getting into the compound and stealing whatever they could. They used a searchlight, which used to pick out the eyes of the wild dogs, besides the local Egyptians. They operated a two hours on and two hours off system, but they still had to be inspected before duty!

If Stan had stayed in the Green Howards he would have been sent to Korea, as the platoon he had been in at Richmond were sent there, and on his way home from Egypt on the *Empire Trooper*, he met a lot of the lads he had got to know in basic training 18 months previously.

After his time in Egypt Stan went back home to Barton Stacey for demob. for about three weeks. He returned to the railways for about six months, before working as a postman, and then tried his hand at local government, finishing up as Area Housing Manager.

Asked whether National Service was a waste of time or not, Stan was of the opinion that it built up his character with the discipline etc. At the time he did not think much of it, especially the basic training, but later he began to realise the benefits.

Stan is now a committee member of the Middlesbrough branch of the Combined Services, holding monthly meetings and arranging social evenings, dances and outings, etc.

JOHN FAWCETT

Royal Air Force, 1955-57

Being an RAF radar mechanic in 1955, it seemed to John that every camp he was sent to after his training in England was in the process of being closed down. He went to Egypt in 1956 when they were leaving, because the government were closing down all the Middle-East bases, and he was in transit for about six weeks.

While he was there John met an Army lad, a typical East-ender, who said he was near the end of his service, while John was just starting. This lad had been in for five-and-a-half years, and still had not finished his National Service! On the troopship going over to Egypt, the sergeant had been objectionable to the new recruits, so a few of them had thrown him overboard, which had been spotted, and they all served an extra three years for it. As a result he had not been home all that time.

Ironically, when he went in, the length of service was only eighteen months, but while all this was going on it had increased to two years. *(See also, Iraq, Cyprus).*

ALBERT WILSON

Catering Corps, 1954-56

Albert Wilson was at Aldershot for a few weeks basic training in 1954, and his trade training for the Catering Corps was at Catterick, for six months, before he went on embarkation leave. While he was at Catterick he developed a poisoned finger, and as a result he just missed his draft. The orderly clerk asked him where in the world he would like to go, because there had been a demand for home postings, and Albert said Egypt, somewhere he had always wanted to go. 'No bother,' said the clerk, so it happened, and he was probably the only National Serviceman who ever volunteered for *that* posting!

After his trip to Egypt, Albert disembarked at Port Said, after travelling on a passenger liner, the *Georgic* with waiters, the very opposite of the normal troopship, but it was on its last voyage before going to the scrapyard. Albert then went to a transit camp, with hundreds of soldiers there, while he waited for his posting. During this time he had to go for a haircut, and the stuff the hairdresser put on the lads' hair had a terrible smell – but he had a shipload of the stuff to get rid of, so everyone had to have it on their hair.

Albert met a sergeant on a train going to Aldershot one day, and he gave him three dirty old 10p Asta Egyptian banknotes, as he had no further use for them. Much later, on his way to a transit camp at Port Said, with 20 others, in the back of a covered truck, they stopped for refreshments, where Albert produced these notes and just one of them paid for three chocolate biscuits, three cups of coffee, and 20 cigarettes!

Albert was based 30 miles from Fayed, spending over a year in Egypt. After this he went on a troopship on this occasion, the *'Empire Ken'* to spend his last five months National Service in Libya, as all the troops in Egypt had to leave at this time. Libya was civilised, compared to Egypt, bearing in mind that in Egypt they were a little camp, an Ordnance Field Park, with only 89 of them there, and attached to them was a mobile laundry, and the canteen was a tent. The only local people they saw were the lads that worked on the camp. Libya though was ten camps in one, with a proper NAAFI, where you could buy meals, and have a game of table tennis or snooker, and was much better in every way. (*See Pic. No. 12*).

Like most National Servicemen, Albert thought that at the time it was a shocking waste of two years, but as he and his mates led comparatively boring lives in England, he later realised that he had had a smashing time, and he would not have missed it for the world.

KEN COAN

When Ken had completed his training he was posted to Egypt, and found himself at the Moascar dental centre in the Canal Zone, which had three surgeries. He was surprised to find one of them being operated by a German officer for the remaining German troops still in the area, a year after the Second World War had finished. Late one afternoon he had to assist the dental officer in an operation at the local RAMC hospital to extract all of an officer's teeth, and Ken had to take all the necessary instruments over from the dental centre. The operation started and Ken was requested to stand near with the kidney dish to collect the teeth as they were extracted. When Ken admitted that he had forgotten to bring the kidney dish, the annoyed officer told him to stand near and cup his hands to receive the rotten, stinking, revolting teeth into his hands, one by one. Ken never forgot the kidney dish ever again, *or that smell!*

Just as Ken was expecting demob. he was promoted to lance corporal and sent to Khartoum for a few weeks, and was then posted to Eritrea, before the authorities discovered their mistake and flew him back to Khartoum, and by train and ship back to England.

After his career as a commercial artist, Ken keeps his hand in by drawing cartoons for his friends. A fine example of his work is shown by Picture No. 25.

ALUN REES
Royal Engineers, 1946-48

Alun was stationed at Fayed, Middle East HQ and while he was there the authorities asked for volunteers to get the thousands of British soldiers out of Palestine to Egypt, when the mandate in Palestine was finished. As Alun was a driver he volunteered because he wanted to see some action. He went to eight different units in two years, because he was always on the lookout for something different.

When they got to Palestine, the British Army was in the process of moving everything out, men and equipment, so they trashed the barracks they were leaving, so as not to leave it for the Jews and the Arabs.

Being nosy Alun went around the barracks and came across lots of adult books, so he filled the sides of his wagon with these books. In the convoy there was a corporal sitting next to him, and in 1946 not many soldiers could drive. Ten miles out, stopping and starting, this corporal said to him: 'I wish I could drive,' to which Alun replied: 'Now's your chance.' So they swapped seats and Alun let him drive. These lorries had a turret on the top and Alun used to go up and watch the Jews fighting the Arabs. He reckoned that the Jews had modern weaponry, while the poor old Arabs were using 1914 guns.

When they got to Palestine the corporal could drive quite well by then, and the RSM came out and said: 'All right you drivers, off you go, dinners ready for you.' They had a nice meal, but when they went back to the lorry, they found it had been stolen – together with the dirty books!

Alun turned round to the RSM one day and insulted him, saying that he had never known his father – he was so polite that the RSM didn't catch on!

When Alun was stationed at Aldershot there was always a tell-tale, and he had told the RSM of one of Alun's misdemeanours, and Alun was furious with him. Alun had done his usual playing about, and he shopped him to the sergeant. A PTI nearby suggested settling it in the boxing ring and Alun agreed. The tell-tale was 25 and a giant, while Alun was 19 and smallish. Now Alun had done a bit of boxing previously, and he was determined to give this lad a pasting – and he did – much to the delight of the WRENS cheering him on. There were no rounds, just a fight to the finish, with the PTI acting as referee.

While in the Army Alun did all sorts of daft things, and was always in trouble, and causing trouble, etc, and had some fun and a good laugh. The officer in charge used to say when he was wheeled in yet again: *'Oh, not you again – get him out of here ...'*

KENYA

Between 1947 and 1950 Mackinnon Road, a small town in Coast Province, Kenya, was the site of a large British Engineering and Ordnance Depot designed to hold 200,000 tonnes of military stores. The British had anticipated the loss of military bases in Egypt due to a rise in nationalism in that country, and decided to create another base that was able to serve their military needs in the western Indian Ocean. The plan was abandoned and the base became a detention camp for Mau Mau suspects until 1955.

IVOR THOMAS
Royal Army Ordnance Corps, 1949-51

Basic training in the RAOC in 1949 for Ivor was at Aldershot, then he was sent to Hilsea Barracks, Southsea, before being posted overseas. When Ivor first went to West Africa, he arrived at McKinnon Road, and after he told them he was a bricklayer by trade they posted him to Mombasa, at a camp called Shamanzi, which to a young Ivor strongly resembled a Butlins Holiday Camp. This was however before the Mau Mau came onto the scene. There were only one or two corporals and sergeants, and it was all very easy going, with the NCOs being addressed as 'Bill' or 'Jack.'

It was that easy going, as demonstrated by a young soldier who threw the contents of a can of beer out of a railway carriage window one day coming back to camp, which just happened to hit an officer in the face, who at that moment was looking out of the next carriage window. The culprit was sentenced to 21 days detention, but there was no-one guarding the cell, so he used to carry his own key to let himself in and out of his cell. He used to go out with the rest of the lads for a nightly drink, and then let himself back into his cell again for the rest of the night. This went on for the whole 21 days.

They were so short of NCO's that Ivor and his mates used to have to go and inspect the native guards, taking it in turns about every fortnight. What makes that incredible was that Ivor and his mates were all PRIVATES! The native guards from the depot, were supposed to be guarding the generating plant stored there.

There used to be about four other privates with Ivor, and ten natives in the shed. They used to tell them what to do, sweep this and move that, etc., and then Ivor and his mates played cards for the rest of the day, while these natives did all the work. There was very little work to be done, and they had been told not to do anything, in any case, which they obeyed to the letter! Native workers used to take orders for breakfast, lunch and dinner each day; serve the meals in the dining room, and take away the used plates and utensils after the meals, and then wash up. All Ivor and his mates had to do was to eat, sunbathe, and play cards during the day, and then go out on the night. *Definitely a holiday camp!*

Five nights a week Ivor and his chums went out to the Seamen's Mission Angel Club in Mombasa, to watch films. The other two nights, Friday and Saturday, used to be drinking nights. To break the routine they occasionally went out on safari, but didn't kill anything.

There were only about 60 soldiers in this camp, including Signals, Engineers, etc., and Ivor only went on parade twice in his two years.

Needless to say, National Service was fantastic for Ivor in Shimanzi, and he was sorry when it all came to end, and he had to go back to bricklaying. *(See also, Last Thoughts)*.

ALAN SERGINSON

Royal Signals, 1951-53

Training for the Royal Signals at Catterick Camp for six months in 1951, seemed like the end of the world to Alan. He found that he was going to Nairobi, Kenya, and was posted to Newton Abbott on embarkation leave, and spent time with his pal who lived there. He sailed from Southampton on the *Empire Ken*, for six weeks to Mombasa, but out into the Red Sea the ship docked in the middle of the ocean for a burial, because the cook had died from heatstroke.

The Ship's Officer wanted someone in the cookhouse to serve the rest of the lads – that was Alan in the cookhouse for the next fortnight. He got to Mombasa after the most appalling fortnight of his life. As he was so weak from his cookhouse duties, his friend Ken lifted Alan and his kitbag plus his own, and dragged him down the gangplank and put him on the lorry, then onto the train from Mombasa to Nairobi, which took 20 hours. Apartheid was rampant, with blacks only toilets, and whites only toilets. The train chugged away up to Nairobi, with natives running alongside and jumping on.

Finally they arrived at Nairobi, to a compound which comprised of only a few huts, just outside the National Park.

Alan was posted to RAF Eastleigh for the rest of his time in Kenya,
and they were short of manpower there, with no infantry, just technical staff, such as Signals and Engineers, etc. The Mau Mau terrorism campaign had started after his first few months, quietly at first, but serious latterly. In 1953 native bodies were found in camp, so the authorities started taking more care, and the Mau Mau threat as serious. Alan was helping to look after weapons, and got the call one night to go out with the REME and Signals on patrol to a village to clear out the Mau Mau that were thought to be there. They all got ready with fixed bayonets and one round up the spout, and off they went, around 100 of them; cooks, clerks, etc., with rifles, and all of them terrified, with an officer into the bush and into an African compound. They were told by the officer: 'If anyone comes out *shoot the buggers.*' But mercifully the African police arrived at that moment and stopped them, and asked them to watch while they dealt with the Mau Mau.

As the terrorist threat got worse and farms with white settlers were being burned, and the settlers killed, everyone on camp had to take their turn in guarding those farms from the terror of the Mau Mau, four to a farm, with rifles and ammunition. The infantry came in three months later, and they were very glad to get back to normal duties.

Each billet had a dhobi boy who did the washing and cleaning, etc, and the members of Alan's billet grew to trust and like theirs, as they had known him for months now. One day the Military Police came and demanded to see their dhobi boy, because he was a suspected member of the Mau Mau, at which they all protested his innocence. The MP lifted up the dhobi boy's arm to reveal three slashes, proof of his allegiance to the Mau Mau, and took him away – he was one of them.

BOAC had a route from London to Eastleigh, and an order came out that crews of civilian airliners had to report to the RAF armoury to be issued with revolvers and ammunition. There was a long aluminium bench in the armoury, and the firearms were laid out on this. The Webley revolvers were broken in half and the rounds put in the chamber. Unbeknown to Alan and George, the armourer, the BOAC captain had pulled the trigger, and this meant that the firing pin was through the firing plate. When the revolver was snapped shut it fired a round which ricocheted off the table and went round the room. They all dived for the floor and the sergeant rushed in and they were both put on a charge. After this episode they took the crews to the firing range, and taught them how to load and shoot a revolver properly.

It was the RAF armourers' job to put the bomb racks up with four bombs under each wing of every aircraft going on anti-terrorist operations. One day Alan and George went on their bikes as usual to collect bombs from a bomb dump in a hut away from camp. George opened the door of the hut to go inside and turned round and told Alan to: *'Clear off.'* The bombs were leaking and the stuff in them was turning into nitro-glycerine, because they were very old World War Two bombs. They sent for men from England to deal with it, and a bomb squad flew in to clear up all the old ammunition.

National Service gave Alan more confidence. He went in as a meek little boy, but he was a man when he came back, and he will remember his experiences in Kenya for the rest of his life.

REX STRAWSON

The next posting for Rex after Somaliland in the summer of 1949, involved an overland journey of several hundred miles from Mogadishu to Nairobi in Kenya in a wooden seated bus. They spent two weeks there, in a camp opposite the airport, before they were off again to Mombasa by train, powered by two wood burning steam engines, with two natives sitting outside at the front with spears to keep the animals off the track. On arrival at the transit camp Rex was put on the camp staff checking meal tickets and going round with the orderly officer, a two-hour day, with the rest of the time spent on the lovely white beach.

At the end of their time in Mombasa they passed through the great Kenya National Game Park, seeing all the exotic wild game animals, and stayed in the same camp as before for ten days with no duties, and being waited on by native soldiers. However, the feeling of the Africans towards British troops was not good, and later turned into the Mau Mau uprising. It was found to be safer to move around in groups of five or more.

They were now just waiting for their unusual method of transport home – by Short Sunderland Flying Boat from Lake Naivasha, 70 miles from Nairobi. The journey took them first to Khartoum, then Luxor in Egypt, and landing on the sea in Sicily. They later circled Mount Etna twice to see the smoke erupting from the top, before landing in the South of France, and then came home to England at last.

Rex thought his National Service had been a great learning curve, having travelled extensively and visited many countries, and he had numerous adventures on the way. The friends he made during it became lifelong friends.

Until illness last year, Rex used to paint miniatures which sold well enough to pay for the annual holidays, but he now collects military medals and badges.

JOHN BOHME
Black Watch, 1953-55

With the Mau Mau creating massive problems in Kenya, John Bohm's Black Watch Battalion were sent there from Korea on the *Empire Orwell*, because they were an up and running battalion, and they were told the Mau Mau terrorists still used bows and arrows. When they arrived at Nairobi racecourse they found that they had thrown the racehorses out of their stalls and intended to put the Black Watch in them instead, and that is what happened. Then they moved up country to Gill Gill, over three thousand feet high, to get acclimatised for going up country to the Aberdares which was over seven thousand feet.

For two years the only time they did not sleep outside was when they were at Pusan for a Remembrance Service, when they slept in tin huts. Other than that they slept in holes in the ground and tents for the whole of their National Service.

SUDAN

In March 1954 British troops in the Sudan consisted of one battalion stationed in Khartoum, reporting to the Governor-General, whose military commander was the Major-General Commanding British Troops in the Sudan, Major General

Reginald 'Cully' Scoons. The last British troops, 1st Battalion Royal Leicestershire Regiment, left the country on August 16, 1955. Sudan became independent from Egypt and the UK on January 1, 1956.

PHILIP HIRONS

Royal Army Medical Corps, 1951-53

Working at the British Medical Hospital at Khartoum in 1951, Philip spent most of his National Service there, apart from four months training in England and a short time in Egypt.

He had a little time on the wards, and was then put in charge of the medical inspection unit. At that time they were based in the hospital grounds, and some of the civilians used to come into the battalion gatehouse to do work for them. They had this particular Sudanese who used to wash the floors down in the wards, and he treated the lads badly, playing tricks on them. So they came in to see Philip one day and asked him to do something.

Soon after this Sudanese went in to see Philip and said that he couldn't go to the toilet, and could he help him. At that time they had a pill called the Army No. 9, which had devastating results. Philip gave him **three,** which he took straightaway, and where he was there was a pathway going down to the main gate. All of a sudden he got hold of his backside and he ran, and later they heard that he didn't stop going to the toilet for three days! They never saw him again.

If they went out at night into Khartoum itself they used to get a taxi and go for a meal or visit the cinema. This particular time was in the rainy season, and they were sitting in the open-air cinema watching *Superman*, and the heavens opened and all the Sudanese went home, leaving Philip and his mates to watch the rest of the film, holding the seats over their heads. When they came out they had to find the pavement because there was so much water about, so they got the taxi back to camp, and on the way they had the windows open when the rain stopped. If you did that you got a nasty 'whiff,' and this came from what they called the 'Midnight Express,' a flat backed trailer pulled by two camels, with a Sudanese sitting there whipping them. He used to go round to the different houses, collecting all the toilet waste, and putting it into open bins on top of the trailer.

There were no flush toilets either in the hospital or anywhere else, so this was the only means of disposing of the stuff. Phil was on night duty one night at the hospital and he had only just arrived, so he did not know about this scheme, and he was sitting on the balcony. He heard a noise, saw a shadowy figure getting longer and longer, and his hair started to stand up at the back of his neck. This Sudanese had one of these toilet bins on his head, before changing the full ones for empty ones.

Another thing that happened in the hospital. In Khartoum there is the Blue Nile river and the White Nile river. If any European goes into the White Nile for a swim, they get what they call the guinea worm, unseen by the naked eye. It gets into the body fluids and feeds off the fluids of the muscles, and when any of the lads came in and said what they had been doing they had to keep an eye on them. The biggest worm Phil fetched out of a muscle was over two feet long, because it just keeps feeding on the muscle fluids. What Phil had to do was to put the victim into a cold bath, and the worm would come out of his bottom and make to the surface, and then Phil would get two matchsticks and put one on either side of the head as it came out, and just keep rolling the worm out with the two sticks. If the worm broke it would immediately grow another head. The Blue Nile on the other hand was quite clean, going down to Omdurman, before changing into the White Nile.

The new Comet jet airliner, a world leader in its time, was taken to Khartoum for its trials, and a special brick wall was built so that the noise of the engines' thrust on take-off could be reduced by blowing against this wall.

National Service was not a waste of time for Philip, because he learned discipline, and it taught him to respect other people.

KEN KIRBY
Royal Army Service Corps, 1946-48

After his initial basic training with the Green Howards in 1946, Ken joined the RASC, before being posted abroad. First stop was Dieppe, and then by rail to Toulon, and ship to Port Said, Egypt. He subsequently went on to a transit camp at Fayed, followed by a journey with a Parachute Regiment across the Sinai desert to Haifa, where he was by himself for ten days. While he was in Haifa the first illegal immigrant ship arrived full of Jewish immigrants. From April 1946 to Christmas, they were closing the camp down, which was the time when the King David hotel was blown up in Jerusalem, and two British sergeants were hanged by Jewish terrorists at Rafa, during the on-going war in Palestine,

From there Ken went down to Cairo for ten days, and received orders to go to Khartoum by paddle steamer and barge. After that his journey took him by rail to the Sudanese border at Wadi Halfa, and finally to Khartoum, where he stayed from December 1946 until May, 1948.

When Khartoum is viewed from the air it resembles the Union Flag, all the main streets form that pattern, a relic of General Gordon's headquarters in that city. While there Ken went to Omdurman, where the white and blue Nile rivers meet, and he remembers crossing the bridge and having a close look at it, and discovering that the steel was from Dorman Long in Middlesbrough!

Khartoum was not like an Army camp, more like a transit camp, where people used to come and stop for a few days and go off, and there was no regime at all, working in the HQ in Khartoum, from eight till one, because of the great heat. Ken used to go in at 7 a.m. working on Part Two orders, and seeing to men going on leave and demobilisation.

Unlike Egypt, Ken was able to go out on a night in Khartoum quite safely, and go round the market during the day. If you wanted a shirt making or a suit, that could easily be done, and relations between the locals and the Army lads was quite good. Ken played football for the local team, and also the Combined Army/R.A.F team, maybe three or four times a week, and because of all this football activity he was recognised by the local people quite often.

Ken remembers spending a day swimming in the Sea of Galilee, a memorable experience. This was a good posting for Ken, with an outdoor swimming pool, and tennis courts, not to mention the football, and Ken enjoyed his stay there.

None of this would have happened if, while at Thetford, Ken had mentioned that he was a more than useful footballer, with Northern League experience. He would have been kept at Thetford, and would have experienced that dreadful 1947 winter, instead of the sun of Khartoum, and he would have missed all the experiences that he had along the way.

LIBYA

In its foreign policy, Libya maintained a pro-Western stance in the 1950s, and was recognized as belonging to the conservative traditionalist bloc in the League of Arab States (Arab League), of which it became a member in 1953. The same year Libya concluded a twenty-year treaty of friendship and alliance with Britain under which the latter received military bases in exchange for financial and military assistance. Reservations set aside in the desert were used by British and American military aircraft and units based in Europe as firing ranges.

KEN HARDMAN
Royal Signals, 1954-56

Basic training for Ken during his time in the Royal Signals was at Catterick Camp in 1954, which he enjoyed in a strange sort of way. The harshness of it at times did not bother him at all, because he was very fit, due to the amount of cycling he had been used to before conscription. What did bother him though was the thieving he encountered early on, and so he dealt with this straight away and it never occurred again.

He remembers one very big lad not wanting to wash or shower at all, and it took six of them to drag him into the showers and scrub him down. It was the sergeant's idea to punish all of the lads in the room for this lad being smelly, and he instructed the rest of them to put this right. If this was the lad's deliberate policy to get out of the Army, then it worked, because shortly after this incident he was dismissed.

From Catterick Ken was posted to the LAC Centre in London, an underground holding station at Goodge Street, for a week, which he did not enjoy, and from there he was sent to R.A.F. Bobbington for a flight to Malta. They landed en-route in France for refuelling, when he remembers climbing up over the wing to get in and out of the plane, a very unusual experience. For a while Ken enjoyed his time in Malta where he stayed for a couple of months, but eventually grew tired of sunbathing, and waiting for his posting with nothing else to do, and being restricted in his movements on the island.

Ken's next port of call was to Benghazi, in Libya, landing at RAF El Adem, and he was stationed there for about five months, being employed as a service despatch security guard for the mail when it arrived by air, to make sure that it arrived safely back at the camp. There were three of them, one driving, one guarding the front, and Ken riding shotgun at the back of a fifteen-hundred-weight truck piled high with bags of mail. Amazingly, considering that the local Libyans knew exactly what times they were driving back to the camp each day, they encountered few problems during their stay there, despite using the same route and times on every occasion.

Benghazi Palace was the unlikely final resting place for a British aeroplane, coming to grief against the palace walls, and covered with the desert sands. Try as he might, Ken could not find out exactly what had happened, whether or not it had been shot down, or had suffered engine failure, etc.

Ken's final posting was to Tobruk, where one day he was diving into the sea from some rocks with several of his mates. Another two lads came along and started throwing bottles in and diving, but they could not see Ken and his pals, because of an overhanging rock separating them. As Ken resurfaced from one of his dives he was hit on the forehead with one of these bottles and suffered a nasty gash, with blood pouring from it, which required stitching. When they went up before the officer he threatened to charge all of them for fighting, and he took a lot of convincing not to do this.

Ken feels that his National Service was definitely not a waste of time, because it made him more of a man, learning to give and take, broadening his outlook, and was part of his growing up process, being only 18 when he joined.

BARRIE SHEPHERDSON

Stationed in Gibraltar for about 18 months, Barrie's time there included a three month spell in Libya doing manoeuvres, because there was nowhere to use their mortars and anti-tank guns in Gibraltar. During their stay in Libya, with no cash, in an old Italian Army barracks at Tahuna the locals used to come outside the wire perimeter with bundles of their cash wanting to buy stuff. A few of the lads sold them some pyjamas, because no one wore pyjamas in that heat, and they were the least missed items. So quite a few Army striped pyjamas went through the wire in exchange for 'Ackers.' Next morning however, a lot of the locals had been taken on as casual workers, and they not only came in their pyjamas, but the name and number of the soldiers concerned were emblazoned across their shoulders in very large bold letters. That stopped any more trading!

Barrie loved the desert while he was there, even though everything had to be nailed down, or the locals stole it. This was the time of King Idris, before Gadaffi, in 1961. One of the lads had found a snake while on manoeuvres, and as they all wore hats, everyone wanted a snake band, like 'Crocodile Dundee.' Two of them were skinning the snake, a horned viper, but it was striking at them. Barrie told them to kill it, and he chopped it in half with a spade; but as he bent to pick it up, the half that he picked up struck at him, but just missed his hand. Considering they were miles from anywhere at the time, it could have been very nasty indeed.

An officer was directing a section attack, also during manoeuvres, but Barrie warned him about using live ammunition, putting an attack in on an old building. With a light machine gun firing on an old broken down blockhouse from 90 degrees, they could get some ricochets, but he was told to get on with it. As the attack went in there was the sound just like a bumble bee, and he felt a wind waft his face - a very close call indeed. (*See also, Germany*).

SOMALILAND

Treaties made with local chieftains from about 1880 onwards gave control of the northern coast of the Horn of Africa to the British. The reason was to make sure no other European power could control it and threaten the route to India. It was all administered together and called the British Somaliland

Protectorate. After Prime Minister MacMillan's 'Wind of Change' speech, indicating an intention to give independence to all countries of the British Empire, British Somaliland became independent on June 26, 1960.

CAPTAIN BILL GOLDTHORP

As a student Bill had neither the money nor the time to pass his driving licence. In Somaliland, by now a captain in the RAMC, with little traffic, he started driving anything that was available, and everyone assumed he had a licence, until he informed them that he hadn't. Told to go to see the adjutant about this problem he did, and was amazed to see him pick one up from his desk, sign it and give him it. Bill had both sat and passed his Army driving test all within a few minutes!

While in the Army Bill developed a talent for dealing with what he describes as '*bumf*.' He had to travel around and survey, then decide what was needed in the various outposts. Having carried out the survey, he used to present a massive report to his CO, together with demands for equipment and extra drugs. For the rest of his life Bill used to put up a large barrage of '*bumf*' and then did whatever he wanted behind it, which stood him in good stead later on when dealing with NHS administrators!

As sidelines to his medical skills Bill was called upon on many occasions to be mess butcher, dentist, veterinary surgeon and choirmaster. Whenever he was called upon to visit some outpost in Somaliland he took a rifle with him, and usually shot a gazelle on the way, taking it to the officers' mess, thus making a change from the usual menu of goat, sheep or camel.

The dentistry started in Aden, when an Arab soldier with bad toothache asked him to remove the offending tooth. Bill explained to him that he was not a dentist, but the Arab pointed out that the previous MO had done it, so why not him? Bill reluctantly told him to come back at 11.0 a.m. and after he had found the appropriate tools, and had downed a double gin, the lower right molar was pulled out. From then on, wherever he visited, he was regarded as a fully qualified dentist.

As there wasn't a veterinary surgeon in Somaliland Bill had to deal with that too. He could cope with dogs and horses, provided it was the usual cuts needing stitching, or antibiotics for infections, but he drew the line when he was asked to cure Captain Payne's riding camel. It had massive biting teeth, and it spat if anyone went near, and it smelt.

One of Bill's early evening duties after dinner was as choirmaster. He had practised choral singing at university at the students' union and rugby club, so he was considered suitable to lead such cultured numbers as *The Ball of Kerrymuir* and *These Foolish Things,* etc. Bill grew attached to the country and its people during his stay in Somaliland, and was sorry to leave when the time came to finish off his remaining period of National Service in Aden.

REX STRAWSON

With the rest of the DCLI battalion Rex sailed on the *Empire Helford* from Cyprus to Hargeysa in 1948, a wild desolate place they found, 4,200feet up in British Somaliland. They had no sooner settled in than they heard of another move that was coming, this time a thousand miles south by sea on the

Empire Pride to Mogadishu in Italian Somaliland, as troops of occupation. This was a beautiful city on the coast, with beaches, shops and restaurants, and laid out with tarmac roads, a cathedral and many shops and hotels. Inside their camp the break-ins by the natives were causing major upsets, happening nightly, so everyone in the camp would turn out and form a human chain around the camp perimeter, and there were no attempted entries. But as soon as they were stood down the pilfering natives came back again.

The Italian barber within the camp employed a 15-year-old Somali boy to sweep the floor, and he spoke very good English. Talking one day about his life there, he told Rex that he was married with two wives, and was very much looking forward to the time when he could afford to buy some more!

There were two very upsetting casualties while Rex was there. The first involved a soldier cleaning his rifle after doing guard duty, and he fired it not knowing it was loaded. The bullet passed through the wall of his barrack room and killed a soldier resting on his bed in another room. The other casualty was when some of the lads were sitting at the water's edge, and a wave washed one of them into the water. Three of them dived in but were unable to find him; in fact he was never found. As they were shark infested waters he had little chance of survival. (*See also, Kenya*).

JACK TURNER

Jack recalls a time in Somaliland with the DCLI in 1947, where there was a chap always bragging that the natives couldn't steal his bedding, as they had done to many others, by sneaking into their tent, as most lads slept naked. Some of the lads got 'Yorkie' drunk one night, brought him back to the billet and stripped him. His bum was painted like a face with black boot polish, he was then turned over and a face painted on the front, after being shaved down below. This made it look like a face with the tongue hanging out. Next day all hell broke loose, as black boot polish takes some getting off, but there was no more bragging – and no one ever told who did it.

One day they were asked to kill three lions that were eating local livestock, so it was decided officers only would do the job, along with an Askari scout. That night the lions were heard roaring, so a young goat was tethered in a clearing near some trees. Three wagons were to face the clearing, and when the lions came their headlights would illuminate the area. The lions closed in, the officers got in position, and the goat started to bleat in fear. Suddenly, out of some scrubs the lioness came and grabbed the goat, followed by another lioness. The headlights came on, bang went the guns, and one lioness was dead, with the wounded one running off, and no sign of the third lion. The Askari said that the wounded lion would have to be killed, but they would need to wait until daylight, follow the trail and finish it off.

Next day the trail led to a copse of scrub bushes thickly covered with leaves, and a movement was heard inside. The officers set up position on one side while the locals beat the scrub on the other. All of a sudden something came rushing out near one of the officers. He took off like a shot, and climbed up the tailboard of a truck as fast as any monkey. All guns blasted away to reveal a small gazelle shot to pieces. It was decided to give the job of killing the wounded lion to the Askari, who shot it the next day. There was great rejoicing in the village, and officers standing with one leg on the lions and having their photos taken, as if they had shot them.

CHAPTER SEVEN

Far East

BURMA

The British drove the Japanese out of Burma in early 1945 at the end of World War Two. However by mid-1945 it was clear that the British could no longer keep her hold on to that country, and in early 1947 they agreed to make Burma independent. Elections for a constituent assembly were held in April 1947 and work began on drawing up a new constitution, with Burma becoming independent on January 4, 1948.

SID THOMPSON
Royal Air Force, 1946-48

Being an airframes mechanic, Sid worked mainly on Dakotas, with 52 Squadron at Changi, Singapore, and in Burma in 1947. The CO decided that he wanted his white Avro York aeroplane polished aluminium, to make it look more aerodynamic, so they had to strip all the white paint off to make it aluminium again, which took weeks to do.

One of the lads in Burma had a pet monkey, which he kept in a tree. The monkey wore a collar, and had a chain attached to a cable, so that the monkey could run up and down the tree. However, when they were walking back from the cookhouse the monkey used to slide down the tree and snatch whatever they had in their hands. One day Sid and his mates were walking past and noticed that the cable had been cut, and the monkey had vanished. The monkey had tried his tricks once too often!

At Mingladon, near Rangoon, all the buildings there were bashirs, a sort of four-foot high wickerwork building, open to the elements, and everything was always damp. You had to get used to putting damp socks and damp shoes on, etc., and everything eventually turned green mouldy. Sid was there from the beginning of the monsoon to about half way through it.

The cooks used to make a lot of curry for the Indian soldiers and themselves, and the utensils were then used for cooking whatever they were giving Sid and his mates that day. This meant that the cookhouse always smelled of curry, and the food had a taste of curry too. It was 40 years before our obsession with curry had started, so it didn't go down too well at the time, and it was many years before Sid tasted curry again. (*See also, Singapore*).

TOM KANE

Royal Air Force Bomb Disposal, 1946-48

Trained as an armourer after his RAF square bashing in 1946, Tom was shipped to Singapore with 84 Squadron, then posted to Mingladon bomb disposal unit, just outside Rangoon, as an armourer, and was told to make his will. When Tom asked whether it was because he was replacing the previous armourer who had been blown up, the answer was: 'No, it's because you are going up in a Dakota.'

Tom stayed for a while in Penang, Malaya, a recreation place for the troops, and was then sent straight to Rangoon at an old disused rubber plantation. Their job was to get rid of all the bombs left over from World War Two by the Japanese and the Allies. Tom had to load the bombs onto trucks to be taken away and blown up every day. Most of the bombs were British and American shipped over during the war, but too expensive to send back. So the armourer at the other end used to blow up about ten truckloads of 500lb bombs every day. They had to send rockets up to warn off any planes going over the area. Previously they used to throw the ammunition into a lake, but ambitious locals used to dredge it up at night and sell it to their own police. The solution was to ask the Gurkhas to sort it out, and six of them did just that, and there was no more trouble.

They used to have an old gramophone player which they had to wind up, because the spring had gone. They only had one needle and one record, Dinah Shore, singing *Smoke gets in your eyes*. One particular day the rest of the team had all gone off with the bombs, and this Indian appeared on a bike, and asked Tom if he had anything that he wanted mending. So Tom told him what was needed, and after giving him a receipt, off he cycled with the gramophone. When the rest of the lads got back they wanted to have a tune, but Tom told them what had happened, and that it had gone for repairs, and he had a receipt to prove it.

He told them that he looked a nice enough chap, but they chased him up a tree and hosed him down, because it looked obvious that was the last they would see of the Indian – and the gramophone player. The next day off they went again, leaving Tom, as on the previous day, and who should come back but the Indian with the gramophone all fixed, and no more winding up needed. Did his mates say sorry about getting it all wrong? – *not a bit of it*!

The only unexploded bomb Tom was aware of was the one which had killed his predecessor and the five women who were with him, when they drove over a Japanese landmine. When he first arrived at Rangoon they were still making the coffins for these women. Tom was shown to his bed, but he asked what was the bit of rag hanging on the bedpost, and the answer was that was all they had found of the man he was replacing.

Having plenty of lorries and drivers at their disposal, Tom and his mates went to different places each night. One night they all went to a pub used by the Army, Navy and the RAF. One of them got involved in an argument with some of the Army lads, and was chucked in the river by some of them, who then drove off. So they gave chase in their lorry until the Army lorry suddenly stopped after about four miles, and Tom knew they were going to have a set-to right there. One of the Army lads stepped out ready to square up to them, and so did Tom and his mates, but his lorry drove away and left him on his own! Tom and his mates didn't know what to do with him – so they just gave him a lift back to his camp!

Tom was a decorator before and after National Service, and now after retirement paints water colours which he sells, and he has a permanent exhibition in Coventry - at the age of 83!

CEYLON *(Now Sri Lanka)*

Following the establishment of the Dominion of Ceylon, with Britain granting independence in 1948, work began to establish a regular military force. From the outset Britain played a significant role in helping the Ceylon government in developing its armed forces.

JOE CLOUGH
Royal Navy, 1945-47

After his Royal Navy basic training in 1945 Joe was sent to Portsmouth Barracks, and two days later sailed on HMS *Berwick*, the bromide in their tea suggesting they were bound for warmer climes. Arriving at Gibraltar for refuelling, the sea was so rough that the Lighter was smashing against the ship and they had to move round to the lee side of the island to complete the exercise. They later tied up in Valetta harbour, Malta, after a *'little'* incident when the hawser, which had been secured to a buoy was being drawn nearer by the capstan, and snapped. Fortunately, it just dropped flat, and didn't whip, otherwise the crew lining the fo'c'sle in their whites, could have been badly injured.

Joe was on look-out duty on the bridge whilst sailing to Port Said, into the Red Sea, and on to Colombo, Ceylon, (now Sri Lanka), and he experienced the phosphorous lighting up the bow wave, and shoals of flying fish during the day. On reaching Colombo Joe disembarked to a camp outside the city, before being transported to Trincomalee to become part of the Commander-in-Chief, East Indies staff.

Trincomalee is a natural harbour and dockyard, and the headquarters were in a concrete building, but the living quarters were very basic, straw roofed but open, the only protection against the mosquito's being individual mosquito nets at night. The amenities were very crude, the toilets were simply boards with a hole carved out. The work at HQ for Joe was simply to distribute typed signals to the various offices in the building.

For recreation they enjoyed sailing, swimming, hockey, and playing football against teams from crews of visiting ships, while at night it meant a couple of beers in the canteen. One highlight was being rum bosun for the mess, which involved picking up tots of rum in a stainless steel can from the purser's office for the 20 ratings in the mess. After sharing the rum out and having 20 sippers or occasional *gulpers*, plus your own tot, you needed the rest of the day off!

In July 1947 after 15 months in Trinco, Joe was sent back to Colombo and embarked on a Dutch troop ship going home to Southampton. He then worked on a farm in Wensleydale until October, before going into industry with ICI.

Joe's opinion of his National Service in the Royal Navy is that he felt it was a complete waste of two years of his life, and it put paid to any plans for entering Agricultural College back home.

INDIA

Knowing that Britain intended to pull out of their colonial rule soon, India was bound up in a religious civil war between the

Hindus and Muslims in 1946 and 1947, killing each other by the thousands. Britain tried to maintain some kind of order, but had to leave in a hurry in July, 1948, after over 200 years of colonial rule.

ARTHUR STONEHOUSE
Green Howards, 1946-48

After his initial Green Howards training, Arthur did his National Service in India. He remembers going over on the boat from England, where the soldiers had to sleep in hammocks, and a great many of them being seasick. Arthur's remedy for that was to lie flat on his back on the deck, but only a few men remained well – which meant that Arthur and his pals got all their rations! He also maintained that you could smell India many miles out to sea.

He was warned by the older soldiers when he arrived to keep his food covered when leaving the cookhouse – and he soon learned why. He went for his lunch with the rest of the squaddies up in the Indian foothills. He was one of the new ones, and they were all watching him, and the cookhouse was in the centre of the quadrangle. Arthur knew they were all still watching him as he stepped out of the cookhouse with his tray containing different receptacles on it. He hadn't got very far before this huge bird the size of a seagull, swooped down and stole his dinner in just a few seconds, and it then dawned on him what they had all been looking at. As soon as anyone stepped outside the cookhouse the 's… hawks' as they called them, (because of their presence around latrines), would be waiting for the unwary to steal the food from their plates. Of course the other soldiers were well used to the scavengers. A lesson learned!

India at this time was the scene of the riots between the Hindus and the Muslims, and he found himself being called out to many a riot in Calcutta to separate them, and he found it quite scary. When there were riots the Army were called out because they needed someone in charge. They were thrown in at the deep end, and several of the armoured cars were set on fire and the soldiers killed. So the Army started to put shocking coils on the armoured cars, and if anyone touched them they got a nasty shock. This move made life for the soldiers inside the armoured vehicles a lot safer.

The local 'tea wallah' became quite friendly with Arthur, and asked him where he came from. He answered: 'England,' to which the man replied: 'Where in England?' Arthur said: 'Why ask, you wouldn't know the area in a thousand years?' The tea wallah said: 'Try me,' so Arthur replied: 'Middlesbrough.' 'Ah, yes,' said the Indian: 'South Bank, Grangetown, Cargo Fleet, Dorman Long,' which amazed Arthur to hear.

Arthur hated getting up early for parade, he was always either late, or improperly dressed. His sergeant despaired of him, because he in turn was getting into trouble with his officer, because of this. He realised that the only way to save face was to put Arthur in charge of stores. So everyone was happy – and there no more early mornings for Arthur!

He always maintained that he was more intelligent than his superiors. He could also drive, which kept him in good stead with the officers and his mates. He would often take the officers into Calcutta, and then borrow the truck to take his mates out, thus keeping his feet in both camps. Arthur was also a good boxer, so once again he became a favourite with officers and men, winning quite a few trophies for his Regiment. This also kept him away from menial guard duties.

Disturbing a hornet's nest one day by accident, they attacked him vigorously, and he ran and ran to a stream to get away from them, and this worked up to a point. They put him in hospital, but that night the bites were driving him mad.

The golden rule was to always carry a torch with you when visiting the latrines. He was once sat on the toilet seat, dressed only in shorts, when a great big lizard landed on his back. He didn't need laxatives that night!

Sneaking back into camp one night with a friend, it was pitch black, and they heard a funny snorting sound, followed by a plop, plop, plop. Arthur's hair stood out at the back of his neck, as he pulled his pal behind some bushes, and peered out. He could see this enormous shape coming towards them – it was his first encounter with a camel. He said he didn't need laxatives that night either!

Arthur loved his time in the Army, being in at the latter part of the Indian disturbances, usually to quell riots. He made lots of friends, and saw lots of places. He managed to send money home to his mother, and also saved enough to buy a motorbike.

KOREA

Korea was divided at the 38th Parallel after the Second World War, with the defeated Japanese occupation forces being replaced by Russian troops in the Communist north of the country, and American troops in the south. In a surprise attack on June 25, 1950 the North Koreans intended to take over the whole of Korea by force, with the backing of Stalin's Russia, who provided them with tanks, heavy artillery and modern jet aircraft, and later on the Chinese, who committed a million-and-a-half soldiers to the North Korean cause.

Commital of mostly US, British Commonwealth and South Korean Forces enabled the hard-pressed United Nations force to defend the perimeter around Pusan, and when Gen. MacArthur the US Supreme Commander in the Far East launched a successful amphibious landing at Inchon, behind the enemy lines, the North Koreans were sent into a headlong retreat.

The Chinese became extremely alarmed at the collapse of its near neighbour, and as the UN force came ever nearer their border they attacked in huge numbers, and the UN forces were pushed back to the 38th Parallel once again. The front line became stabilized by early 1951, and the war became one of trench warfare, with only occasional offensives by either side.

The Korean war ended on July 27, 1953 with a huge loss of lives. Both sides signed an armistice, but a peace treaty was never reached. Often called the Forgotten War, it nevertheless brought the world to the very brink of a Third World War, with the threat of the use of the newly invented nuclear weapons a possibility at one stage.

The United Kingdom sent 63,000 troops to the Korean war, around 60% of whom were National Servicemen. Over 1,000 UK troops died in the conflict and around the same number were taken prisoner, and badly mistreated, of whom 82 were never seen again.

DERRY RAWLINGS MM
Durham Light Infantry, 1952-54

Stationed with the Duke of Cornwall's Regiment since the start of his National Service in 1952, Derry and some other DCLI men had gone up to the King's Own Yorkshire Light Infantry (KOYLI) Barracks to do their training with them before being posted to Hong Kong. Derry did more training in the Cantonese mountains of the New Territories in Hong Kong with the Gurkhas, and he enjoyed his stay there, being fit and well fed, before sailing to Kure in Japan to get kitted out before going to Korea. Then they went up the line to meet their new regiment, the Durham Light Infantry.

Derry was in Korea from November 1952 to July 1953, and he remembers an officer picking out so many men to go on an ambush up on Hill 355, and being left at the bottom of the hill for some reason. The Chinese had already ambushed two of their patrols that day, and had killed and wounded some of them. The DLI had an ambush party at the top of Hill 355, and this lad was at the top, and he came down the hill screaming his head off that he had been shot in the head, with blood pouring out of the wound at the side, so Derry grabbed hold of him and took him back up the four-in-one hill, with the lad helping himself as well. As they approached the top there were bullets flying around their heads, nevertheless, Derry eventually got him into the trench, but the Chinese were still firing at them from Hill 227, until he got the injured man into the hands of the medics.

Derry had run up the hill not knowing where the next man was, and went straight into a load of barbed wire in the dark, and was sent flying back down the hill on the back of his head; so when he came across the wounded man he was not really with it himself, but he got the lad up there somehow. Derry then reported to the sergeant at the command post who had two other wounded men there. They couldn't get down the trench because it was full of water, then Derry pushed the two wounded men up on the top of the trench and got himself out the best he could. The captain came up to him from the hill bottom and he gave them to the officer, who told Derry to stay where he was.

When the officer returned he got Derry to help him with a lad just killed by a mortar bomb. They put him into the back of a jeep and raced to the dressing station, being under constant fire all the time. The medic also examined Derry and asked him some questions, whereupon Derry passed out, concussed, and cannot remember any more about it. He did not know the names of the wounded men, and never heard of them again. Derry received his Military Medal a year later from the captain who had given him a lift in the jeep going back to the battalion, and he had told Derry in the dressing station that: '*He had won a medal,*' but he did not attach any importance to this at the time.

Before this Derry had lost his best mate who he joined up with, on Hill 159, and caught him in his hands as he fell. They got him on a stretcher but couldn't get him out of the trench, so they carried him 500 yards up the hill to Company HQ. Derry had very little action on this hill other than some shelling and mortaring from the Chinese, and by going out on patrols.

Derry was on Hill 355 twice, once on the left hand side, and later on the right, with the South Korean Army beside them, and then there was Pork Chop Ridge, and Old Baldy with Americans on it, and there were many fire-fights there, he remembers. When Derry was on the left hand side they had a bunker facing Hill 227, and he and two other lads had a browning machine gun, and the Chinese were firing down on their outpost. They were firing back at the Chinese all night to try and keep their heads down and stop the enemy from firing at them.

The next morning Derry was told to clean one of the guns on the parapet, and just as he took it down and was taking the barrel out of it he saw some Chinese coming up out of the ground with a 75mm cannon aiming at them. Derry screamed out a warning to his mates, but just then a nearby shot blasted him off the firing step and exploded into the top corner of the bunker, and he finished up 15 feet down on his face at the bottom of the trench. The noise of the attack was deafening and a few more shots were fired at them before they put the cannon out of action, and fortunately they all survived.

Another time Derry and another lad were in a bunker and ready to put their heads down to sleep, when the Chinese dropped an 81mm mortar bomb on them, but it stuck in the mud at the bottom of their trench and miraculously didn't go off. When the sergeant got them out of there he told them to go to another bunker where they would find a bed with two bunks. The other lad got the top bunk and Derry finished up with the bottom bunk which was standing in a foot of water, but he was so tired that he went to sleep with his bottom submerged in water, and was frozen stiff when he woke up next morning.

When on listening patrols from their position they had to slip down a rope to the bottom of the hill into the valley between

Hills 355 and 237, which were about 500 yards apart. The first two patrols were uneventful, but on the third one the lad in front whispered that the Chinese were coming about 50 strong straight for them, but at the last moment turned to the right and went down the valley. This was just as well, because the DLI could easily have been overrun by the enemy. Derry reckons that they were suicide squads doing that job, having to radio back to the company and warn them. The patrol was in a very vulnerable position however, because by this time they would not have been able to have got up the rope again, and would have been shot or taken prisoner. Derry found those patrols terrifying. He went out on ambush and fighting patrols, but it was the listening patrols he did not like.

Derry Rawlings, like all the other brave men who have won military awards, does not talk about how he won his Military Medal, but according to his citation he earned it for holding the mine gap with his bren gun when the Chinese would otherwise have broken through, and carried on firing even though wounded, thus saving the lives of the rest of his platoon. *(See also, Egypt)*.

2nd Lt. JOHN CAPITO

Royal Marines, 1950-52

Commissioned into the Royal Marines in May 1951, John was posted to CSRM Bickleigh and attached to a Regular recruit squad, to do the course and help out. He later took over as instructor and took one other squad through the complete commando course before being posted to 41 Commando in Korea. John joined the unit at Sasebo, (the main US Army port supplying Korea, via Pusan), where they were trained briefly in the use of US weapons and equipment.

It was late October when he joined the forward unit on islands in Wonsan harbour, North Korea, meeting up with Capt. 'Pat' Shuldham on Modo Island. It was from Modo that their 'B' troop embarked aboard a US Navy destroyer. Their intention was to make two landings on consecutive nights, further north up the coast, and cut off the railway which ran along the coast, by blowing up a train in one of the many railway tunnels.

They embarked at night in landing craft and landed in a small bay, surrounded by steep looming hills. The CO was hovering offshore when a few of them clambering up the steep hillside, met automatic fire and grenades from above. He ordered a withdrawal, for the men's safety, and shortly after guided a direct hit from their bazooka rocket launcher onto the enemy positions. Because of the opposition met that night it was decided not to land the following night, but to wait silently offshore in LCAs in the hope of shooting up a train.

Under the command of Pat Shuldham John was ordered to occupy the island of Taedo, sharing it with a few South Korean troops, but being rather near Wonsan harbour they were subject to enemy mortar fire, and enemy night raids from there were a strong possibility. The main task for them there was to improve the defensive positions by felling trees with plastic charges and carrying out defensive patrols. As their tent did not have a heater, John constructed one from two empty tin cans, some tubing, and a lot of faith, and it worked!

(See also, Malaya).

RONALD SHAW

Duke of Wellington's, 1952-54

On the night of May 12/13, 1953, Ron, along with other members of the 1ˢᵗ Btn. 'D' Co. Duke of Wellington's was sent to relieve the Black Watch, at a hill in Korea known as The Hook, a small crescent-shaped ridge, about 300 yards long and 150 yards wide. (*See Pic. No. 24*). Their position was at the top of the hill, around the Ronson tunnel, but a place of great tactical importance to both sides in the conflict.

By May 17 the Chinese were using probing patrols on the approaches to the Hook, with close quarter fighting against the Dukes' patrol outposts on Ronson, Green Finger, Warsaw and Long Finger. As they were greatly outnumbered the Dukes' patrols withdrew.

Very soon the Dukes experienced some heavy initial artillery and mortar fire as they were being heavily shelled every day. 10 platoon lived in the tunnel, the remainder were in hoochies cut out of the sides of the trenches. 'D' Company's position was on the Hook for two weeks, and they guarded patrols. During one of these patrols on May 18 a Chinese soldier, Private Hua Hong gave himself up and passed on vital information about an attack due to take place. This included the facts that the Chinese would outnumber them by five to one, and their way of approach would guarantee them protection from the planned Allied artillery fire, but he did not know when.

Ron found the mortars the worst, usually at meal times, and they suffered 58 casualties as a result. They then came under some of the heaviest shelling since World War One, as 30,000 shells were fired at their position in a week.

After May 18 the tension on the Hook mounted and the Chinese shelling increased dramatically, as did the Dukes' casualties. (*See Pic. No. 22*). The Chinese grew bolder by day, and by night they were constantly probing the Dukes' defences, and their nerves were stretched to breaking point with having to stay awake. This continued for the next ten days. By May 28 the Chinese had completed their preparations, and the full fury of their artillery was turned onto the Hook. Just before 2 a.m. their heavy guns started to pick off individual weapons pits and dug-outs. Bunkers collapsed and men were buried alive. On the right of 'D' Company's forward sector the platoon HQ bunker received four direct hits and the occupants were entombed. There were nine casualties, including two out of the three section commanders.

At 'stand to' in the trenches when the patrols went out on night patrol it was Ron's job to give them cover, and he was looking out over Ronson patrol on a nice light night and they got really shelled. They went to the observation post position, set the bren gun up and a corporal from 11 platoon (later to win the military medal) came up and said: 'Lt. Kirk sent me to tell you to try and get to the tunnels.' After their observation post was blown up, they moved out fast. They found out later this was about five minutes before the attack. Ron and his mate tried to get into the tunnel from the trenches but couldn't reach it in time, as their previous position was shelled. They looked over the trench and saw masses of enemy troops coming up towards them, about 7.30 at night. There were 10, 11 and 12 platoons on the hilltop guarding the Hook position, about 40 of them at the time, as the Chinese overran the barbed wire perimeter, so they now *had* to get into the tunnels, and Ron and his mate were the last two to get in.

The Chinese got as far as the tunnel entrance, with firing and shells going off, then everything went quiet, and the Chinese shouted at them to come out and surrender, but they refused. Ron couldn't see any way out of the mess they were in, fearful of the Chinese using flame-throwers or throwing explosives down the tunnel. Someone moved to the tunnel entrance after a while and discovered that the Chinese had blown it up, and had done the same at the other end. The Chinese had thrown satchel bombs full of high explosives at both ends of the tunnel. *'Thank God for that'* said Ron, realising that with the tunnel blocked at both ends they now had a chance of surviving.

On the crest of the Hook two occupants of a browning machine-gun post were killed and the remaining three wounded when a shell slammed straight into its embrasure. Weapons pits and fire bays were badly damaged and some communication trenches almost obliterated. The incessant shelling caused great gaps in the communication system, and the outlook was grim. Two hours later the situation had deteriorated, with the Ronson standing patrol being caught by a blast of mortar bombs. With one man killed and five seriously wounded the patrol was virtually destroyed for the second time in 48 hours.

At 7.45 p.m. the Third Battle of the Hook began in fading light and slight drizzle. Five minutes later the bombardment rose to another height on the Hook, and faded away three minutes later. Then came the attack, with the Chinese infantry carrying pole charges and petrol bombs swarming up Green Finger, and two minutes later they were on top of the forward positions. A message from a gunner in an observation post ceased abruptly after reporting that the Chinese were clambering over the trenches in front of him.

His body was found next morning beside his wrecked radio. Two observers in No Man's Land, Glen and Taylor, sent one final message on their radio set. *'This is it!'* said Glen, before the radio faded out forever.

In one of the forward positions Major Kershaw was manning the wireless intended to control Glen and Taylor in 10 platoon's HQ dugout. Platoon Commander 2nd Lieutenant Kirk was a National Serviceman due for demobilisation in a few weeks time. When the Chinese charged up the Green Finger ridge Kershaw was with Kirk in his platoon HQ dugout. One of the tunnels connected it with an observation post in the forward communication trench, and it was in this tunnel that Kirk, Kershaw and the men with them took shelter. After three direct hits by heavy shells on the platoon bunker Kershaw ordered everyone back into the tunnel. The earth was shaking, the noise indescribable, and from what he could see outside a giant plough seemed to be chewing up the hillside. The tunnel they had taken refuge in was then attacked from both ends at the same time, and 2nd Lt. Kirk at the HQ end was cut down by a burst of burp gun fire. Maj. Kershaw and his men replied with automatic gunfire, amidst the screams and hysterical yells of their attackers. Although wounded in the foot Kershaw hurled grenades at the Chinese until they grew tired of the fight, threw a petrol bomb at the defenders and blew in the entrance.

The Chinese gained a foothold on the Hook within minutes of the start of the attack. While the first attackers were trying to mop up Kirk's platoon area, fresh waves of Chinese raced along Ronson, circled round and broke on what remained of the wire on Dasent's position. However, they were decimated by airburst shells and small arms fire. Every gun and mortar possible was now firing its lethal projectiles on the approaches to the Hook, as fast as men could load and reload. The Black Watch were firing across the front from Yong Dong, and the Turks the same from the other side. Hand to hand fighting was taking place all over the Hook, with fresh waves of Chinese infantry arriving all the time. An Allied counter-attack was planned to take place at midnight, but it did not go according to plan, with mortar bombs straddling the first section going over the top, killing every man. Despite this being a slow process, the Hook was back in the Dukes' hands by 3.30 a.m.

During the morning Ron and his fellow survivors in the tunnel heard digging, and some soil trickled through, and a major in the Engineers with a big moustache was lowered down and asked: *'Everyone all right, chaps?'* They were pulled up one at a time, right on the top of the hill into a mist of cordite smoke. As Ron and his comrades went through the trenches, they found that there were only 14 Dukes remaining out of 40.

When dawn broke on May 29 the full extent of the devastation on the Hook was revealed. Thousands of Chinese shells had ploughed six-foot furrows in the hillside and levelled it. Trenches had been smashed in, weapons pits had ceased to exist, and the bunkers had filled with rubble. Shredded sandbags and tangled bundles of wire littered the area. *(See Pic. No. 23)*. Amongst all this debris the remains of Chinese soldiers testified to the murderous effect of the steel rain from the Dukes' positions, and in the dull grey early morning light the scene was gruesome. Chinese casualties were estimated at 250 dead, with 800 wounded, while the Dukes suffered 149 casualties, of whom 28 were killed. The 16 men taken prisoner were released when the cease-fire was signed in July.

The Americans were over the moon with the Dukes because of their actions on the Hook, and when 2nd Lieutenant Kirk was killed, General Mark Clark, in charge of the UN forces, sent a letter to his parents giving his condolences, and signed it personally – a very unusual occurrence.

The Third Battle of the Hook was probably the last full-scale infantry battle the world will ever see. It was the biggest battle of the Korean War, and the most concentrated barrage of artillery since the First World War. In it the Dukes defeated and routed a fanatical Chinese Army who attacked them over 15 days with incredible ferocity. [1]

57 years later Ron went back to Korea, with many other Korean war veterans, to receive inscribed medals commemorating 60 years since the Korean War began in 1950, as guests of a grateful South Korean government. Ron is seen at Panmunjon with his friend Bill Speakman VC. (*See Pic. No. 36*).

FRED WILLIAMS

After their tour of duty in Berlin the DLI arrived in Korea on September 8, and Fred spent his 19th birthday on the front line on September 25.

Two 'volunteer' stretcher-bearers were needed for a raiding party to blow up some enemy tunnels, and take some prisoners; one was Fred, and the other was his mate, Mervyn Bence, and they found themselves on *Operation Blaydon.* They had to go on a three-day course to study first aid etc., and train to put stretchers on their backs and get them off again as quickly as possible. They were obviously expecting casualties, because there was a make-shift operating theatre ready for action.

There were seven west countrymen, six Shropshire light infantry, six King's Own and eight DLI lads, and about 30 went up the hill with some assault Pioneers. They had practised carrying men on stretchers, two and four at a time for three days, and were timed how long it took to get them off again. On the actual attack they soon had a casualty. Fred had him on the stretcher, and he was pretty badly wounded. He was a Regular soldier, called Hodge, and he tried to get up to rejoin the attack, because he didn't know how badly wounded he was. He went right across the front of the Chinese trenches, and he fell down. Fred ran after him and got him onto his feet, and by this time they were under fire with bullets and grenades being fired in their direction, and he said to Fred: *'You're National Service, just leave it!'*

Fred wasn't about to leave him, because they didn't do that in the DLI, though he had to abandon the stretcher, because he was now alone with him, his friend Mervyn having been killed. Fred managed to drag him more than halfway down the hill, then with the help of the radio operator and another lad he got the wounded man back to base. There was a little river between the two hills and it was frozen over, but soon broke with the men going over it, and they then had to go through three feet of water. Fred and the other two got him across the river and he decided to try and bandage him up as best as he could. It was a moonlit night, and he couldn't see the injury, but he could feel the blood running down the wounded man's legs as he bandaged him.

When they got back to the trenches the wounded were all laid out on stretchers, and Fred thought he was the last back, with stopping to bandage the wounded man. However, Corporal Moore (on his way to earning the Military Medal) had gone back looking for a severely wounded man, Private Dolman, so there were two missing at that time. Fred's wounded man was cold, so he got a blanket for him until they were ready for him in the operating theatre. They were then told to go back, as this was the reserve company. The next day in the trenches was terrible because they had lost a lot of men, either killed or wounded. About half the platoon were affected, and it was as if no one was there, and they were taken out of the line soon after. Private Hodge never returned to the battalion, and was not heard of again.

Fred reckoned that as they got level with the enemy trenches they didn't hang back. When they got on top of the trenches they were equally matched, but when they were walking up the hill they were sitting ducks. They were not actually frightened when on the hills; they had to go up to the forward enemy trenches in the first 15 minutes, about 40 yards from the top, and were expected to keep to that time.

Fred was there right to the end, and went out on standing patrols, consisting of three privates and an NCO, halfway down the hill, listening for Chinese coming through the minefields in front of their positions. Several platoons in different positions were doing the same, in radio contact with the front line. In summer, it got up to 40 degrees centigrade, and they used to get eaten alive by mosquitoes, but in winter, often well over minus 30 degrees, they froze. They used to go out as soon as it was getting dark, so the Chinese wouldn't shell them, and in winter stay for three hours before another crew would take over. In summer they couldn't go out until 10.30 p.m. and then stayed until 5.30 a.m., timing it just right or they would be caught out in the open. They also used ambush patrols, consisting of 14 bren gunners and an officer, lying in wait where they thought the enemy were going to come. Fighting patrols also consisted of 15 men, but they went round looking for the enemy, moving around all the time

One day Fred was on one of the observation posts, and the sun was shining on the back of the hill. One of the lads was running through the trenches, and the Chinese must have seen his movement, and for the next half hour they shelled Fred's position. The next weapons pit was shelled out of the ground and all the debris went over him, and he was knocked to the trench floor.

Fred was one of those who didn't smoke or drink, and he used to give his share away. The American food packs contained 20 cigarettes a day, 140 a week, together with 50 Craven A English cigarettes, so he was never short of friends. The food was not good, mostly American in the front line, consisting of things that they would not normally eat, like Lima beans and pineapple chunks, and sometimes a bit of butter and bread, and they used to fry it in their mess tins. They had around six weeks in the line and then maybe three weeks in reserve.

Around six months after returning home from his National Service Fred became very ill, with his weight going down to eight stone, and was eventually diagnosed as suffering from malaria. He later discovered that his friend Derry Rawlings MM had fallen off scaffolding while at work, and Sir Michael Caine the actor, had collapsed on stage one day, both having contracted malaria after serving in Korea. There were many others too who contracted malaria after being bitten by mosquitoes, while serving in Korea, but did not show any symptoms until a few months after they returned home.

To this day Fred feels privileged to have been with, and accepted by the DLI, during his National Service. They were all working class lads together, and were more like brothers, and he was helped by the fact that he was the son of a Welsh coal miner.

JOHN SCOTT

On their way to Korea John remembers the DLI stopping at Aden, and being told to do a six-mile route march uphill in full kit, and in 130 degrees heat, but he never found out why. John recalls carrying his bren gun and looking down on the Yemen below, going back down again and straight back onto the boat. From Aden they sailed to Hong Kong and then Pusan, and went straight into the front line at Hill 355, and stayed there for a few weeks. While they were there they fought the North Koreans, Mongolians, and Chinese, and found that the enemy were being supplied by the Russians. John took a toy popgun off the wire one night with 'Made in Russia' printed on the side, and various others things were frequently stuck onto the perimeter wire to make the lads think of home. In winter the Chinese used to come at night time to fasten Christmas cards and presents onto the wire – a brainwashing exercise.

Operation Blaydon involved the task of entering the Chinese positions at Point 133, destroying their tunnels and bringing back a prisoner. The Chinese were bringing tanks up and they didn't know were they were coming from, so Capt. Burini and a corporal stayed out two nights and watched and saw enemy tanks coming out of a tunnel. The order was given for John's platoon and some sappers to try and blow the tunnel up, which they did. The platoon went down, and were supposed to get the area lit up with searchlights by the Americans, but they used star shells instead, which illuminated not only the area, but John's platoon as well. After they had blown the tunnel the Chinese opened fire on them and they suffered two men killed, one still missing, and 13 injured. Asked where he did his battle training, John replied: 'On Beverley Moors, Yorkshire,' which is exactly the opposite of what the conditions were like in Korea!

Standing patrols were used, comprised of four men, one with a CD set; three would lie down and the fourth would stamp on the ice around them to stop them sticking to the ice. You could fill a jerry can full of water and halfway up the hill it would be frozen solid. What they had to do was to fill a shell case with diesel oil in the trenches, light it and thaw the frozen water out. At times the temperature dropped to minus 40 degrees centigrade, and there were several cases of frostbite, and the conditions in a Korean winter were really terrible. The parkas they were given were warm, as were the lining for their boots but they had to rely on gloves sent from home. For beds they had to improvise by pinching bits of steel, and fixing them with signal wire, for springs. The food was rubbish according to John, and had to be supplemented by American tins of Lima beans, tins of soup and self-warming tins. When the beer came it was always frozen, so they used to smash the neck off and hold it near the hot shell casing.

The only way that food could reach them on Hill 355 was by the 'flying fox,' a platform hoisted up and down the mountain to keep them supplied. The only time they had a reasonable meal was when they came out of the line. They slept in hoochies cut out of the side of the trenches, and tried to keep warm in the winter by using a shell casing with a few holes in it, and filled it full of diesel and some sand and set fire to it, and the fumes used to come out of the makeshift funnel they made. However, the hoochies also kept the rats warm too. They were twice the size of rats they had ever seen before, attracted to them by the scraps of food as well as the warmth, so they used to kill them by using their sten guns, but to little effect. The American soldiers had been badly affected by disease from these rats, but John and his mates seemed to escape all that. Just as well because the British authorities were not interested.

John spent a lot of his time on Hill 355, the highest position, and a good vantage point, which is why the Chinese wanted if from them, but the Commonwealth position was kept all the time. He saw a lot of Chinese patrols coming up at night, and they beat them off, but they never left any dead or wounded, and the DLI thought they were fighting ghosts, because there were rarely any bodies left the following morning. Also disturbing at first were the messages they kept sending over the tannoy, like: *'Go home British soldiers.'* On their first night in the line, it was pouring down with rain, and they were taking over from the Australians' 3rd RAR. The Chinese searchlight came on from an enemy spotter plane, and over the tannoy came: *'Welcome to the 1st DLI, your first time in the line.'*

At times they had to stay a month in the line, then came a week or so respite in reserve at Camp Casey, which had a decent NAAFI, and they slept in tents, but they still couldn't get a proper wash, unless they used the Americans' shower facilities down the road. The idea was to relax, but one time an officer made them practise a night patrol. After a while John had a five-day rest and recuperation time in Tokyo with Barry, and they were determined to get drunk every night.

During the day they cleaned their weapons or put barbed wire fences up, which involved a big roll of barbed wire, with a man either side, walking down the hill and rolling it off. John and his mate Barry were walking down one day, and there was a shout from above that one was loose and rolling down towards them. They both ran like hell, and the roll just missed them by inches – a narrow escape from death. They were always busy doing outside duties.

When the Chinese patrols got right in close at night they used to blow their bugles and whistles to frighten them, then use their Russian-made 'burp' guns, rather like the British 'tommy' guns, and to an 18-year-old first time in the line, it worked, but not later. Because he was one of the oldest at 21, John was made up to corporal in the line, there was no other option.

Frankie Howerd was due out there to entertain the troops one snowy winter's night, but the comedian failed to turn up. Instead, they were shown a film called, unbelievably, *Hell Below Zero*. Frankie did turn up later, but John was out on patrol that night.

Eventually the time arrived for John to leave Korea, and he and a few others went to Kure in Japan, for transport home. (*See Pic. No. 21*). Coming back home on the *Dilwara* John and four lads from the Black Watch, fresh from the Battle of the Hook were sent down to the galley washing up pots for the entire five-day trip. John was a corporal but was asked if he had been made up between 1939 and 1945, and when he said 'no,' he was told by the ship's RSM to take his stripes off. Before this John was going to join up as a Regular, but this stupid and arrogant RSM's attitude sickened him, and he told them to stuff it.

TOM FERGUSON

Duke of Wellington's, 1951-53

A member of 'C' company of the Duke of Wellington's Regiment, Tom Ferguson was doing his National Service in Korea. They all had standing patrols to do, and just before dark half a dozen would go out so that they could see anyone coming, giving the company an extra 200 yards warning to know that the enemy were there, and they would phone back on the 88 sets to base. Tom had a night sight weapon which enabled him to see in the dark for about 70 yards, but it only had one half-full magazine, so he used to take his sten gun as well into no-man's land over the other side of the hill. Strict silence was kept, unless they saw something, in which case they gave a whispered message back. Before first light they had to come back in, so as not to give themselves away, or they would get mortared or shelled.

The Dukes knew the Battle of the Hook was coming, because their spotter planes had detected a huge build-up of enemy troops on the other side of the hill. They had rows and rows of 3ft high barbed wire in front of their trenches, just like in the First World War. If the Chinese did reach the wire they could bring their defensive fire down onto the line. On that particular night the first wave of Chinese came over, making a huge noise, banging and screaming, but they had no weapons of real power, and the next wave would come, until the third wave would come really armed to the teeth. The Chinese always managed to take their own dead back with them, and Tom reckons they must have had men just doing that while the battle was going on.

'D' company, near the top of the hill and in the very front line, were being overrun by the Chinese, who had broken through their wire defensive perimeter. They had to get out of their trenches and enter Ronson tunnel, only broad enough to get one man through at a time, and the last man only just made it. When the Chinese arrived outside the tunnel and told them to: 'Come out and you will be all right,' they answered by firing back at them, but were aware that they were in a very vulnerable position if the Chinese were to throw grenades or napalm into the tunnel.

Tom was further down the hill at the time, and he and the rest of his 'C' company could see their comrades being overwhelmed by the sheer weight of numbers of the Chinese. Though themselves exhausted, they fired thousands of rounds at the Chinese that night in support of their fellow Duke of Wellington's, especially after the Chinese blew up both ends of the tunnel, which of course entombed the lads left trapped inside. They now *had* to get those Chinese off the top of the hill as quickly as possible, before a rescue operation could take place to get those lads out of there.   Reinforcements soon arrived, and a few hours later the Chinese had been driven off or killed, and early next morning the buried alive survivors of the attack were pulled out of the top of the tunnel.

The reason for this ferocious attack was that the Chinese needed to capture the Hook and advance beyond it, to get a better bargaining power at the on-going peace talks in Panmunjon, and it turned out later that this was their last major assault in three years of bitter fighting.

You had to be 19 to fight in Korea, and Tom Ferguson was 19 on the boat going over in 1953, and stayed there for ten months before the Duke of Wellingtons were relieved by the

Staffordshire Regiment. The 'Dukes' were leaving Korea for Gibraltar, with Tom only having three months service to do then.

He enjoyed his National Service, in spite of the cold gruelling conditions, because he was surrounded by a wonderful set of lads who fought for each other, and got on well together during those two years of his life. He still keeps in touch with some of them, by being a member of the Cleveland branch of the Korean Veterans Society.

Tom has been invited back to both Korea and Gibraltar, and while he was in Korea he was taken to where the Armistice was signed by both sides in the conflict 60 years ago.

LES BAYLES

Royal Army Medical Corps, 1951-53

Basic training for Les was at Keogh Barracks, Aldershot, which was followed by a posting to Minchington, Surrey, which he enjoyed, but found a bit rough at times. One day he was found talking in the Square, so he had to run around it with a weapon above his head for what seemed ages. Les was later posted to Catterick Camp, then to Fenham Barracks, Newcastle, with the Royal Artillery and Northumberland Fusiliers. He contracted pneumonia there, and was shipped back to Catterick to recover. Later he was asked if he wanted to go abroad, and Les replied that Hong Kong or Singapore would do nicely – so naturally they sent him to Korea! He did go to both of those places, but only en-route to Korea, embarking finally at Pusan.

Les was sent straight up to the front line at Imjin. and was there when the Black Watch suffered badly at the Battle of the Hook, and the medical team had to work 48 hours without a break treating serious injuries (*See Pic. No. 34*). Les had the job of landing the US Dragonfly 'choppers,' which had a casket on each side, with a perspex dome, using smoke bombs and fluorescent strips. They sent some of their wounded to the US Mash, and he reckoned that those 'chopper' pilots were very brave guys, and added: 'But we were all *bonkers.*' (*See Pic. No. 33*).

Getting tropical ringworm (*Tinea Pedis*) on your buttocks was a problem in Korea. They used to form a circle and paint on gentian violet on each other's buttocks. Les reckoned that they used to make many new friends that way!

The Imjin River was frozen over, and they drove across it. Les suffered pneumonia again and was dropped back to the Normash unit, down near Seoul, where he stayed two weeks, and was sent back to the front again. He was asked to go on a fortnight's work in Japan and he accepted, as he was working at a Command Post at the time as a field medic. So off he went down to Pusan, then on to Kure, with the Pay Corps. When he returned he was told he had done very well indeed, and was asked to stay on with the Field Ambulance, to which Les firmly declined, even though he was offered sergeant's stripes straight away if he did. His reply was: 'No thanks – just let me get out of here!'

There were plenty of bullets flying about where Les was on the front line. The Norfolk Regiment were going home the next day and news came through that the Chinese had killed one of their medics, which devastated the going home celebrations, and many more National Servicemen were killed in Korea during the three years conflict.

Les came home on demob, and after that he did three lots of 'Z' training at Keogh Barracks, Aldershot, Salisbury Plain and Wyke Regis, Weymouth.

Some pals of Les's persuaded him to go along with them one day to the Recruiting Office and enlist again, but when the Army found out that they were all 24 years of age, they were told that they were too old for Army service then!

Les thought National Service was a waste of time when he was doing it, but when he came out he realised that it had been the best time of his life! He reckons that it would do the 18-year-olds of today a world of good if National Service was to make a comeback.

RONALD TAYLOR

Durham Light Infantry, 1952-54

Basic training for Ronald was at Borden, in 1952, but he was later posted to Strensall, before his overseas posting to Berlin, where the DLI took their turn in guarding Rudolph Hess and other German war criminals in Spandau prison. After a few months the battalion was sent to Korea in September 1952 and took over seven front line positions in the area held by the Commonwealth Divisions, and Ron served in every one of them. The front line had become static when they got there, with a trench system similar to that used in the First World War, except that they were fighting mainly on hillsides.

Lookouts were in operation during daylight hours, but most of the action in patrols, etc. took place at night. Whilst in the line they lived in underground cabins called hoochies, cut out of the sides of the trenches, usually for three to four weeks at a time. They were then moved to a reserve area for two to three weeks before returning to the front line. Ron was the HQ Co. 88 set wireless operator, and whenever the CSM or Company 2 i/c led a patrol he was with them. These patrols were mainly 'fighting' or 'ambush', and most of the patrols had skirmishes with the enemy, but luck was always on Ron's side whenever he went out.

One of the most scary nights was when the DLI mounted a raid on the enemy positions, with the objectives being to capture a prisoner and blow up a tunnel which the Chinese were constructing. 'A' company was chosen for this task, with half going up the hill to attack the enemy positions, while the remainder (including Ron) occupied a firm base. UN tanks, mortars and machine guns were firing at the enemy positions, and the whole hill was lit up, but after only a few minutes the withdrawal signal was sent, while the objective was still under heavy fire. The raid was declared a 'success,' even though three DLI men were missing. One was found dead the following day, another was discovered later, but the third member was never found, and 14 were wounded – with no enemy prisoner being taken.

Another night whilst on a fighting patrol they came across a dead British soldier, and rather than leave him there the officer decided to take him back to their lines. Unfortunately, the dead man was frozen and very difficult to carry. They managed to get him back, but instead of being praised for doing so the officer told them that they had made more noise doing it than a herd of wild elephants, and so they would be doing the next night's patrol as well.

During the winter months in Korea it can be as cold as –40 degrees centigrade, but all they had to wear were string vests, inner trousers, sweaters and parkas, nothing like the clothing the Americans and Canadians had. If they were on Hill 355 (Little Gibraltar), the highest point in the Commonwealth sector, they had one hot meal a day brought up at night time by the 'flying fox,' a pulley system from the bottom of the hill to the top, but they lived mostly on American 'C' packs. These consisted of beans, hamburgers, chicken, etc., some cookies, chewing gum, 10 Lucky Strike cigarettes, and toilet paper. Other forward sections were not so high, and supplies had to be brought up by army vehicles.

They had a medical orderly attached to them in the line, with a larger hoochie to keep his medical equipment in. Most of the hoochies had the roof covered in cardboard from the 'C' packs, to keep rat droppings from falling onto them, because they were all overrun with rats. The medical orderly was so sick of the rats that he obtained an Australian bayonet, and every time he heard a noise or movement he would charge around the hoochie stabbing at the cardboard, but no-one ever saw him kill a rat!

Sometimes they occupied the hoochies that the Americans had just left, and they found medals, hand grenades, boxes of cookies, boxes of ammunition and worst of all, napalm, booby-trapped to go off at the slightest touch.

During his time in Korea Ron did manage some time away from hostilities, and that was when he went for five days rest and recuperation in Tokyo, which he enjoyed to the full. He left Korea in July 1953 to complete his National Service in Egypt, before returning home in September.

ALAN MAGGS

Durham Light Infantry, 1952-54

Alan was unimpressed when he had to report to the DLI Brancepeth camp in 1952, when he saw the primitive accommodation with old wooden huts, and toilets hundreds of yards away, and no hot water, for his National Service basic training. After that, Alan was sent to Strensall for two weeks coal fatigues, where he and three others had to deliver coal to married families, during which the rest were sent to fight the Communists in Malaya. After ten weeks basic training, he sailed from Southampton on the *Asturias* to Korea, calling at Hong Kong, and joined the Royal Worcester Rifles, of which 'A' Company consisted of soldiers too young to go to Korea; marking time for three months to reach 19 years of age. Alan was subsequently sent to Kure in Japan, and later by the aircraft carrier *Unicorn* to a holding camp. He did a signals course there and gained a 100% pass – being something he was really interested in. The Army were short of signallers in Korea, so Alan and two others went over a few weeks before his 19th birthday.

The battalion were in the line at this time, in trenches on Hill 355. Alan and the other two travelled from Pusan to the railhead, the end of the line, with no station, and arrived at battalion after 10 p.m., too late to be allocated quarters. They had to sleep in a marquee on the ground in what was called a death blanket, an oversized blanket which you were sewn up in if you were killed. They found six trestle tables side by side when they woke up in the morning, and realised later that they had been sleeping in the morgue!

The next morning Alan was taken to HQ and he remembers an MP controlling the traffic on the road there, not far from HQ as they passed. A shell then landed right on the spot where this MP was on, and he disappeared from view, but he just jumped up from the ditch at the side of the road, and carried on signalling as if nothing had happened! Alan could see our 3-inch mortars down in the dip firing on the Chinese positions, while the Chinese mortar bombs were falling on them at the same time.

One night when he was up at the top walking down the road, Alan heard the sound of mortars coming, and was hit in the right leg by a mortar shell, through not getting out of the way quickly enough. Another time he was nearly killed by a Chinese shell, but it landed on the other side of a Centurion tank, which shielded him from the red-hot shards of metallic shrapnel whizzing past.

The Chinese were on the tops of the hills facing the Allies and the valleys in between were no-man's land, and they used to brainwash their prisoners of war. The 'human wave' was the Chinese way of attacking with bugles and flags and plenty of noise, and the whole hill seemed to come alive like ants when they were coming over. This worked at first in unnerving the Allies, but later on the Americans used their artillery as a meat-grinder which blew them to pieces, hundreds at a time.

There were three major battles of The Hook, a key position for both sides, involving the Black Watch and the Duke of Wellingtons, plus the Royal Australian Regiment, when they were overrun by the Chinese. One incident at Yom Dom involving Alan's battalion was when some of their men got buried alive by the Chinese blowing up an escape tunnel, but they were quickly dug out. The Chinese were adept at tunnelling and used to pop up unexpectedly quite often, sometimes tunnelling from one side of a hill to the other.

Britain's Army was the third largest contingent, after the US and South Korea, and has 300 missing men from the Korean war, some still believed to be alive in North Korea, while America has 20,000 unaccounted for.

In those days there were many instances of 'Friendly Fire' – but the media were not there to report them though. 'A' Co. of the Argyll and Sutherland Highlanders and the Middlesex Regiment, the two main British regiments in Korea got hit by the US Air Force, when 120 men were napalmed and wiped out, but it went unreported at the time.

US troops if under attack would retreat without telling anyone, leaving whoever was next to them exposed on one flank. One US General was reported as saying that the only time in Korea when he slept peacefully, was when he had the sea on his left flank and a Commonwealth Division on his right flank - because he was sure that they would still be there in the morning! The US own casualties were far too high, because of their gung-ho tactics and a head-on approach.

JOHN FORSTER
Royal Signals, 1950-52

Serving with the Royal Signals at Vimy Lines, Catterick Camp, in 1950, John finished his basic training, and then went on to Aisne and Burlon Lines, for his radio operators' trade training for five months very intensive training. From there he was posted to the 3rd Infantry Division, Signals, at Harwich, a transit camp, before being posted abroad on the *Empire Orwell* to Korea. When they arrived in Pusan they were just developing a base called Brittania Camp, getting their things together there. They were unloading vehicles from ships and putting them in the port, and one of those freighters was the *Poplar Hill* from Stockton. Some even came from Tripoli, used in World War Two.

They had all their vehicles parked up at Brittania Camp and mobilized and then made their way up country making various stops up towards Seoul, through the badly damaged gateway, seeing all the badly damaged buildings there. After that they went over the Han river which was full of old knocked out tanks. In winter apparently the river was frozen over, and many of these tanks had been crossing over the ice.

John then went up towards the main division, just north of the Imjin river, and maybe a couple of miles from the front line British Infantry battalions. The main division's code name was Fort George – after King George, who died in 1952. In fact John took the message over the radio from the main division telling of his death. He was attached to an English company of the RASC, No. 78 Co, at Uijong Bu, and the main railhead was at Chokchon, run by American engineers, who dealt with all the supplies.

The Allies used to put artillery onto the hills and bombard the Chinese for a week at a time, while the Americans used Sabre jets to napalm their communication trenches. The British used land based Meteors, and also carrier based Sea Furies, which were propeller aeroplanes. During monsoons everywhere was deep in mud, and no one moved unless there was an offensive.

While John was there the Chinese mounted their winter 1951 Offensive, with 70,000 attacking the British emplacement, who were greatly outnumbered, but still mowed them down. The same area and time as Bill Speakman's remarkable VC, in November, 1951. This was hand-to-hand action, and when they ran out of ammunition they threw rocks at the enemy. The Glosters had around 900 men to start with, but only 290 or so answered the following morning roll call, with many taken prisoner. The action involving the Glosters happened a month before John landed in April 1951. John was camped between hills on the paddy fields; the hills in Allied possession had markers on them to stop 'friendly fire' from the air.

As men were recalled to go home, 78 Co. RASC were relieved by a New Zealand 10 Co. Transport, and John was then attached to them to provide communications between the company and main division.

John regarded Korea as an experience that he would not have really missed, coming out unscathed, when hundreds did not. He reckoned that National Service gave them all a code to live by, an outlook on life that you would never have seen, especially the discipline. They had lads who were out of control in civilian life, but once they were under military order they had to knuckle down, or face punishment.

JOHN POLLARD

Royal Electrical and Mechanical Engineers, 1951-53

On his way to Korea from Liverpool John was on the *Empire Halladale,* after his basic REME training in 1951, and the sea was very rough crossing the Bay of Biscay. The ship's officers went round looking for someone to do picket duty to prevent anyone from falling overboard, and as John was the only one not seasick, he was given the job. He was assigned to the ship's top deck, and given a picket stick, and told not to let anyone out on deck in case they fell overboard, and to use the picket handle if they became violent.

He was there all night from 10 p.m. to 6 a.m., and about 2 a.m. the door opened, and an older man in a dressing gown came out, and John promptly told him that no one was allowed out on deck. The man told him that he had only come out for a pipe of tobacco, and as he seemed steady on his feet on the swaying ship, John decided on prudence, and allowed him to stay. They talked for a while, until the man said goodnight and went in, and John was left wondering just who he was. Later, as the ship docked in Gibraltar, John saw the man leave the ship – he was a Major-General.

While in Korea John was posted to the 1st Infantry Troops Recovery Unit at Inchon, to assist with vehicle recovery, but occasionally acted as duty driver. One day he drove the cook to Seoul to collect their supply of rations, but also to the RASC bakery to collect bread. They drove back to Inchon via some back roads, and called in at a farm to collect some eggs, and then went to a large American base and drove straight in, because they were expected. They went to their cookhouse, where they were welcomed with open arms, as cook gave them the bread and several dozen eggs - they only had dried eggs and hard tack biscuits. In return the Americans loaded them up with tins of fruit and chicken, ham, and loads of wonderful food. Good old cook, no wonder they were the best-fed unit in Korea!

One day John was called into the CO's office to be told that his father was very ill, and that he would be sent home immediately. He was taken to Seoul to get papers processed for his leave home, and then flew to Tokyo, where he didn't know where to go, until he met an American soldier going home on compassionate leave, who suggested going with him to the American Embassy. After failing to contact a British counterpart, *they* decided to send him home that day, and kitted him out with a beautiful suit, shirt and tie, etc. John was waiting for transport to the airport when two British MPs turned up, saying they had been looking for him everywhere, and took him to Isubu, where they gave him a medical, and an old ill-fitting demob. suit. Five days later he was put on a KLM flight to London, where he had to give all the civilian clothing back, in exchange for an army uniform, some money and a ration card. He was sent to an army camp near his home, and was there when his father died shortly afterwards.

John had a wonderful time in the Army, and found it a very exciting part of his life, and recommends it to any 18-year-old.

HONG KONG

Hong Kong was always regarded as the best overseas posting, with duties being generally light, and training only minimal, with sport and travel available to be taken advantage of. The various regiments stationed there were to look after British interests, and those put in the New Territories were there to prevent a possible Chinese invasion of the Island, however remote a possibility that was. As had been agreed many years previously, there was a transfer of sovereignty to the Peoples' Republic of China on July 1 1997, as Britain made a tearful withdrawal.

PETER YEATES

Royal Navy, 1955-57

Joining the Royal Navy at 18 in 1955 after enjoying a course at the Outward Bound Sea School in Aberdovey, and then serving in the Bath Sea Cadets on TS *Avon,* Peter was no stranger to being shouted at, early morning cold showers, and learning to look after his hygiene and kit. Before his draft to Hong Kong whilst in the midst of training, in early September 1955, HMS *Ocean* had left Devonport on a high security emergency sailing to the Mediterranean. The Cyprus crisis had erupted, and she was withdrawn from training duties, and quickly loaded up military personnel, vehicles and supplies and sailed for Malta. There more Royal Marine Commandos embarked, and they went on a war footing to Cyprus via Crete, and then down to Port Said, returning to the UK via Gibraltar in November 1955.

ML 3510 was one of ten boats in the Hong Kong Flotilla (*See Picture Back Page*), and Peter joined her in 1955 after a marvellous six weeks voyage on the troopship *Empire Clyde,* having departed in November from a dirty, dank Fifties Liverpool docks. Most of that 1955 glorious summer Peter had been trained as a seaman. His first harsh training reality was HMS *Victory* and Victoria Barracks, Portsmouth, before joining HMS *Ocean* a light fleet carrier at Rosyth. As a National Serviceman Peter had started with lots of sea time, and then in late 1955 he arrived in Hong Kong on HMS

Tamar, and was drafted into the Hong Kong Flotilla. For almost two years they did many three-day patrols around the waters of Hong Kong, where two boats were always at sea on patrol. The duties were the prevention of strategic goods reaching Communist China, piracy, and controlling the rising illegal immigration from Red China. Peter's service was unique, because he was on one of ten gunboats that were supposed to protect Hong Kong. In 1953 the Red Chinese had shot up ML 1323, and seven men had been killed, so the draft was no picnic.

There were six of them who were OD's; Hugh Mann, Michael Naysmith-Miller, Pat Wilson, Michael Tooze, Peter Yeates, and a Newcastle lad. These National Servicemen certainly were the very last to serve in the flotilla, because from late 1956 onwards the motor launches were gradually converted from European to locally enlisted crews. All the National Servicemen named were Spring 1955 new entries at HMS *Victory,* Victoria Barracks Portsmouth, where they were accommodated in those old Victorian former Army barracks, now housing the Museum of Portsmouth.

Peter was really an Able Seaman, and finally those National Servicemen did achieve respect from their regular shipmates because after long months they had learned their jobs, and then they, Peter in particular, assumed the role as 'real Jacks' and acted like it. He had 'let go springs, let go aft, let go forward, stood with fenders ready, rigged a collision mat,' etc. He had lived for a good part of every week for nearly two years aboard his ML 3510. He was to start with second, then became first operator on the 20mm Oerlikon gun they had aft, exactly as HMS *Medusa* has now, then later he was gun layer for the heavy six-pounder anti-tank gun. This gun replaced the earlier Bofors fitted to the Hong Kong ML's, necessary to take on armed junks. The Royal Navy equipped Peter to get on and make some sort of success of life. He owes the Royal Navy for everything, teaching him self-reliance and so much more. Most of this collection of National Servicemen served well over two years, and they were all demobbed together at Guzz Barracks in 1957. They joined together, and departed together. It was a very special time in a very special place, serving in a very special flotilla.

Of course, Peter never dreamt that he would, one day, step back on board another short harbour defence motor launch, and some 47 years since his very last ML patrol. On that last patrol in 1957 he was just 20 years old, and had been aboard HMML 3510 for two years. But now here was HMS *Medusa* ML 1387, the first ML he had seen in nearly half a century. It was an early cold Sunday morning in January 2004 when he first sighted her alongside the jetty in Southampton dock; just the same, but painted dark grey now, but the familiar lines so welcome to see after so many years. It was an emotional return for him after all that time. He knew every inch of ML 3510, and comparing his time in her with his January visit 47 years later was a real experience, because every plank of timber was familiar. His hours of scrubbing decks, and painting, left him with an indelible memory of every part of an ML, and here on board one again, on HMS *Medusa,* it all came back.

These were great adventures for a young sailor of just eighteen, steaming through the many small islands in Hong Kong waters, being nervously allowed to stay on the wheel as they took a short cut through the treacherous rocky seas where many islands were so close together. But returning to ML 1387 has brought it all back, like the morning sounds from the Chinese Junks anchored close by or fishing close to. And now Peter has a whole new opportunity to visit and to maybe be part of another ML. 1955-1957 has come alive again, full circle. The Hong Kong Flotilla and ML3510 was such an important part of his life; apart from family they were the *best* years of his life. *(See also, Last Thoughts)*.

HARRY WILSON

After Harry's first posting to Minden in Germany and subsequent leave, came the order for getting ready for embarkation. Hong Kong was regarded as *the* plum posting – and that was where they were going, and they sailed from Southampton on the troopship *Empire Fowey* in 1956. (*See Pic. No. 46*)

On their way to Hong Kong they made a stop at Colombo, Ceylon (now Sri Lanka), where they had a strange interlude. One of the company officers was engaged to the daughter of a tea planter there, so the entire Company was bussed up country to play them at cricket, and enjoy high tea and drinks in the club house. The Raj still ruled, even in 1956. (*See Pic. No. 45*).

When Harry first arrived in Hong Kong it seemed a strange camp they were allocated to, called Fan Gardens. This was given to the British Army by a rich Chinese businessman – having been a trading post, with house and gardens and high walls, and then of course the Nissen huts the Army had put up since. There had always been a battalion of Gurkhas and a British battalion, because the Establishment had been there since the inception of Hong Kong, and they wanted to keep it that way, and they needed to have some back-up to call upon.

After a period at Fan Gardens, the battalion had to go back to their camp in the New Territories. The British manned a look-out post on top of a mountain ridge overlooking China. When Harry's platoon was detailed to go up the mountain they found that they had binoculars and telescopes there – and a detailed panoramic view already marked with any military items in the area they overlooked. Instead of looking at those of course, they spent their time looking at every good looking girl who lived in the area, and every couple who went into the fields.

There was a great uprising by the Nationalists in the colony in October 1956, so serious that the British government decided to close it down for a time, using all available troops to do this. Harry's battalion were called in when the rioting was at its height, and were ordered to get out onto the streets, patrolling as a platoon. As they entered the area of rioting, there was a lot of smoke, noise and movement and burning buildings. At this point they had to cross a bridge, and were ordered to fix bayonets, put a round up and take the safety catches off.

They were ordered to get into skirmish order and advance over the bridge into the centre of the rioting, and Harry noticed a great number of bodies lying about in the darkness. As they advanced the rioters retreated, leaving the Green Howards in possession of the area. The following morning the city was closed down completely, and nothing was allowed to move, neither people or transport; it was utterly still and silent. The Howards mounted road-blocks and eventually ended up on the railway line running through the city. They started everything moving again by blowing a siren at noon on a given day, and the residents were allowed to carry on with their lives.

As the city resumed its routine the Howards were told to report to the large transit camp, and mount guard on all entrances, and not to let anyone in without a pass. Harry demanded passes from a large group of permanent staff and wives going into the NAAFI on a Saturday night, but no one had a pass. Harry played dumb, they got mad, and the wives demanded the most senior rank to order him to let them through. Harry raised his weapon, and the men calmed down, but the wives poured a torrent of Anglo-Saxon over him. They returned to the married quarters for passes, and Harry had a good laugh.

As a result of the great upheaval caused by the riots, the Governor of Hong Kong decided to hold a great parade through the streets of Kowloon, involving the Green Howards and the Gurkhas, and designed to make a statement to the locals. On the day of the parade they wore their all-white dress uniforms, and did a version of Trooping the Colour, with marching, counter marching and slow marching; ending the exhibition with a *'Feu de Joie.'* They stood to attention, firing in order, so the shots made one rippling sound, and did this three times. They then grounded their weapons, gave three cheers for the Queen and threw their hats in the air. It felt as if this was from another age - and it was. (*See Pic. Nos. 47 & 48*).

Harry realised that he had been very lucky in getting the two plum postings available to National Servicemen; Germany and Hong Kong. To illustrate this, on the troopship going to Hong Kong, he bumped into a lad he had served his time with, who was on his way to the Korean Garrison - not a good posting. Harry later saw Bill Speakman in Kowloon one day, famous for his extraordinarily brave Victoria Cross winning exploits in Korea. (*See Pic. No. 49*).

ARTHUR WATSON

Royal Artillery, 1951-53

The first two weeks of basic training for Arthur in the Royal Artillery was at Oswestry in 1951, and he was then posted to Tonfana, near Barmouth, for anti-aircraft training. Arthur found his basic training hard but fair. One thing which stands out though, was when they all got punished for a couple of incidents. PTIs rounded them up one evening after they had finished, marched them to the gym, shut the doors, and made them run round and round with 56 lb. dummy rounds held above their heads, and in an enclosed area in the middle of summer for half an hour, which totally exhausted them.

His overseas posting was to Hong Kong, and he sailed from Liverpool in September 1951, and was in Hong Kong a month later, based at Stonecutter's Island in the middle of Hong Kong Harbour. (*See Pic. No. 13*). One day two education sergeants asked for volunteers to spend a weekend in the New Territories, so six of them, including Arthur went with them by ferry to Lan Tau Island, landing at Silvermine Bay. They walked up over Sunset Peak to Tung Chung (*See Pic. No. 14*), to what had been a walled courtyard, with six or seven old canon. They spent Saturday and Sunday morning there, then walked up to a Buddhist temple, before coming to a place called Po Lin, before going back down to get the return ferry to Hong Kong. However, it had gone, so they had to use a sampan to reach the ferry. Asking for tickets to Hong Kong, they were told they were: 'Going to Tai Ho, no Hong Kong – *Hong Kong tomorr*ow'! So they were all now AWOL – they should have been back on Sunday night, but they were not back until Monday morning. However, the two sergeants carried the can and the rest got off any punishment.

Occasionally they had to do border patrols in the New Territories. These were for three or four days at a time, stretching from Kowloon to the border with China, about 18 miles away. Arthur explained that Britain always maintained a garrison in all of its colonies, in this case protecting Hong Kong from the Chinese.

One lad with Arthur called Ormerod was out one night and missed the transport home to 'C' troop, the other troop in Arthur's battery, at Brickhill, above Aberdeen on Hong Kong Island. Faced with a six-mile walk back to camp, he 'took' a bicycle from a passing Chinaman, and rode back to camp. He was picked up next morning and received six months hard labour from the City court, which was added on to his two years service. He was locked up in Stanley jail with people who were doing 20 years for collaboration with the Japanese during the Occupation in World War Two.

When the Communists finally took over China between 1947 and 1949, the population of Hong Kong almost doubled, because of the large number of refugees coming over from China. Squatter camps, with shanties, made out of anything, were all built up the hillsides. Near the town of Victoria, fire one day swept through them. A relief fund was opened in Canton, and a deputation set off to bring relief down. There was a rumour that this deputation had been stopped at the border by the British troops; a Communist inspired plot, because no such thing had happened. But this rumour started a riot with the Chinese and Chinese squatters. Police quelled it but the Army were all on standby. This was the only time they were threatened with any violence. In all 12 people were shot during the rioting.

Arthur got something out of National Service, in that he saw something of the world and learned about other people and how they lived. He was amazed that you could get anything you wanted to eat there, while there was rationing back home when he left – and even when he got back! They could get steak, other meats, and all the fruit and vegetables etc, and things like bananas we had forgotten existed in England. Arthur was in Hong Kong for about 16 months, and he came home in February 1953.

Stonecutter's Island was later reclaimed by Hong Kong, as part of the New Territories.

ARTHUR MORGAN
Royal Army Service Corps, 1955-57

Posted overseas to Hong Kong, after his RASC basic and trade training in 1955, Arthur was based at Whitfield Barracks, Kowloon, New Territories, to start with. After a while he was moved as a heavy goods vehicle driver to Kaitac airport, delivering to all the other regiments all over Hong Kong, and the New Territories. Arthur regarded this posting as a glorified holiday camp, despite having to do regular guard duties, because being a driver he had the next day off.

The Gurkhas had their camp in the New Territories guarding the border with China, possibly as a deterrent to any Chinese incursions into Hong Kong. There was a hill that ran along the border for about 600 metres, and Arthur was delivering food rations there one day in summer, 1956. Colonel Nasser was about to shut the Suez Canal, and Arthur was astounded to see on the hillside, about 800 metres from the British barracks, a line of over 40 pure black Chinese tanks, all lined up with their guns facing towards Hong Kong, in a very menacing way. Usually Arthur stayed for a meal after a delivery, but not on this day – he just got back into his cab quickly and drove off back to his camp! Very possibly this was just a show of power, and a backing for Nasser. Whatever the reason for it, the next day they were all gone without trace. At that time there was still 50 years to go before Britain had to hand Hong Kong back to China.

He used to go over on the ferry to Hong Kong to deliver. There were three Gurkha regiments out there, and Arthur remembers stopping at the docks in Malaya and being greeted by the Gurkhas. There was one particular fellow standing there who had just recently won the Victoria Cross. Later on he was on guard duty for a week at Whitfield Barracks, Kowloon, Hong Kong, and every person that went in or out of the camp when he was on duty had to salute him as they passed. He had won it by rushing a machine gun nest after his platoon was ambushed, and had wiped out the five men in the nest, two with his bayonet.

Arthur and his mates were shocked when they heard that Nasser had shut the Suez Canal, because they were told that they were now not going home when their time was up, and they would have to stay on until an agreement had been reached. Eventually, what happened was that the Australians supplied a cruise ship to take them home, called the SS *Navasa*, and it picked them up in late November, 1956, and went round South Africa, stopping at Durban overnight. The *'Lady in White'* was waiting for them there, and she sang to them. She had done this to every troopship that had docked in Durban during World War Two, and until after the last troopship had docked there after the war, including all those who had fought in the Far East. However, this was 12 years after the war; nevertheless she still came out, an old lady then, and sang to them that day.

PETER WESTWOOD
Royal Air Force, 1955-57

After his trade training as an RAF electrical fitter at Melksham for four months in 1955, Peter was stationed just outside Hong Kong, at a valley called Sekong, 30 miles in on the Chinese mainland. The nearest point to the Chinese mainland is Kowloon, and they were in what was known as the New Territories, an area the British owned under a Treaty with China.   Peter joined a group of six electrical engineers/fitters servicing Venoms and Vampires. There were only about 120 people altogether on the base, including the pilots, sharing it with the Gurkhas.

He went out there on the *Empire Fowey*, with around 150 RAF people. No-one knew where they were going, but after stopping at South Africa, they finished up at the International Airport at Hong Kong. They were then taken to an old Japanese airstrip and two of them joined 28 Squadron, the very last RAF squadron to fly Spitfires. Six months prior to him going there in 1955, they got rid of the last ones. No sooner had they done that, than they had a visit from Douglas Bader, the World War Two fighter ace, who had come especially to see the last Spitfires, but he was too late. They ended up with a squadron of 16 fighter aircraft, Venoms and Vampires, and later on the Squadron itself was disbanded in Hong Kong – it never came home.

They were told by the Squadron Leader not to wear uniforms while on the base, so Peter spent 18 months there in a pair of shorts and wore flip-flops, as did everyone else. Further north there was a range of hills and the number of British pilots who had ploughed into these hills was six – the only time they ever wore a uniform was for the funeral parades.

They were told that just over the hill were six squadrons of Chinese fighter bombers. 208 Squadron were only there to show a presence, but they wouldn't have lasted long if hostilities had broken out.

STAN CROOK

1ST Btn. Royal Warwickshire Regt, 58-60

As previously stated, Stan had been given a posting to stay in Aden in order to drive a Brigadier General of the Education Corps. However, he had a temperature of 104 on the day he was supposed to have his kit checked before going to his new posting, and finished up in hospital for 21 days with malaria. On leaving hospital he was informed that he had missed his posting and was going to Hong Kong instead, which pleased him immensely. They set sail for Hong Kong and stopped at Singapore for a while, but while walking around Stan felt unwell again, so he hired a rickshaw bike back to the ship. On board was a Queen's Royal Army Nursing Corps major, and after examining him she told him he would have to go to hospital in Singapore. He remembered being lowered over the side of the ship into an ambulance, and the next thing he knew he was being treated in the hospital in Singapore, told he had a relapse of his malaria and remained there for another three weeks. From the hospital Stan was sent to Nee Soon transit camp on the Malaysian border where he stayed for yet another three weeks before being flown to Fan Ling Barracks, New Territories in Hong Kong, at long last.

This posting turned out to be every bit as good as he imagined it would be, and Stan enjoyed every minute of it, swimming at Lai Chi Kok, sunbathing on the beach, and drinking at the Red Dragon Club, Kowloon, besides meeting old friends and making new ones. All good things have to come to an end, and he sailed home on the *Oxfordshire* with his best pal Alan Barnet in October 1960. However, they both had a fortnight's leave together before they left the Island.

MALAYA

In Malaya the British retook control of the country from the Japanese occupiers at the end of the Second World War, but the local people no longer accepted the right of the British to rule them. The Chinese Communists formed a guerrilla army, operating against them from the jungle, but always near a village, so that they could demand food and information about British Army activity from the Malay-Chinese villagers.

This was a successful policy at first, and a State of Emergency was declared by the British in 1948 to counteract the terrorists. It was done in two ways. Firstly, Lt. General Sir Harold Briggs was appointed in 1950 to direct operations against the CTs (Communist Terrorists), and he set about integrating the police and the military, and reorganised his intelligence forces to give a better picture of terrorist whereabouts. He then directed the infantry to move into the jungle and drive the CTs deeper still into the jungle, killing as many as possible in the process.

Secondly, the villagers were forcibly removed and their crops destroyed, and were moved by lorry and resettled many miles away from any terrorist activity. This took away from the terrorists their methods of gaining food but also their means of gleaning valuable information about where exactly the British troops were.

The worst of the war was over by 1954, and Malaya was granted independence in 1957, but pockets of terrorist activity dragged on until August 1, 1960, and the Emergency was finally over. This long drawn out 12-year war remains the only successful post-war counter-insurgency campaign against terrorists, due to the expertise and enthusiasm of the infantry battalions, some with over 65% National Servicemen, who flushed them out of the jungle.

2nd Lt. MIKE GREGSON
Queen's Own Royal West Kent Regiment, 1950-52

Called up in early 1950 into the QORWKR Mike did his basic training at Shorncliffe. Side events included a week strike-breaking in the Smithfield meat market, and providing a guard of honour for Princess Margaret. He went before a War Office Selection Board (WOSBE), and obviously held his knife and fork correctly, because he soon arrived at Eaton Hall, living in the Duke of Westminster's large mansion.

They were soon busy on tactics, assault courses, lectures, and in Mike's case, rugger and boxing. He graduated, and went back to Shorncliffe as a Second Lieutenant, and the officers' mess of the 1st battalion QORWK, prior to them sailing for Malaya. They sailed on the *Devonshire,* arriving at Singapore to be greeted by an Army band playing '*A hunting we will go.*'

The battalion went to Nee Soon for jungle training, but Mike with others went to the School of Jungle Warfare at Ulu Tiram in Johore. After several weeks Mike rejoined the battalion, and they all went by train to Kuala Kubu Bahru in north Selangor. The bandits were quite active in this area, and the battalion had rifle companies in four different locations. Mike went to 'A' company Trolac on the border of Perac and practised patrolling and laying ambushes. He soon left 'A' company and went to KKB where he took a fresh draft off a troopship for training, and when trained they would go to 'D' company at Kerling, north of KKB. Training kept them all busy, but soon they went to 'D' company to be 11 platoon, and met their two Iban trackers, from Sarawak.

Kerling was very busy for Mike, because the other two platoons were new with new officers, and he sometimes had to come back off patrol to go out again to keep an eye on and help a new officer. They were later sent on platoon detachment to Tanjong Malim, where he used to plan their patrolling schedule with the police, as they had the best intelligence as to what was going on. They had their first casualties there, but later got the bandit who had killed their leading scout and wounded the man behind.

One morning Mike and the rest of 11 platoon were just completing an uneventful patrol in the North Selangor jungle, just like all the other patrols they had undertaken recently, simply finding no trace of the enemy, and were on their way back to camp. The majority of the men were in the leading 3-

ton lorry, ten more in the 15-hundredweight truck that followed, and another two in the scout car bringing up the rear. They were negotiating a twisting stretch in the road when they were ambushed, a hail of fire from above them killing the officer in charge and several others instantly.

Mike took charge and ordered them out of the vehicles, but was immediately hit in the arms and legs. The surviving 12 men were all taking cover, most of them wounded, but still able to throw a grenade and fire a rifle. Mike spotted a bandit and aimed at him, but his adversary fired first, and Mike sustained a head wound and was unconscious and out of the battle.

Very soon, Mike found out later, they were down to only four men, and private Pannell, an old soldier took charge. He reorganised the other three so that the gaps in the defences were covered, moving from one position to another, firing from each, to prevent the enemy from realizing just how small a defence force they were. Just when all seemed lost an American car appeared and pulled up sharply with a scream of brakes. It was the planter with three Malay policemen, who started firing at the enemy until they slunk away back into the rubber trees. [2]

When relief arrived later from Battalion HQ they saw that 11 of their regiment and three Iban trackers were dead, among the destroyed vehicles, and most of the rest were wounded, some badly. However, not one weapon had been lost to the enemy, nor any ammunition, and they found six dead terrorists. [3]

Mike recovered in the British military hospital at Kinrara outside Kuala Lumpur; was invalided home and served the rest of his National Service at the regimental depot in

Maidstone. As he now lives in Australia, he finds it difficult to keep in touch with the remaining members of 11 platoon.

(See also, Last Thoughts).

2nd Lt. PETER MORLEY-JACOB

Queen's Own Royal West Kent Regiment, 1952-54

After being called up in 1952 into the QORWKR at Maidstone, Peter completed his basic training at Canterbury. After passing the War Office Selection Board he went to Eaton Hall Officer Cadet School for four months, during which time he marched on the Queen's Coronation Parade in London, as an officer cadet. Peter was commissioned into the QORWK, and reported to the depot at Maidstone to await the troopship to take him to 1 Battalion, based at Kuala Kuba Bahru, Selangor, in Malaya. All the officers and about 30 other ranks who sailed on the *Empire Clyde* went on a training course laid on by the CO, because they were the last intake to join the battalion before the end of its tour of duty. On the course they were shown how to react instinctively if caught in a trap by the enemy, and practised what to do.

They arrived at KKB in September 1953, but very soon after the battalion was moved to Bentong, in Pahang, where he stayed until the following March. Peter's 'A' Company was 15 miles away, at Karah where 100 of them were in a tented camp, and they did their operations from there. Information used to come through to Battalion HQ, and as a result of that someone would get detailed off to do the job. Most of the operations consisted of ambushes, 14-day jungle patrols, or patrolling rubber estates for half a day. For ambushes it was often near a village, or in a rubber plantation, and the information was usually that someone was coming in to collect food or to contact someone. In Peter's case no CTs (Communist terrorists) were caught in that way, because the information was often poor. Peter once spent a week in a banana grove with his platoon, and set up ambush positions, based on information received. After a week it was decided that the CTs had found out about them, probably through the rubber tappers who would tell the bandits that they were there. When they were going on an operation they had to start ahead of the tappers, who started between 6 a.m. and 7 a.m. The tappers were more frightened of the bandits than they were of them, and used to give the CTs information because of this.

The only operation which was a complete success was an attack on a bandit camp, to which they were directed by a surrendered terrorist, and involved a tracker, who was a Sarawak Ranger. These were great trackers and two of them were attached to each platoon, and were so good that they could tell just by looking at a track who and how many had been along it, and how long ago. This particular tracker was very good, and when two of the bandits ran out in his direction he killed them. Two platoons were involved in this particular exercise. Everywhere in the jungle they went single file, with about nine yards apart between men, so they could just see the person in front.

The difficulty of having to rely on a surrendered terrorist was whether he was leading them into a trap, but this one was believed. He was anxious that no-one should escape from the camp, or his position would be untenable. They positioned men all around the camp, and then three or four men, including 2/Lt. Tony Follet Smith, who was in overall charge, attacked and killed one bandit, and the only other two in the camp ran out and were killed by the tracker. When the shooting stopped everyone then had to close in on the camp, but none of them knew if there were other bandits lying undercover. But fortunately there were not. The operation had been a success, but as it was nearly dark by then they had to set up a quick position in the camp itself – a dangerous situation, but better than floundering about in the dark. The next day orders came in to photograph the dead bandits for identification purposes.

Most of the operations were of platoon strength, consisting of 30 men, with a 2nd Lieutenant in charge, a sergeant and three corporals, and once they were in the jungle no-one else knew where they were. They had a signaller with them and he could usually communicate with HQ. As they could only carry about three days food rations, they had to have airdrops to replenish food, batteries and clothing etc. Unless they could find a clearing and identify it and direct the aircraft onto it, they had to cut a clearing themselves. The idea was to start a bonfire, put some smoke up and use smoke grenades to attract the pilot's attention. The CTs kept away, unless outnumbering them.

The Malay campaign was a battle won, because the local people wanted them to win, in preference to the Communist terrorists, who were brutal towards them if they did not feed them. There were lots of atrocities committed by the CTs against the locals as well as planters, so the idea was to win over the hearts and minds of the people first. The operations in Malaya were a natural progression from the 'Briggs plan,' under which the locals had been resettled into villages or compounds surrounded by high fences, and were forbidden to take food out to the rubber estates. Thus operations centred mainly around the control of food. The jungle was photographed regularly, and any new clearings were visited by troops, who destroyed any food crops growing there. This prompted the CTs to come into the villages to get food, but they were guarded, and when warranted certain paths to the villages were ambushed.

The platoon weapons were mainly .303 Lee Enfield No. 5 rifles and three bren guns, and as the range of 2 inch mortars they were trained on had a 200 yards minimum range, there were not many opportunities to fire, it needed something with a much shorter range. The solution was to use World War One Lee Enfield rifles turned into grenade launchers. Unlike the .303 rifles No. 5, with flash eliminators on them, rather like a bren gun, which they normally used, these older rifles could fire a ballistite cartridge which was like a blank, and 'blew' the grenade out of the discharger cup which fitted on top of the rifle. You could lob a grenade with a seven seconds fuse about 75 to 100 yards with this weapon, and these rifles were thus converted into a kind of mini mortar.

Peter's platoon also manned road blocks with the police to check ID cards and stop villagers taking food out to the CTs. They also did the occasional village search for bandits, but in neither case did they see any during the time he was there. The battalion as a whole were in Malaya for three years, and in that time killed over 100 terrorists, but themselves suffered 25 fatalities.

He was there from September to March, and was allowed to come home with the battalion then, when they reformed the battalion and were sent to Luneburg in Germany, by which time he had only two months to do.

Lt. JOHN CAPITO

Ordered to leave Korea, John and a few others embarked once again for Sasebo, where they celebrated Christmas, before being told they were bound for 3 Commando Brigade in Malaya. That ended John's short membership of 41 Commando, and he had been the only National Service officer in the unit, and the youngest officer, and was proud to have been associated with them.

Disembarking at Singapore they travelled by train to Ipoh, and then transported to 'Y' troop location, at Tanjung Rambutan. The next day John set out with a half troop into primary jungle and saw two bandits, but they were too far away to engage. A few days later the unit was transferred south to the Kuala Lumpur area, with the HQ at Kajang, south of KL. 'Y' troop was detached to an isolated location, based at a vacant rubber plantation house, Bukit Darah, half way on the road from KL to Kuala Selangor.

The following day John went out again with two sections, patrolling along the boundary of the rubber plantation, one section in the rubber, and John's section outside, where the going was thicker and slower, so the section in the rubber forged well ahead. They heard shooting a few hundred yards in front, and moved as fast as possible to join them. By the time they got there the shooting had ended and they found four dead bandits and one hurt marine. Apparently, the other section had encountered impassable terrain and had crossed outside the rubber. Their Iban trackers had found fresh tracks, and followed them back into the rubber, where they came across four terrorists, who, having stopped to rest, had heard the section and had taken up ambush positions, using draining ditches as cover. In the fire-fight the marine with the grenade launcher fired accurate grenades into the terrorists' position, enabling the patrol to pick off each one of the enemy. Unfortunately, the marine with the grenade launcher dived into cover while he still had a grenade in the launcher, and it fell out and exploded next to his thigh.

The radio was unusable, so they could not summon help, and they had the task of carrying four dead bodies, one wounded marine, and numerous heavy terrorist back packs. This required considerable physical effort, and progress through the steeply sloping rubber was horribly slow, and they were still in 'bandit' country. They eventually made radio contact and transport was soon there. This incident made an impact in the national newspapers, but the police chief was not pleased, because the Iban trackers had removed the scalps of the dead bodies, so they were less useful for identification purposes. He was also annoyed that none of the terrorists had survived for questioning, and was sure that some had been 'finished off' illegally. However, the information contained in the back-packs contained very useful intelligence.

The unit was withdrawn in June, and went first to Singapore, then Malta, and on demob. John hitch-hiked home through Sicily, Italy and France.

A typical National Service Malaysian jungle patrol, 1950.

(Photo courtesy of Roy Follows)

EDDIE MACK

SAS/Royal Hampshire Regiment, 1954-56

Starting his National Service at 18 with the SAS/Royal Hampshire Regiment in 1954, Eddie trained for six weeks at Winchester, then sailed from Liverpool to Malaya, taking six weeks to arrive in Singapore. He went by train to Malaya, and started his six weeks jungle warfare training, and was put into 'D' Co. with 10 others, to work as a rifleman in the jungles of Jahore.

They fought in swamps for two years, with water up to their waists, day and night, carrying their rifles above their heads. There was no shaving and no proper leave for two years, with malaria tablets to be taken every day, and the blood-sucking leeches had to be burned off with a cigarette end. They slept outdoors in hammocks every night, and monsoons were a daily occurrence, with their clothes drying on their bodies. There were also snakes, tigers and wild boar to contend with. Occasionally they were allowed out of the jungle for three days to have a wash and shave and write their letters home, then it was back into the jungle again for them.

Eddie was based around the jungles of Jahore, with the HQ in Kuala Lumpur. Sporadically they went about ten days without any action, then it would all start up again, after having a tip-off about the enemy activity in their vicinity. On and off, Eddie survived his jungle experience, with only leech marks on his legs after burning the creatures off, but he was nearly shot between the eyes by a terrorist sniper hiding up a tree, as they picked their way through the jungle, with Eddie as lead man in the terrorist's sights. The soldier behind him saw the sniper about to press the trigger and shot him out of the tree, just in time!

Food parcels had to be dropped by the RAF, so the clearing of trees to accommodate this was a must. They were fighting terrorists, and the ones they killed they brought out of the jungle, while the British soldiers that were killed were buried at a graveyard on a hill.

Eddie was in the SAS, but attached to the Royal Hampshire Regiment. All the Companies, A, B, C and D had their kills and surrenders and were in competition with each other as to who killed the most terrorists. Besides hunting terrorists and killing as many as possible, they had other duties too, such as checking on the villages for terrorists in hiding, etc., and for any information regarding the terrorists' whereabouts.

The Communists used to set fire to the rubber trees, which caused a lot of smoke to be made, to impede their progress, and to stop them going in and finding them. This of course also had an effect on the local natives, because the manufacture of rubber was their livelihood.

The villagers used to be frightened of the Communist terrorists and would give them food and protection, or suffer the consequences if they did not. In fact, the villagers used to come out at night and give food to the terrorists, so petrified were they after being surrounded and threatened by them.

They used German Shepherd tracker dogs to hunt down the Communist terrorists, by picking up their scent, and Eddie's best friend was one of the dog handlers. There was one tracker from Borneo, but in the main it was all done by the Royal Hampshires, and their dogs.

In Eddie's opinion National Service was not a waste of time, because he went in as a boy, but came out a man, after two tough years in Malaya, doing the job he was trained for.

(See also, Last Thoughts).

STAN YOUNG

Scots Guards, 1949-51

Always wanting to be in the Coldstream Guards, Stan got to the depot at Caterham on St. Patrick's Day, 1949, and was told he was going into the Scots Guards, so Stan asked: *'Do I get a kilt?'*

Stan did 16 weeks square bashing at Caterham, which was followed by eight weeks weapons training, and then to Edinburgh for six weeks. He arrived at Pirbright just in time for his 19th birthday, his first one away from home.

He was on the first Trooping of the Colour in full dress after the war, in 1949. Only three months in the Army and there he was, marching up the Mall with the drums and band of the Regiment. He then went back to the Guards depot, and later Edinburgh, for what was to become the Edinburgh Tattoo. Stan was the right hand sentry as they did the changing of the guard, giving out all the signals and working hard as one of a pair.

Stan was one of the original virgin soldiers, and saw quite a bit of action in Malaya. When they captured any terrorist camps and took their ammunition and guns, etc, it was always better and newer stuff than they had. Stan was using 1943/44 ammunition, whereas the CTs (Communist terrorists) were using 1947 ammunition, so where was it coming from?

They were on patrol in Malaya and could see that when the Japanese left they wrecked a lot of places. There was only one coal mine in Malaya, so the Japs had set it on fire, and slashed the rubber trees, etc, and did a lot of damage. They came across an old tin mine in the jungle, and the manager's house was still standing in Mentacab, so they camped there. Stan has always been a good cook, and downstairs in the kitchen was an old stove, and as he had some tins of sardines he traded them for some rice, boiled the rice, found some Carnation milk and sugar, and put it in the oven. It made a fantastic rice pudding. In the Guards the officers are all Lords and Earls, etc. They had a young subaltern with them called Lord Melgin and after they had the stew, Stan told the lads there was a pudding to come. Later on the officer came up to Stan and asked: *'Geordie, is there any more of that beautiful rice pudding?'* Think about it - a Lord asking a guardsman for some more rice pudding!

Stan was stationed at Kuala Kubu Bahra, a town in Hula Selangor, and went to Kuala Lumpur to go swimming on his day off, to a private beach belonging to Hollywood, with beautiful white sands. He wasn't bothered about the Communists, it was the wild life he didn't like, such as rats, monkeys, snakes, elephants, ants, etc. Everyone suffered from prickly heat, as it used to rain every day, and when in camp the lads used to strip off – the rain was the only relief.

When they were in training they were told to dig themselves in with their trenching tool to get cover. However, when ambushed instinct tells you to hit the deck, and dig yourselves in with your bare hands (the earth being very soft in the jungle). If ambushed they were told to fire to the left and right of them, as some of their own lads could be in front. At one point early on, as Stan was hitting the deck (through fear), he fired off a full sten gun magazine, and he would not have been the only one to have done this.

When they arrived at the training base they had to do a basic three weeks training, and at that time volunteers were requested to sweep the training area looking for bandits. A platoon went in, but the Communists had set a bren gun up on the track on fixed lines. Two of the three men in the advance party went forward, and the front man, Guardsman Holland, the Company storeman, was shot between the eyes, and they blew the top of his head off. The platoon withdrew to review the situation, as the rules were not to run into an ambush, but to withdraw, come out to make plans, and get organised. When they went to recover the body they found that Guardsman Holland had been stripped of uniform and weapons, and he had a water bottle cork screwed into his head wound at the front. This was just a clearance patrol in an area where they were going to do some training in.

They used to go out at night with the Malay police into the villages, and on one occasion they went to a wood village, what we would call lumberjacks. The police used to separate the men away from the women and. take the children behind the bashirs, or huts, and fire a couple of rounds into the ground, to get the women to talk about where the terrorists were, and this usually worked. On one of their patrols one of the lads was killed and a local native was seen running away into the jungle, but he was caught and given a beating by a couple of the lads in retaliation, which distressed Stan.

Stan was a carpenter by trade, and after his National Service he went back to doing that, and now at 81 he still keeps his hand in making rocking horses. He is also still a member of the Scots Guards, of which he is very proud.

JACK POWELL
York and Lancaster Regiment, 1945-47

In the 2nd Battalion of the YLR from 1945 to 1947, Jack was driving an American Jeep in a district of Kelantam, South Malaya, when the radiator started to overheat and boil, so he stopped the jeep, as there was a stream just by the side of the tracks. He had a collapsible, canvas bucket in the jeep for carrying water, so he took the bucket down to the stream and put it into the water. After the bucket was half full he looked up and on the other side of the stream looking at him, was a tiger, barely ten feet away. So Jack grabbed his rifle and ran, faster than he had ever done before, and totally forgot about the jeep needing water. On reflection, he realised the tiger had just been thirsty and had gone to the stream for a drink, but at exactly the same time as Jack was filling up. They had both wanted the same thing at the same time, but for different reasons.

While he was in India they could not go out alone, because of the strong anti-British feeling with a lot of them, even after having been freed by the British from the Japanese a little earlier. The Hindu high class Indians were all right because they had all the important jobs, but it was such a religiously divided country that things were difficult for the British soldiers there. Jack's Regiment were only there to be taken forward to join their Battalion in Burma.

Incredibly, Jack was still rounding up remnants of the Japanese in 1947, because there were units of Japanese in the jungle that had not heard of their surrender in 1945. Jack was in action around the village of Timmin, on the main road from Mandalay to Mitkiana, on the Cambodian border, and after this they reorganised and prepared to move forward. The headman of the local village went up to Jack, because he was the section leader, and presented him with two tapestries, for chasing the Japanese out of the village, and he still has them in his dining room at home today. The Japanese had committed an atrocity in the village before Jack's unit had got there and Jack did not want to elaborate, because the memory of what he saw that day is still too painful for him to discuss.

When Jack was in action in the rice paddies they never got their feet wet, but the Yanks that came later on used to jump straight in and were up to their chests in mud. Jack's lot used to run along the clay banks instead. He reckons the Yanks were the most undisciplined Army he ever served with.

KENNETH COY

13th\18th Hussars, 1959-61.

National Service was delayed until 1959 for Kenneth until he finished his apprenticeship at 21. He trained with the 15th/19th Hussars, and was then posted to the 13th/18th Hussars at Ipoh, Malaya.

On their final inspection before embarkation to Malaya, one of the lads was missing a fork, so he ran down to the NAAFI for one of their forks, unaware that they were mark laying it out for inspection, and he got 14 days for that. Due to the fact that they were being shipped out the next day, two of the lads were made up to corporal, so that they could escort him to the ship. On the way down by train they got out at one of the stations to buy some drinks, and nearly left him behind, and when they arrived at the ship he was put in the brig for 12 days.

Ken volunteered for a trip to deliver vehicles to 221 camp, hoping to see his brother based there before he returned to the UK. On arrival at 221 late at night he checked into the guard house, and on seeing his name he was told that his brother had left that morning, and that he should go to the bedding store to draw out bedding for himself, and then find a hut with a spare bed. After lugging the mattress around the camp he finally found a bed, and looking at the bed card it still had his brother's name on it, with the words 'Gone home to England.' Ken then sent it home by post – and it arrived before his brother.

On the return trip from camp 221, based over the causeway from Singapore, the sleeper civilian train journey was expected to take 12 hours, but at times it travelled at slower than walking pace. After about two hours into the journey the need to use the toilet was getting to be a high priority, but knowing it was used by locals filled Ken with horror. Eventually he went into the cubicle, and before him was just a hole on a platform only 18 inches off the floor, but as the train was shaking so much he knew that he would never have made an accurate deposit. He returned to his seat, but after a further hour, with the situation now desperate, he tried again, and looking around the cubicle he found a large lever, which he operated. The whole platform then raised up into the air, exposing a normal toilet with a brass plate with the words:

'Made in Birmingham.' Being from Birmingham, Ken found it very comforting.

On one afternoon off from camp Ken and some of the lads went to see the movie *Ben Hur* in Ipoh. After the film they lined up five tri-shaws for a chariot race back to camp – one lap round the town, and then the main road back. The only trouble was that their Chinese tri-shaw rider looked half dead before they started, and they had no chance of winning.

(See also, Germany).

LESLIE IVES
Green Howards, 1949-51

After his training for the Green Howards in 1949, Leslie spent most of his National Service in Malaya. The rifles that the squaddies used in Malaya were the R.E. No. 5, a shorter version, with a flash eliminator on the barrel and it was made so that when in the jungle it was not too cumbersome. Les's sergeant carried his Extra Yield rifle - the woodwork and the barrel were banded up with wire. Because these World War One rifles were so accurate, the sergeant dispensed with the cup which fired the grenade, and carried it as his personal weapon, and was good with it.

The whole battalion were on a long jungle operation lasting 28 days, called *Operation Jackpot*, the idea being to drive the Communist bandits into a particular area, called a killing ground, where they were going to be attacked by them and strafed by the RAF.

They were going along this jungle track with the platoon, and the guy at the front raised his hands; the sergeant went forward and there was the biggest cobra snake Les had ever seen, coiled around a branch of the tree. Only the sergeant knew that these cobras could spit venom into your eye from a short distance. With no medical assistance in the middle of the jungle, it could prove fatal. So the sergeant put up his trusty .303 and got it right between the eyes. They all passed the stricken snake very quickly in case it had a mate.

When they got back off this reconnaissance trip in the state of Pahang, where the company base was, there was this poor dead squaddie, tied to a pole, wrapped up in parachute silk, just about to be taken out of the jungle. They had tried out a new idea of sending a squad of guys down a track and came across concealed bandits. There was a fire-fight and this poor chap was killed. It took three days to take him out because there were no roads – you went out the way you came in. The sergeant major in charge of this party got mentioned in despatches because the sheer weight of someone being carried on a pole in turns through the jungle made it very hard work, extremely slow and dangerous.

BILL DAVIES
13th/18th Royal Hussars, 1950-52

Being an apprentice joiner by trade, Bill knew nothing about cars, so in 1950 the Army in its wisdom decided to train him up as a vehicle mechanic, and at Bovington he was taught everything there was to know about cars. He was then posted to the 13th/18th Royal Hussars as a vehicle mechanic in Malaya.

The 13/18 Royal Hussars was a regiment of armoured cars, whose job was to keep the roads open. They were in Malaya at a place called Kluang and the Hussars had a base there, in the bottom end of Malaya at Jahore. They had a small camp out in the wilds, on The Old Lady's Coast, and it was called Jema Luang, an Army camp with three tents. They only had a wind-up gramophone, and just a few records for entertainment, but no radio.

Bill and his mate had been out on a job one particular day, and ended up in a convoy from Kluang, to get back to their place at Jema Luang. They came across a big battery wireless in a wrecked car, and got it back to camp, where they had a Signals friend who was a genius with such things. He rigged it up with an aerial and loudspeaker, etc., and very soon they were receiving the Forces network from Tokyo and all over. After a few days word got around and the tent was always full of people wanting to listen in, and it became very untidy, and they all got barred, except for Bill and his mate.

A few days later they were both out on a job together again repairing a pick-up. When they got back to camp they were informed that they were in dire trouble, going to be shot at dawn, etc., and they got a telling off about this wireless from their sergeant. A convoy of MPs had arrived, marched in, grabbed the wireless, and went off again. Strangely, they never heard any more about it

Years later, working in a hospital as an assistant nurse in the late 1980's, on night shift, Bill was reading a story in the *Reader's Digest* about the dirty tricks the British military got up to in Malaya. 'For example, leaving wirelesses about where they knew they would be picked up and handed over to the terrorists. These wirelesses had a homing device fitted, but it backfired on them one day at a British Army camp. Two enterprising squaddies had picked one up, taken it back to their camp, and fixed it up in their tent.' Bill went cold. After all these years he had found out why they never really got a rollicking. He realised they couldn't – it was a secret! His mate came in with a cup of tea, and asked him what was the matter, because his face was white? Bill explained that the article referred to him and his Army pal.

While most of the terrorists were in the jungle, some were in camps. There were Malayans called the Minuen, civilian terrorists, money collectors in towns, and they collected things and handed them over to the terrorists. Kluan, where they found the wireless was a very active place for them, and the military were hoping the Minuen would hand them over to the bandits, and as each one had a homing device they would be able to track it with their spotter planes. As regards Bill's radio, they spotted it all right – but it was in Bill's tent! The MPs went into Bill's camp, grabbed the wireless, and nothing further was said for obvious reasons.

Bill was of the opinion that they were not trained properly beforehand for what they were up against in Malaya. The jungle was frightening, you never knew whether you were looking for them, or they were looking for you!

On a training session they were using World War One equipment, what was called an EY, an old Lee Enfield rifle wound round with copper wire to strengthen it. A canister on the end fired a 36-type hand grenade and it had a ballistite cartridge which was a blank, and you loaded that and the butt went on the ground. You put the hand grenade in the cup, pulled the pin out and the hand grenade dropped into the cup. Then you pressed the trigger with your thumb and it blew the hand grenade out 50 yards or more. It was a grenade launcher, as used in the trenches from 1914 to 1918, firing from one trench to another. One lad from Liverpool was killed when something went wrong, and the handle came off as he slipped the hand grenade in, and it went off and killed him, and after that the rest of the lads refused to use them anymore. Bessie Braddock, an influential Labour MP from Liverpool herself was informed of this, and their use was suspended almost straight away.

If anyone was killed, and there were three in Bill's unit during his spell in Malaya, their equipment was rounded up and taken away, and if anything was missing, any part of their equipment, the money to pay for the missing article was taken away from their credits before it was sent to their parents. This appalled Bill, and quite rightly so.

In Singapore there was a club called 'Raffles,' but ordinary soldiers were not allowed in there, because only officers and NCOs could gain admittance. The very short haircut gave the game away, you looked like a squaddie. There were many other similar instances like this – it was just how things were in those days – you just took it and said nothing.

Bill reckoned his National Service was a waste of time, taking two years out of his life. All he learned was how to service a car; and comprehensive though that was, currently useless information, because they are now computerised.

HOWARD DUDDLES
Royal Signals, 1957-59

Doing his basic and trade training at Catterick for the Royal Signals in 1957 as a teleprinter operator, Howard went later to Brighton Cypher School to train to become a cipher operator, before sailing from Southampton for Malaya. Life on board ship was one big holiday for him. He was in charge of a group of lads cleaning brasses in the hospital on the ship going out, and the MO told him there was no need for him to go down, as long as the rest did. So every time the ship berthed he was able to get off and see the sights.

Shortly after arriving in Malaya, Howard had an invitation to witness the Gurkha Christmas, Dashira. They have a ceremony, with the High Priest officiating. They bring on a bull and tie it to a pole, and the Gurkha has to cut its head off in one action with a kukri knife. Howard was too close to the action in taking a photograph of it, and was splashed with the bull's blood. The Gurkhas then cut the heads off chickens, sheep, etc., and it was time to depart!

In Malaya whenever near Communist terrorist activity the local inhabitants were encouraged to leave their villages and go to purpose-built villages with high wire fencing surrounding them, well away from the CTs. This move cut off the food supply for the terrorists, and they also lost their influence over the Malaysians.

The cook just wanted to make curry and rice, but in those days it was not part of our favourite diet. He just had a dirty pair of shorts on and bare feet, working in the cookhouse, but in the end he succeeded in making them eat curry and chips and curry and rice – many years before they became popular in Britain.

Howard started a cub pack as Arkayla, and later on had an officer to help. They were all Army officer's children, and occasionally one of them would say to another cub that his father was a major or a captain, but Howard used to point out that he was just a corporal, but he was running the show. One of the cubs was always late, so he had a word with him to ask his father to drop him off at the proper time. The errant parent happened to be the Brigadier, who was soon on the phone to apologise, saying he would try and improve his child's timekeeping! Howard got a lot of pleasure out of running this cub pack, even though he had to work shifts.

They took a message one night about a soldier being attacked by a tiger, while he was draped in his hammock. He was screaming at his mates to shoot the thing, but they didn't dare, in case they shot him, as they were entwined together. However, the tiger gave up when one of his mates fired into the air, and the soldier survived the very deep wounds in his back.

Another time Howard was on an island off the coast of Singapore, called Blabka Mati, (now called Sentosa, with its theme park, etc.). That is where all our guns were pointing the wrong way in the Second World War, out to sea, expecting a seaborne invasion, but the Japanese came down the mainland in Malaya, and took Singapore from the rear, rendering our guns useless. While he was there Howard got talking to a nun who was on the *Walk of the Sixth Happiness,* taking all those children over the mountains to safety, away from the Nazis. The film of that walk depicted one nun, whereas there were actually five or six. Howard was amazed that she did not want to get away from all that and go back to England, but she just loved being there, and had no intention of going home.

There was a chap there from New Zealand, who had been imprisoned in Changhi jail, the infamous Japanese prisoner of war camp, during World War Two. He was still in the Army, a sergeant now, and was coming back to Singapore, and dreading it, but the first thing he did was to go back to Changhi. Someone informed the authorities and he was given a grand tour of the prison, and he told Howard that he had finally got rid of that dreadful experience. Howard went back to Singapore in 1996 with his wife, and visited Changhi jail, around 50 years after the Japanese surrender, and saw letters from relatives, like: 'We've been to see where you spent your last days, dad' etc. They found this very moving.

He was guard commander for one 24-hour duty on the ship coming home at the end of his National Service, down in the bowels of the ship, and there were two Glorious Glosters in prison, and a chap from World War Two. The Glosters told Howard that they had been napalmed by the US in Korea (friendly fire) and had been badly burned. They went to hospital in Japan, and decided they had had enough, and were not going back to Korea, so they had skipped hospital. The other chap had escaped from the Japanese during the war, gone to Australia, and come back to Singapore later. He was picked up, and they were taking him and the other two back to England to face courts martial.

Howard thought his National Service experience was marvellous, and realised that he was lucky to go abroad at such a young age, and see the interesting things that he did; meeting some extraordinary people on the way, rather than having a boring home posting for two years. *(See also, Last Thoughts)*.

STAN HAWTHORN

Royal Engineers, 1947-49

Starting off at Brancepeth camp for his six weeks basic training with the DLI in 1947, Stan was then posted to

Aldershot for a 12-week Royal Engineers administration course. He was later sent to Barton Stacey for drafting to the Far East, sailing on the *Dunera* from Southampton to Singapore, calling at all the usual places, as well as Rangoon in Burma, to bring out the 1st Btn. 6th Gurkha Rifles, still in service to the British Army. The ship sailed on to Penang, to offload the Gurkhas, and Stan finally arrived at Singapore and eventually Nee Soon transit camp, where the conditions were dreadful. After only three days his posting came through to 126 plant troop, Ayer Rajah Road, Singapore, to take over administration, where the lieutenant could not wait for him to arrive, and after only two days instruction he left for England.

Stan then moved to Kuala Lumpur in Malaya, with 126 Plant Troop to take over the work of 733 Indian Mechanical Troop, who left all their equipment, and earth moving equipment etc., on the outskirts of Kuala Lumpur. The troop was used to clear scrub jungle, build roads, lay water and sewage pipes for a civilian hospital. (*See Pic. Nos. 15 and 16*). Stan's unit and others were then disbanded to make up a work squadron, and they were moved to a new unit at the end of May. It had been an RAF camp before the war, was under Japanese occupation for three years, and became British again by 1945.

By this time the Emergency had broken out, with Chinese Communist insurgents killing planters. They were not allowed out of camp, and slept in tents, fully dressed with a rifle and 50 rounds to each man, because the Chinese had boasted of being in Singapore by the end of the week, making it a very bad weekend. But fortunately nothing happened, and then Stan was posted to Taiping, Perak, 200 miles from Kuala Lumpur, to take over administration up there, also a working unit.

At Taiping some of the lads had gone down to Tapah but nothing was heard of them for days. The sergeant at Taiping was going to change with the sergeant at Tapah, but there was no knowledge of them being paid, or wear and tear of uniforms, etc., so the person in charge of stores was going down to see what was happening, and Stan was to go and see what the pay situation was. Stopping outside Ipoh for a break, the wagon broke down completely, with rubber plantations on either side, not good in terms of a possible enemy ambush. They phoned HQ to ask for assistance, and were told to wait for help to arrive, and keep a lookout – which just had to be Stan, because he was the only National Serviceman there!

Eventually a Buick automobile pulled up beside him driven by a lady, and she offered to take him to the nearest village where there was a police post. She had a .37 service revolver on the passenger seat, and was possibly a rubber planter's wife, and she drove Stan to the police post at Gopeng, and they sent a truck out and pulled them back. They eventually finished up at Ipoh with the Gurkhas, then the next day they went back to Tapah and found the men were OK, having been looked after by the Coldstream Guards.

Young National Servicemen in North Malaya were used as forward scouts in jungle fighting at first, then head-hunters from Borneo were used instead, because they knew the jungle better. Taiping was right in the middle of two Communist bands.

Like so many other National Servicemen on leaving Singapore, Stan vowed never to return to that part of the world – ever! However, like many others he got the urge to return again in the 1990s, and took his wife with him to reminisce and see again the places he had not seen for over 50 years. *(See also, Last Thoughts)*.

ARTHUR JAMES

Royal Army Ordnance Corps, 1947-49

Doing his basic training at Brancepeth Castle with the DLI in 1947, before joining the RAOC at Hilsea Barracks at Southsea, Arthur sailed from Southampton on the *Strathnaber*, taking four weeks to reach Malaya, his overseas posting. Going into the Red Sea the Ships Orders gave the order for all portholes to be kept closed, but on this particular day it was exceptionally hot and overpowering, so someone shouted: *'Open that bloody porthole,'* another repeated the order to keep them shut, while another bright spark decided to open both of them, and the breeze coming through was wonderful. They must have got too close to a huge wave however, because it was just like two giant hoses coming through the portholes. There were shouts and screams before they were closed, but by then the damage was done. The rest of the night was spent with a mop and bucket, and Arthur has never seen so much water, and everyone was absolutely drenched. There were about 40 affected, but they only had half a dozen mops and buckets between them, and it took until 3 a.m. in the morning before they bottomed it. No one else noticed all this activity, and so they got away with it.

In Malaya they were just mopping up the war surplus stuff, like tanks, jeeps, etc, left over from the Second World War. They used to get paid about 15 dollars a week. After spending on the usual essentials, they used to keep the rest on credit for the end of the month, which used to amount to around 40 odd dollars. On the Friday night they went straight over the Causeway at Johore Baru to Singapore, and then into the Union Jack Club. Many a time they did not have the taxi fare between them for the return journey, so they just ran like hell when they got out of the taxi back at Tebra camp, Johore Baru. Arthur stayed there for the whole of his service, and at one time was the youngest soldier in Malaya.

Two of the Scots lads had been down to Johore Baru, and they brought a prostitute back with them. They were based in billets like two storey flats, with a maximum of four people to a room, and the corporal in his own room. They brought the girl in while the Regimental Police were on the ground floor, without being seen or heard by anyone.

She started at one end of the block, and went right to the end of the other before she went. The lads paid her off with Japanese money, and she went off her head, screaming abuse at them before she left, which of course brought the RPs into action, and the inevitable recriminations followed.

Arthur enjoyed his National Service and wouldn't have missed it for the world, because he came from a military family anyway.

TREVOR SHIELD

Serving for six months in Aden with the 1st Royal Dragoons, before arriving at his posting at Ipoh, northern Malaya, Trevor stayed there for the rest of his service. Because there was no call for gunners at that time, he was posted to the officers' mess for eight months. While he was there the Hussars celebrated their tri-centenary, the regiment being formed in 1661.

Trevor was in charge of the silver which was very valuable, and there was a tremendous amount of it, and whenever they had any big dinners which was often, Trevor had to make sure that it was always cleaned. On one occasion two items went missing from the safe, and from the inventory when they had a stock take. The officer of the day would choose what pieces of silver they were going to use, and when the losses were discovered Trevor got the blame, because he was in charge of it, but he was not the only one with a key, there were also two officers. One of them had taken the silver – and they never saw him again, or found out what happened to him, and the items were never found either.

There was a special parade for the Regimental tri-centenary, and they sent to London for uniforms of that period for the occasion, and they were duly sent out to them in Malaya; all the relevant tunics and helmets etc. They had horses at Ipoh, because some of the officers owned them, and so many men were chosen to wear these uniforms and go on parade for this tri-centenary, and Trevor was one of those selected. After it was all over, following a week of celebrations, they gathered all the uniforms and equipment together and destroyed the lot; because they said there was no point doing otherwise, because it would be too costly to send them back – a terrible waste.

Princess Margaret who was Colonel-in-Chief of the Regiment, was to come over to inspect them, and they all paraded and stood out in the blazing sun for over four hours waiting for her to appear one particular day. It was terribly hot standing still there, particularly in those uniforms, Trevor remembers - and she didn't even bother to turn up!

Trevor reckons his National Service was the longest two years of his life, and he just wanted to get home. He enjoyed the experience overall, though, and from that point of view it was not a waste of time.

He was a landscape gardener before he was conscripted, but he went into sales when he came back, and stayed in sales for the rest of his career. (*See also, Aden*).

CLIVE KING
13th/18th Royal Hussars, 1958-60

Hadrian's Camp, Carlisle was where Clive did his basic training with the 11th Hussars in 1958. He did six weeks basic and then six weeks basic radio operating, before being sent straight out to Malaya, as a driver/signaller. He first went to Singapore on the *Oxfordshire*, and stayed at the Nee-Soon transit camp overnight, then travelled by train to Epoh, where the Regimental HQ was. Most of the time Clive was situated in Jahore Baru, at a camp called Majeedi Barracks, the last town at the bottom of Malaya. He was subsequently posted out to the King's Dragoon Guards there, before being sent back to Singapore to Nee-Soon camp for three months, after which he had to drive up Malaya to Epoh.

One of Clive's mates was a bit embarrassed at getting dressed in company, and one day while they were out on an exercise, he tried to get undressed under a blanket. He pulled his trousers on and put his jungle boots on and fastened them the best way he could. However, when he got out of the blanket he found out that he had put his trousers on back to front. At seeing that everyone laughed, which made him a bit more embarrassed.

Later on the lads all went to the pictures to see the film *The Pyjama Game*, and there was an incident in that film where one of the actors had to model some new designer pyjamas. When he had finished modelling he got his trousers on the best way he could, and he was trying to pull his zip up which was at the back again. A few of them were sitting near the lad who had already done that back on exercises, and he was sitting uncomfortably, and they all just burst out laughing. The lad in question just slouched a bit further down in his seat.

SINGAPORE

Singapore had a clear strategic importance during the Malayan Emergency, from 1948 to 1960, and the Korean War from 1950-53, but it also represented Britain's desire to retain a presence in the Far East, however unpopular that was to become.

While the infantry battalions were fighting the Communists in the Malayan jungles, they depended on administrative back-up from the large military HQ in Singapore for supplying and feeding them. Those technical clerks and storemen, many of them being National Servicemen, played an important part in our only victory against Communism to date, in that 12-year war.

ALLAN NEWMAN

Royal Army Service Corps, 1947-49

In September 1947 Allan, like all the other 18-year-old lads, received a culture shock doing his RASC basic training at Brancepeth Castle, the DLI HQ for six weeks, and being told to do things by a sergeant, very forcefully, and usually in Anglo Saxon. He was then posted to Blackdown, Aldershot, where an acting unpaid lance corporal was needed, and as Allan was easily the biggest at 6' 3'' he was given the job. Allan next went on embarkation leave, and from there to Thetford transit camp, where the conditions were terrible.

Allan's overseas posting to Singapore on the *Dilwara* took 28 days with 2,000 men crammed into hammocks, with Allan on 'G' deck, way down below. On the journey out they landed at Colombo and were told they needed special injections, which soon took effect, and a lot of them were in no fit state to go ashore, so they stayed on board. Alongside their ship was another, filled with French Foreign Legion troops, a really tough looking lot, on their way back from Vietnam, and Allan reckoned that they made their lot look like Boy Scouts by comparison. Later in Singapore, while he was in hospital, Allan found himself in the next bed to a Legionnaire, who had some great tales to tell, and said it was a good life with a great *esprit de corps*, fighting for each other, with a pension after 15 years service – if you lived that long!

His main off-duty occupation during his time in Singapore was playing rugby, and when those matches were in Malaya he had to go protected – with two bandoliers of rifle bullets, and his rifle on his shoulder, because the campaign against the Communist insurgents was then at its peak. His garrison was based at Nee Soon in Singapore, (*See Pic. No. 26*) a huge camp, and the RASC had to service the records of all the men serving in the Far East, train the local recruits, and do air drops into the jungle. Leslie Thomas of *Virgin Soldiers* fame was in Allan's billet, unfortunately just after he left it!

While he was there Allan's unit lost one man to Communist action, a private Brown, while his pal, l/cpl. Whitehead received seven bullets, but still lived to tell the tale.

Allan travelled all over with the garrison rugby team, which included Pat Drew a DLI officer, and a very good rugby player, but the best was Frank Sykes, later an English International. During his time there they only suffered one defeat – to RAF Changi – infamous for its barbaric treatment of Allied prisoners of war during World War Two, then full of Japanese war criminals. The democracy in the team was tremendous. They had two captains, two lieutenants, and various warrant officers, and off the pitch it was 'Yes sir, no sir,' but on the pitch it was: '*For crying out loud, Pat, get rid of the bloody ball.*'

Allan had walked the same two-mile route to work each morning for three years before call-up. Two years later, having been halfway round the world doing his National Service, to places like Singapore and Malaya; met and played with top rugby players; and on the way to work again, he passed the same people he had always passed before. One of them stopped and said: 'Excuse me, but *have you been off sick?*'

Allan reckoned that National Service broadened a person's life, and taught one how to get on with other people. He still corresponds with comrades he met all those years ago, and now living all over Britain, and joined the Ex-Servicemen's

Fellowship, meeting others once a month who have worn the uniform. *(See also, Last Thoughts)*.

ANTONY MINTON

Royal Signals, 1947-49

Finding himself posted overseas for his National Service in 1947 in the Royal Signals, Antony finished up with the Singapore District Signal Regiment, a unit responsible for the military telephone lines in Singapore. The following year the Malayan Emergency was in full swing, and a few of the unit had to go into the Malayan interior as wireless operators on operation 'Force Ferret.' Antony and the rest of them stayed in their isolated tented camp in a derelict rubber plantation called Yio Chu Kang, where the perimeter defence was a ring of expanded metal all around, which did not prevent the disappearance of the officers' mess piano one night. The fence was completely intact, and the usual night guard had been on duty, but the piano had *gone*!

It was thought a good idea to see if any of them still knew how to shoot, and the chosen ones, including Antony, were sent by truck to the firing range, still in the early morning dark. On the perimeter of Singapore city they were stopped by an armed police patrol, and a young Malayan police officer came to inspect the rear of their truck, and said: 'I have stopped you in accordance with security regulations to ask if any of you are carrying any arms or ammunition.' '*Yes mate*,' came the gleeful chorus, as about a dozen rifles were poked out at him, '*what would you like?*'

They did their shoot with some success, except that the ammunition had been on the seabed at some time, and a lot of the rounds burst in the breach, causing much consternation.

In that same camp a new conscript was approached by his corporal, who told him to: 'Report to the squadron office, ask for Lt. X, and act dumb.' A short time later the lad approached the corporal again and said: 'Corporal, I acted dumb as you said, and got into no end of trouble, what was it all about?' 'I didn't say that,' said the corporal, 'I said _ek dun_.' Unlike the corporal the lad hadn't been in the Indian Army, and didn't know that 'ek dun' meant straight away!

On their way home in 1949 the troopship called in to Ceylon (now Sri Lanka) for a day's shore leave, and Antony and a few of his pals took advantage of a rickshaw tour of Colombo. After a while they arrived at an open square to see a snake charmer who started to tootle his pipe, but as no snakes appeared, he put his hand inside the basket and gave them a good slapping. With angry squeals three deadly looking cobras emerged, and promptly set off towards the crowd to escape, which made Antony and his pals retreat hastily. But they were soon saved by two little brown boys who chased after the snakes, caught them and put them back into the basket. Exit shamed soldiers, those guardians of the Empire!

SID THOMPSON
Royal Air Force, 1946-48

The first RAF National Service posting in 1946 for Sid was near Newcastle airport – for just 24 hours, followed by postings to Inverness for a week, and further north for another week, before finishing up at Warrington Despatch Centre. While he was there Sid volunteered for a draft to Canada, but was put on a draft for South Africa instead, but while on the boat he was told that he was going to Singapore. No sooner had he landed he was told that he was not staying there, because he was bound for Burma!

During Sid's basic training he came across an awkward bod who got everything wrong. When Sid and everyone else shouldered arms in the approved manner, with fixed bayonets on, his bayonet didn't stop on the rifle, it just flew off, and everyone scattered out of the way. Another time his scabbard came off his bayonet on his belt, and the bayonet was flopping around, so everyone else was jumping out of his way again. Unsurprisingly, on Parade Day the awkward bod was made billet orderly, to keep him out of the way.

P-------- turned up again in Changhi as a general duties wallah, in the same billet as Sid. He was one of those lads who liked to wander around with no clothes on all the time. He was sitting on his bunk one day, no mattress, just a derriere, and one of the female Chinese cleaners came in and threw a bucket of water over him for being naked! At this he leaped up, and his 'old man' was caught on the spring on the bed, which left him hopping about in agony, and it needed several stitches putting into it. Undeterred, he carried on wandering around unclothed, with an enormous bandage on his willy, waving it about as he wandered around the billets.

During the monsoon season, they were standing on the parade ground one day, in over two inches or more of water, wearing monsoon capes, on a weekly parade. The CO came down the steps, and the sergeant major ordered: '*Attention!*' The men slammed to attention and a tidal wave hit this CO and drenched him from head to foot. Sid was in the front row right beside the action, when the CO told them they were all: '*A bloody shower*' – and they were all dismissed immediately.

BRIAN GILBERT

Royal Air Force, 1949-51

Starting his National Service in the RAF at Compton Bassett in 1949 as a wireless operator, Brian requested a posting abroad. One weekend the top brass there decided they would have a 'battle' with a nearby radio station, to teach them how to defend themselves.

It was a 24-hour operational thing where they set up at 6 p.m. at night. Everyone was issued with rifles, and they were marched off to defend and observe for a while, until someone came in to relieve them. This went on over the weekend, and the signal that the exercise was over was a flare fired into the air, when they had to go back to the armoury and hand their rifles back. But there was a huge queue and it took over an hour-and-a-half to get rid of the guns. A few days later a message came over the tannoy: 'Would any personnel who still had rifles that were issued for the exercise, please return them to the armoury.' *There were over 200 rifles missing,* and Brian never found out how many they got back, because they had been left in the woods!

Brian's posting abroad turned out to be Changi at first, then Fellita, Singapore, which was a 24-hour operational station, and they needed some vhf/direction finding operators, so Brian went there on the edge of the airfield, near Jahore. Nothing had to be near them because they were monitoring the airborne aircraft at all times. The aircraft were calling for a bearing, and besides Brian at Seleta, there were three others taking measurements at Iricuni, Butterworth and Kaypac, and they each received a signal, took a bearing on it and sent it back to the aircraft, and from that the aircrew could plot where they were.

The Squadron Leader sent for Brian one day and said that they were short of engineers at the transmitter station, and asked him would he go. This turned out to be a good move, because there were no drills involved there. They had three transmitters on each frequency but only one operator on the channels, and were operational 24 hours a day, with sorties coming out all the time. There were also Sunderland flying boats which were going out bombing and strafing the Communist terrorists in Malaya.

The Communist terrorists (CTs), used to come across the Jahore Straits and raid the equipment compound on the camp, even though they had searchlight towers operated enthusiastically by Malaysians.

The only scary experience for Brian was when they had a homer beacon there which was pumping out 10 kw, and they had two 220ft masts, and the area between them had lightning conductors on them. The signal used to come down the transmitter, and where the aerial coil joined the lead to the aerial there was a big fat piece of copper three quarters of an inch in diameter. This had a nut and bolt through it, and taped over and running right throughout the building where the transmitters were, was a storm drain underneath the transmitter. Whenever the lightning hit the aerial it use to arc from the joint to the duct – with Brian only a few feet away. If the transmitter was off more than three minutes they had to send the signal out to all aircraft stations, shut the thing down, go in, rewrap the joint and get it started again within three minutes, with the lightning going on all the time.

Because this thing used to pump out 10kw of power they used to have a length of cable stuck on the bench, with a neon lamp attached to it. If an officer came in they would sit him opposite them at the desk, and when the signal from the transmitter worked, this lamp would light up with the signal speed. They used to pick it up and move it while it was still flashing, with no wires attached to it, and you should have seen the look on their faces. They didn't want to show their ignorance, so they *never* asked how it was done.

All in all, Brian enjoyed his National Service, gaining great experience on the electronics side, and he enjoyed the great camaraderie, doing everything together. He did not do any guard duties in his last year, in fact he only did *one* guard duty altogether, and that was spent asleep in a church!

WILLIAM H GARDNER

ROYAL NAVY, SEPT., 1960-1962.

William Gardner was one of the last ten men to be called up for National Service in the Royal Navy, and was told to report for basic training to HMS *Raleigh* at Torpoint, Cornwall, on September 26, 1960. The last ten joined HMS *Venus* in November at Devonport for a trip to Hamburg, and were taken to Hamburg Zoo and treated to tea and cakes before being taken back to HMS *Raleigh* to complete their training.

After Christmas leave the ten were sent to HMS *Sultan* at Gosport for a six-weeks engineering course, before Bill and three others were assigned to HMS *Lincoln*, a brand new frigate at Portsmouth, in February 1961.

Bill sailed for the Far East, spending Easter in Gibraltar, then through the Mediterranean to Malta. HMS *Lincoln* was in Malta for a fortnight doing gun trials, and he really enjoyed that experience, until a Welshman was sent back to Portsmouth. Bill was detailed as part of a naval party with MP on his wrist and in full blues, with orders to take the prisoner to the Inter Services Prison in Portsmouth. Being in Sulima Creek at the time, he had to go into Grand Harbour to collect the detainee, who had to pay for the escort's fare back to the UK, and for his train fare from London to Portsmouth. Prisoners at Portsmouth Barracks had their hair cut every day, had to run round the yard with their .303 and a sack of sand on their backs. The detainee did his time and had to pay for his and his escort's travel all the way back to Malta, but it was all to no effect, because the Welshman was still the same when he got back.

Relations with the Regulars were not bad for Bill and three other National Servicemen aboard. There were times when they wanted to go ashore on leave like the others, but extra duties were usually found for them to prevent that happening. All four National Servicemen did the same job, and had the same naval rank: ME 1 Stoker 1st class. There were three engine rooms and Bill was in the control room, and the work just normally involved pushing little levers around; not the filthy job it had been.

From Malta they sailed through the Suez Canal to Aden, which was just a stop-off point for a weekend while refuelling took place, so Bill and his mates just went with the RAF lads at Steamer Point. He remembers coming down the Red Sea and the RAF and Army had their own place and NAAFI and made them welcome there. Bill recalls running into the sea, and it was just like going into a hot bath with lots of little fish normally seen swimming around in aquariums, but there was the smell of sewage everywhere.

HMS *Lincoln* stayed at Colombo, Ceylon (now Sri Lanka) for a week, so all the crew took the opportunity to travel up to Candy, and saw the Temple of the Holy Tooth, and the vast tea plantations, and also where the film '*The Bridge over the River Kwai*' was made.

They sailed from Colombo to Singapore, and were all set to go to Hong Kong to join up with HMS *Victorious*, only to be told there was trouble in Kuwait, so they joined her in the Indian Ocean instead, and were all geared up for going up to the Persian Gulf, during the Kuwait-Iraq dispute, because at the time Kuwait was a British protectorate. Told they might be attacked by Iraqi torpedo boats in the Straits of Hormus, nothing happened; just patrolling and boarding the dhows, searching for ammunition. Having patrolled for several weeks Bill's crew mates were allowed R & R in Mombasa for two weeks, and took the opportunity to visit Kilimanjaro. On the tour there came a time when Bill and his pals needed a comfort stop, but were warned not to go near the water hole. Of course Jolly Jack took no notice, until suddenly chased by the biggest elephant they had ever seen – and only just managed to jump on the bus, with the elephant charging down the road after them!

Bill and his National Service mates returned to Kuwait to continue their patrols before being relieved by another frigate, and then came back down the Gulf to the Indian Ocean, arriving at what looked like Treasure Island, but was actually

Gan in the Maldives. In those days Gan was used by all RAF planes going to Australia as a refuelling point, but was hated by the RAF lads stationed there for six months, because it only measured one mile by three miles.

On their return to Singapore the four were told to pack their bags, and were detailed to HMS *Terror*, a stone frigate shore-based in Singapore, and waited for a plane to take them home. This was a new experience for Bill, because he had never flown before, and there was only space for two passengers in the aircraft. He flew home via Mombai, Instanbul and Stanstead, a 24-hour journey, then went on leave, before being sent to HMS *Victory* at Portsmouth. Bill was finally demobbed in late December 1962, just in time for Christmas.

He soon went back to Portsmouth to his previous place of work as a coppersmith, but later applied for a job making torpedo boats outside Portsmouth, near Fareham, and eventually ended up in Portsmouth dockyard for ten years.

Fast forward fifty years, and Bill was asked to take part in the 2010 Remembrance Day Parade, in London, along with two others, representing the Navy, Army and Air Force, who were all in the last intake of conscripts. This was because it marked the 50th anniversary of the termination of National Service conscription. Bill was impressed as Princess Anne stood taking the salute in pouring rain in Horseguards' Parade, Whitehall, London, and later that night he was on TV news for a while after being interviewed following the parade.

CHAPTER EIGHT

How Dared They?

Still aspiring to be a world power after the Second World War ended in 1945, after two atomic bombs were dropped on Hiroshima and Nagasaki in Japan, Britain was determined to join the USA and the USSR as the only atomic powers in the world. Britain duly tested nuclear devices in Australia, and the South Pacific Islands of Christmas, and Malden, and never gave a second thought as to the probable health risks to the thousands of servicemen they asked to witness the series of tests they undertook in the 1950s.

The men were asked to stand with their backs turned to the most destructive weapon then invented. A Top Secret report to the Military Chiefs of Staff dated February 14 1951, and headed 'Atomic Weapons Trials,' stated:

'The Army must discover the detailed effects of various types of explosion on equipment and men, with and without protection.' [1]

The only people '<u>with</u>' protection were the scientists wearing protective suits, and well away from the blast, while those tested '<u>without protection</u>' were the troops, many of them National Servicemen, standing only a few miles away. [2]

The tests involved over 22,000 servicemen from the Army, Navy and the Air Force, about 15,000 of whom were used as observers, and over half of these being National Servicemen. They were told their destination beforehand, but were warned not to tell anyone where they were going, and were never at any stage informed that they were going to be exposed to nuclear radiation. Most of those Servicemen involved regarded it as going on a long sunshine holiday with extra pay, and very little in the way of duties, etc., and were very happy to be going there. They were totally unaware that they were about to be used as human guinea pigs.

Because roads, runways and buildings had to be built wherever the tests took place, both National Servicemen and Regulars spent months over there, with usually a month for rehearsals, when they were taken through the precise course of action that they would have to take on the day. On detonation day they were usually taken between five and fifteen miles away, instructed to sit or stand with their backs to the forthcoming explosion, and to put their hands over their eyes and to shut them. In some cases sunglasses were issued, in most they were not. Protective clothing was non-existent in all of the tests, and their actual clothing consisted mainly of a hat, shorts and sandals. [3]

After the countdown, usually from sixty seconds to zero, came the intense light and complete silence, followed by a dramatic rise in the temperature. After the bang came the wind, which threw men to the ground and overturned vehicles, and soon afterwards they were transported back to camp. Even then the authorities were not satisfied with exposing the men to radiation dust, because soon afterwards some of them were instructed to go back to the detonation area to inspect and clean up. This area was of course the most heavily contaminated of all, and again no protective clothing was provided.

Decontamination procedures after the tests were almost non-existent, and no interest at all has been shown by any succeeding British government since, regarding the medical conditions of the veterans. All British governments since the tests have denied any causation between service at the test areas and ill health. They have always said that if a link can be shown between ill health and service, then a war pension will be paid to the veteran or his widow. No scheme exists for dependants.

In 1993 the National Radiological Protection Board (NRPB) published a study of 21,000 men involved in nuclear tests, according to the Ministry of Defence records. The conclusion was that 'participation in the nuclear testing programme has not had a detectable effect on the participants' expectation of life, nor on their risk of developing cancer or other diseases.' This report has been used by successive governments to refuse any compensation or pensions to the thousands of surviving veterans who witnessed the tests. [4]

No health tests were carried out directly after the tests, or at intervals since that time. All participating servicemen witnesses had to sign the Official Secrets Act when they arrived back home, to make sure they did not talk about what had happened to them, and only much later did the servicemen question what was wrong, when their own health deteriorated rapidly, and mutations appeared in their offspring.

Over 55% of nuclear veterans have suffered degrees of ill health, some of which has been passed down to dependants. The diseases they suffer from range from bowel cancers,

314

leukaemia, ischaemic heart diseases, to multiple myelomas and liver and kidney complaints and mental disorders. However, their children and grandchildren are suffering from diseases such as Alexander's disease, a type of leukodystrophy, a neurological degenerative disease where the white cells in the brain are progressively destroyed over a period of about ten years, spondylitis (inflammation of the spine), rare bone and lung diseases, etc., and various organs being in the wrong places in their bodies. [5]

However, it is almost impossible to prove that exposure to nuclear tests by their forebears caused the diseases which they exhibit, which is what successive governments use as a good enough reason to ignore their duty of care to all the nuclear test participants from 1952 to 1962.

Well over 50 years since the first tests took place at Monte Bello in 1952 the BNTVA (British Nuclear Tests Veterans Association) are still fighting for compensation for the survivors of those tests, their widows and families. The veterans were determined to pursue a lawsuit because it has been scientifically proved that future generations will continue to be affected by the nuclear tests, and that of the other countries also involved in the tests, the United States, Australia and New Zealand governments have accepted responsibility for their veterans and are paying out pensions to them, even knowing that hard and fast proof would be impossible to obtain after such a long time. [6]

When the issue finally came to court in 2008 the judge, whilst being sympathetic, ruled that there was not enough evidence to link health problems to events which happened over 50 years ago. This is because successive governments, both Conservative and Labour, have been determined not to pay out what could come to hundreds of millions of pounds in compensation, and realise that the longer they can delay, the less they will have to pay out eventually.

The following stories all have a light-hearted cavalier feel to them, because the majority of young Servicemen felt that they were doing something different, worthwhile and exciting, and they were curious to find out more.

NUCLEAR TESTS

MIKE ETHELSTON

Royal Marines, 1955-57

In September 1955 Mike reported to the Infantry Training Camp, Royal Marines, at Lympstone, for basic training, and later Poole, for amphibious warfare training, consisting mainly of learning to crew and operate landing craft, both LCAs and LCMs, used to land men and equipment on beaches. Just before the end of the course the colour sergeant called all 30 of them together and asked for two volunteers for a special assignment, and Mike and 'Crutch' Underwood drew the 'short straws.' Only when they boarded HMS *Messina* at Southampton on June 29, 1956, did they discover that out of a total of 50 marines, they were the only National Servicemen, and that they were bound for Christmas Island, to join *Operation Grapple* for the testing of Britain's 'H' bomb.

The trip to Christmas Island took three weeks, stopping off at Kingston, Jamaica for a few days. Because the local men objected to the sailors and marines chatting up the girls, they pulled knives on them, which set off a mini riot, from which the locals came off a very poor second best!

When they finally arrived at their destination they found that the Island was in the shape of a horseshoe, and was an atoll, and the sea surrounding it was very shallow. Their LCMs were needed to go out to the merchant ships, which unloaded everything from cement for building the airfield at the other end of the Island, as well as gas, food, water and NAAFI stores. The latter was very popular, consisting of beer, sweets and tobacco, and never reached the shore in its entirety! The ships were anchored three miles out from the Island, so one trip could take up to three hours there and back. The H-bomb was going to be dropped by a V- bomber, and set to explode at around 20,000 feet, hence the reason for building an airfield.

They lived in tents at the bottom of the Island, and had their own NAAFI canteen and dining tent, etc. There was no fresh water for washing, but it didn't really matter, as they were operating under wartime conditions and they all just wore a sunhat and a pair of shorts. The Island was ten degrees north of the Equator, so it was very warm all the time.

In October Mike was promoted to Marine First Class, and in those days marines and sailors over 21 were entitled to a daily tot of rum, and his crew who were all Regulars, allowed him to have a sip of their tots; 'sippers' as it was known. His promotion meant that he was now paid the princely sum of 24 shillings a month, and as they had just been told that they were going to Honolulu for ten days leave, he looked forward to drinking beer and sitting on the best surf beach at Waikiki and watching the surfers. This turned out to be a great disappointment, as it was very expensive, with the beer costing a pound a pint, and the Waikiki surf was as flat as a millpond.

On their return they were told to hitch up one of the LCMs onto a fairly long tow-rope behind one of the merchant ships. They were destined for Fanning Island, two hundred miles away, where the boffins wanted to put up some equipment to test the fall-out when the bomb was exploded. Shortly before the test took place the Japanese fishing fleet attempted to stop the test by sailing underneath the drop zone, so the British ships formed a circle about ten miles in diameter to prevent any disturbances.

They were taken onboard the aircraft carrier HMS *Bulwark*, sat on the flight deck, and were given dark goggles and anti-flash gear, and told to face away from the epicentre behind them. They had to keep their eyes closed until given permission to turn around. Even with all these precautions they could sense the flash when the bomb exploded, 20,000 feet above them, after being dropped by a V-bomber specifically designed for nuclear warfare. To Mike the noise was more like rolling thunder, but the mushroom cloud was awesome.

They were informed that it was a 'clean' bomb, and the prevailing winds dispersed the cloud over the Pacific Ocean, so no damage was done apparently, and the test was said to be a success, but he does not recall any specific de-contamination procedures after the bomb exploded. (Many years later Mike found out that the wild life in the area had been affected, being blinded by the flash). Shortly afterwards Mike and 'Crutch' Underwood, together with a marine called Ginger Eames, were sent home on the RFA tanker *Brave Warrior*, as their time was up.

Mike was transferred to RM Forces Volunteer Reserve, London branch, to do his four years Reserve training, and during this time he took part in the Somerset to London Bridge, 24-hours non-stop two-man canoe race, coming third. He also did weekend underwater diving courses, and spent a couple of 14-day camps out at Malta, carrying out underwater exercises.

Mike had a brilliant time during his National Service, and very nearly signed on for seven years, but he felt that it was now time to earn a living back home.

During the last ten years Mike has had the privilege on more than one occasion to speak to the Royal Marines Captain General, Prince Philip, who is aware of his service on Christmas Island, and always says: '*I'm glad to see that you are still standing!*'

MICHAEL FULBROOK

Royal Marines, 1958-60

Michael joined the Marines as a National Serviceman in December 1958. After basic training at Lympstone he went to the Joint Services Amphibious Welfare Centre (JCAWC) in Poole harbour, passing out as a stoker on landing craft. This led him to Christmas Island for the last series of atomic and hydrogen bomb tests – two H-bombs and three atom bombs. Michael was based at the port, and the landing craft were used to ferry all the materials delivered by merchant ships, such as cement for the roads, and wooden huts to replace the tents they were living in. There was a company of Royal Engineers, who operated the winches on the ships, and a company from the Fijian Army who operated cranes on shore to unload them. The only goods that did not come into the Island by ship were fresh vegetables, which were collected from Honolulu by the RAF on a regular basis.

During the bomb tests all their landing craft faced out to sea, with engines running and with four marines per craft, with the coxswain and the stoker looking after the engines. All the personnel at the port had to be seated on the ground near the landing craft allocated to them. There was a radio commentary broadcast over a tannoy system, giving details of the aircraft take-off. If it crashed on take-off there was a chance of an atomic explosion, but it was not fused for an H bomb until after take-off. In the event of a crash they were told to put to sea with the Army on board in the well deck.

Contrary to official reports they were dressed in shorts and berets only. Once the aeroplane was up the bomb was fused and released at a certain height, and exploded at around 20,000 feet. As they were not far from the Island they had to have their backs to the explosion, with their eyes in the crook of their arm, because the flash from the bomb would have blinded them if seen with the naked eye. As it was, the light was so bright they could see the bones in their arm, just like an x-ray. Next there was an intense heat on their backs, lasting for a few seconds, as if someone had put an electric fire on their neck.

As far as Michael knows the atom bombs were exploded over the Island, but they were nowhere near as dramatic as the H-bombs. There was no protection, and if they had ever had to put to sea, he reckons that not many would have survived. It was a metal boat, and the temperatures were always well into the 100s.

As the tests were over the authorities decided to offer long weekends for anyone interested in seeing Honolulu, so Michael and a friend went for four days, staying at the YMCA, and they were shown all around the Island.

Michael also applied to go to New Zealand to see his father who lived there. He applied to the Captain of HMS *Resolution*, who granted him '14 days leave on reaching New Zealand, after which he had to make his own way back to Christmas Island as quickly as possible.' He was amazed at having being given such an open-ended pass, and decided to make the most of it. At the end of his leave he had the choice of two ways of returning, by Fiji or Australia. He chose Fiji, and stayed for another two weeks at the RNZAF flying boat base at Luthala Bay. The next RAF plane back to Christmas Island carried the Air Commodore, on his way to conduct his annual inspection of the Island, who announced that they were staying over for the next weekend at Samoa. So Michael's 14-day pass had turned into nearly six weeks by the time he eventually arrived back on Christmas Island!

STAN PEVERLEY

Royal Air Force Balloon Unit, 1954-56

When Stan first went to Maralinga, Australia, the Army were making the roads, and their pay books just had 'overseas posting' on them – not atomic bomb testing – the authorities had no records of them. But the RAF balloon unit, all 84 of them, were classed as an atomic bomb unit. If the authorities wanted RAF lads they said RAF personnel please meet here, but if they wanted Stan's lot they asked for RAF *and* the balloon unit. They were separate altogether.

On a testing day, after breakfast, the winch wagons had to be made ready, then they had to go up to the box site, bring the balloons down and test them to see the ropes etc. were all right, and wait until the Aldermaston scientists came along to tell them what was going to happen. There was lots of hanging about entailed, and sometimes they had to get the balloons mended.

In the box was all the equipment with the bomb, and Stan put the last hook of the balloon on top of them, and away it went. The balloons lifted the atomic box off the ground. Once they had them away in the air they just used to peg them down and then move away as fast as possible, say about ten miles up the track, on a straight road about 30 miles long.

For the last explosion, the balloon unit witnessed it from landing craft and tents, and the wind used to blow right through them. They were on this landing craft as they dropped the bomb and the wind changed as they were coming over the Island. They were told they might have to go out to the ships, but they were hundreds of miles away; just then the wind changed back again, so they were all right and back on the Island. When they finished after the last test they left all the wagons and equipment for the Army to sort out.

There were open air theatres at Maralinga which they went to in their spare time, and it was an altogether better life than in England; much more fun than at Cardington, where he had done his balloon unit training, and better weather too. Driving along the roads kangaroos used to jump straight out in front of you, and could catch you unawares if you were not careful.

Having lost a few balloons, the boss told them to anchor them down extra firmly in future. All explosions were atmospheric, detonated 800 feet up– none at all from the ground. The balloon unit used to allow the balloons to take the basket containing the bomb up to that height, and the scientists used to detonate it from a hideout. Most explosions were atomic, except for the last few which were hydrogen – the *Grapple* ones. Stan did those and the *Antelope* ones too.

Stan started National Service in 1953 but later signed on for nine years to be part of the Christmas Island tests. Stan thought it was a good job, working from Aldermaston at first, their main base, now and again. He was based at Maralinga in Australia, and the aborigines who lived there were just told to clear off. He also went to Christmas Island, between Hawaii and Australia – 1000 miles away, perhaps, where Fiji workers did all the building work.

On the day of the explosion they were all told to: *'Put their backs towards the explosion, close their eyes and pull their hats down.'* After the big flash a few seconds later, say ten, came the big bang. Stan did not see any radiation. However, the personnel at Monte Bello on ships at sea, apparently came off the worst – they did not know anything about it. They received the worst doses of radiation, according to Dr. Rose of Birmingham University, who reckoned that the radiation would not affect them or their first offspring, but would affect subsequent grandchildren.

In 1959, back in England, Stan was sent to Gaydon as a transport driver, but his next posting was to Acklington where Stan was driver to a Group Captain. They were flying down to Topcliffe one day, and the GC could not take his plane down, being foggy, so they flew into Newcastle, and driving back to Topcliffe, Stan followed a bus, and instead of going over the Tyne Bridge, Stan went over the High Level Bridge, so the GC told Stan he had gone the wrong way, but Stan turned round and told him to just read his paper as *he* was doing the driving! There was no reply from the GC – he just did it!

Later the fog lifted and the GC was going down to Dishforth, and from there he flew back to Acklington, while Stan was still at Topcliffe waiting for a call. Eventually Stan was told to make his way back to Acklington, and arrived at 2.0 p.m., and was asked why he had taken so long, but he replied that the GC had a jet, whereas he did not have one on the car.

The day Stan left the RAF he went to the office to say goodbye, and the GC asked him how he was going to get home, and where was it? Stan said: 'By train to Barnard Castle,' so the GC told his new chauffer to: 'Drop Stan off at his front door.' A very nice touch, Stan thought.

RICK SOWERBY

Royal Air Force Balloon Unit, 1954-58

Rick's RAF basic training was at Hunningford, and from there he was posted to Cardington, where he trained for the balloon unit. When the job came up for Australia, he was sent on special training to Aldermaston for six weeks learning about radiation and how to drive heavy D8 track laying vehicles. They received instructions that they were going abroad, but were told not to tell anyone where, so naturally they told *everyone* they were going to Australia!

Rick's journey started by going to New York for a couple of days, then San Francisco for a week, and Hawaii, where they landed at 7.30 a.m., were picked up by a stretch limousine, and had garlands of flowers placed over them by young girls. Leaving Hawaii they went to Fiji for an overnight stop and stayed on the beach all night singing: *All day all night,* etc. with the local girls. From there they flew to Canton Island and Sydney, Australia, and eventually arrived at Adelaide, (*See Pic. No. 57*) before finally going on to Maralinga, their ultimate destination, where their tents were already up waiting for them.

There were three floating balloons and well away from the camp, with huge concrete bases, because the balloons were big. Six men at a time watched over the balloons, doing duties, and then they would swap duties. One day up there they wanted some rations, so they went back to the main camp to get them in a vehicle, through Security Police. They went on this hard road where there were hundreds of kangaroos and drove through them on their way to camp. After collecting their rations one of them suggested catching a kangaroo. They saw them in the distance so stopped the vehicle, and two of them went one way, while the other two went the other, but the kangaroos kept avoiding them by diving away, and they gave up trying. When they got to Security they told them their story, and Security replied that they were the luckiest people alive. Apparently the kangaroos would grab someone by the neck and strangle them – and they had been trying to *catch* one!

At night time they used to have a fire going and play with the scorpions. They had a tent with all the food in it, but they saw a big wildcat go in. But only Rick saw it grab a piece of meat and go out of the back of the tent, so he volunteered to go in and chase this wildcat out, amazing the rest of the lads with his apparent bravery. He grabbed a fire-axe and told the rest of the lads to stay back, while he saw to it. He made lots of noise in the tent, as if fighting the wildcat, and emerged to tell them that he had got it. They all piled into the tent to see, but saw no sign of the wildcat, and soon realised they had been conned!

They had arrived at Maralinga and unpacked all their kit, and the balloons – one metre square when packed – then they saw their first bomb going up. They were told that this was just a one-kiloton bomb to be detonated from a tower 40ft high by another unit, and they could see it clearly. They were put on an observation hill about 20 miles away from the tower and observed it, wearing just dark sunglasses. There was a countdown and then the bomb went off. They were just in normal khaki dress, cotton shorts and vest, nothing special.

They let that one off, then a couple of weeks later they let another one off, a bigger eight kiloton bomb with the normal mushroom and flying cloud. From that day on, *that* bomb radiated fall-out onto the site where they were going to explode their balloon bomb later, and contaminated the whole area. They had to wear special suits, which were short leg combinations with cotton socks, little white woollen boots, cotton gloves and a cotton cap, also a green radiation badge which, if it turned red, showed heavy dangerous contamination. This was while they were practising for their balloon bomb. They were working in a contaminated area, and after 20 minutes their badges had changed to red, but they still had to finish their two-hour shift, practising putting their bomb up with the balloons, and then taking everything down again.

They were rehearsing for the big day. Every day they practised they were ingesting an average of between six and eight roentgens of radiation (a unit measuring a radiation dose). They did all this for about three weeks. Each day they were scrubbed down afterwards in a decontamination unit because of the radiation caused by that eight kiloton bomb exploded previously. The wind had changed during that explosion and this had carried the radiation onto their site, which was called Taranaki.

Rick was operating a D8 track laying vehicle, but his friend Wally Kaye was outside with a crowbar, keeping the cable which led to the bomb out of the contaminated sand. There were little whirlwinds swirling around; it was very hot so he took his hat off, and all this contaminated dust went onto his hair. Later on in the decontamination unit getting washed down, while Rick had six to eight roentgens, his friend had 12 roentgens just in his hair. (A few years ago Rick went to a Civil Defence Day for the police, and the person in charge told him that he should be dead, all the contamination he had ingested!)

The day they put their bomb up it was Rick's job to drive a Leyland Hippo vehicle in convoy. They had put the bomb up and tied it up and their job was done, they then had to get observational distance, about two-and-a-half miles away from the bomb. There were six vehicles in convoy on the road with Rick's second in line, when it suddenly stopped. He was told to get out and let the mechanic look at it, but it took a while for him to find the fault. Nobby McAlvar had switched it off on purpose, just for a laugh, *with a bomb waiting to go off above them!* They got to Observation Hill and they had an hour to wait before detonation, and loudspeakers were nearby telling the men what to do.

They had their backs to the bomb, with their hands over their faces, and there was a countdown every 15 minutes. Then it got to 15 seconds, then 10, 9, etc., and now they felt it. The actual words coming over the loudspeakers were: 3, 2, 1, *flash*, ABOUT TURN! You had to be joking, and no-one did straight away of course. The flash burned them and they felt the heat all down their backs. Light came through their hands, reflections from the clouds, and they all turned around slowly. The sand was just like the waves in the sea. Then the blast hit them and nearly knocked them over – they could hear the blast they were told later, in Adelaide, 500 miles away. They saw a giant fireball going up and up, and then it stopped, and a radiation cloud came in forming the mushroom shape. (*See Pics. Nos. 58 & 59*).

As soon as it went off it looked like a chequer board with rockets flying across so the scientists could do their measurements. This all went on for 20 minutes. Two jet aeroplanes flew into the fireball to get radiation measurements, and some of the mechanics 100 miles away died from cancer later, as a result of servicing the planes when they returned, heavily contaminated.

Because the scientists had detonated the bomb at 800 feet, there were gamma rays, but no radioactive fall-out, two-and-a-half miles from the bomb. They were safe from radiation, but not from gamma rays, blast and heat. Heat comes first, blast second and radiation last. The other bombs were from static towers, over two miles away at Observation Hill, like Nagasaki in 1945, on the ground. The balloon unit was unique, consisting of three Mk. 12 big balloons, with a cable going through.

After the bomb was exploded the job was done, and they were all on their way home within a couple of weeks. Rick cannot remember going through any decontamination procedures afterwards, even though their 23 kiloton bomb was bigger than the 22 kiloton atomic bombs which were exploded at Nagasaki and Hiroshima. They later went into the dropping zone where the bomb went off, which was about as big as Wembley Stadium, and the sand was burnt to a depth of about one metre. All they found was a piece of cable about a foot long from all the balloon unit and lengths of cable. *'Operation Antler,'* the third explosion witnessed by Rick, has been described as the most dangerous test ever, by many people at various veterans' reunions he has attended.

An Australian film crew rang Rick up about making a play, involving him, and what happened at Maralinga, and the Australian ex-servicemen who were dying from the after-effects of it. When the play was ready he was invited to the Civic Hall in Leeds as a VIP, and found it very moving in parts.

Eight years ago Rick had a telephone call from *'News at Ten'* asking him to go down to Leeds to do a link-up with London for the news programme about his part in witnessing *Operation Antler*. His wife told him to phone the Ministry of Defence to get permission, because of the Official Secrets Act, and was given permission to appear on television, providing he did not talk about the name of the Operation. He was given a tour of the studio before being put in a glass cubicle and asked questions through the earphones. When he got home that night his wife did not believe that he had appeared on television earlier, and she got a shock when she saw him being interviewed on the *Ten o'clock News*!

Rick still plays golf at least four times a week, which keeps him active, and gives him the opportunity to socialise.

PORTON DOWN

In the 1950s and early 1960s notices began appearing on Army and RAF camp notice boards all over the country, asking for volunteers to take part in experiments to find a cure for the common cold. Most Regular servicemen were far too experienced to volunteer for anything like that, so it was left mainly to hundreds of National Servicemen to take part in the experiments. The inducement to be included in the experiments was the offer of extra pay, less than one pound, and time off, but as an average week's pay for these lads in those days was in the region of £1, it looked a very attractive proposition indeed.

The experiments took place at the Chemical Defence Experimental Establishment at Porton Down, in Wiltshire, which had been Britain's military research and development facility since the First World War.

The scientists were really trying to find out the amount of sarin (a deadly nerve gas) that could be applied to bare skin before death occurred, and some Servicemen were given as much as 300mm. The volunteers were also subjected to other nerve gases, as well as mustard gas.

As part of this 'common cold' research on May 6 1953, Ronald Maddison, an RAF National Service engineer from County Durham, had 200 milligrams of liquid sarin poured onto clothing attached to his arm. He fell unconscious soon after, and died later on the same day in extreme agony. A coroner's inquest held in secret stated that his death was attributable to 'misadventure.'

Alfred Thornhill, another National Serviceman from Salford was there on a month's posting to Porton Down, attached to the ambulance service the day Ronald Maddison died. He arrived at the gas chamber and witnessed Maddison flailing around on the floor, his whole body convulsing and spewing an obnoxious frogspawn-like liquid out of his mouth. Scientists were standing around Maddison, and it looked to Thornhill as if they did not know what to do next. Eventually Thornhill was helped by three of them to pick Maddison off the floor and put him in the ambulance, to be driven to the medical unit there, which had been cleared of all other patients.

After he helped carry Maddison over to the bed Thornhill saw something that has greatly disturbed him for the last 58 years, with frequent flashbacks of the events that he witnessed. He saw Maddison's leg lift up from the bed and his skin turn blue from the ankle and rise up his leg and continue to rise up until a doctor produced a huge hypodermic needle which he plunged into Maddison's body. At which point Thornhill was told to get out. [7]

The next day he was told that Maddison had died, and that he was to drive his body via some minor roads to the mortuary at Salford General Hospital. When he returned to Porton Down he was asked to report to the medical officer who told him to sign a form, and threatened him not to say anything about what he had seen to anyone, or he would go to prison.

In those days you did not question authority, you just followed orders, which is what Alfred Thornhill did, even though he was very uneasy about what he had seen, the strange behaviour of the medical officer, and also about the strange and prolonged route he had been told to take to the mortuary. [8]

On October 28 1999 a BBC North East & Cumbria documentary called '*A Death at Porton Down*' was shown on BBC North television. In it Alastair Hay, a toxicologist from Leeds University claimed that scientists' briefing notes at Porton Down suggested that they knew that the doses that they were giving young National Servicemen, used as guinea pigs in nerve gas tests, was endangering their lives, and could be fatal. [9]

A wide-ranging police investigation called *Operation Antler* started in the late 1990s, after continued complaints about hundreds of other illnesses related to the Porton Down experiments over the years. A team of detectives started investigating the deaths of a further 25 National Servicemen who took part in tests at Porton Down in the Fifties and Sixties.

Fifty years on, in the summer of 2003, Alfred Thornhill was listening to a local Manchester radio station, and he heard a report about a police inquiry into the death of a young RAF National Serviceman called Ronald Maddison at Porton Down all those years ago. Alfred stopped what he was doing; he knew it was the same lad he had seen dying, and he telephoned the Wiltshire police conducting the inquiry, and they travelled up to Manchester the following day. He gave them all the information they required on what he saw at Porton Down that day, and his eye-witness testimony was the break-through needed in a re-opened inquest into Maddison's death.

A Coroner's Inquest into Maddison's death in November 2004 ruled that he was: 'unlawfully killed' at the hands of the state. The court heard Alfred Thornhill describe what he had seen of Maddison's terrible death at the hands of an unscrupulous secretive chemical establishment, and it also laid bare the sickening experiments on hundreds of other volunteers. Many of them had died prematurely, and countless went on to develop cancer, Parkinson's and Motor Neurone diseases, very early on in life after their experiences at Porton Down. The jury concluded that: 'The application of a nerve agent in a non-therapeutic experiment' was the cause of his death. Finally, Ronald Maddison's family and the Ministry of Defence agreed on a charge of *'gross negligence'* in February 2006, the ruling forming a basis for compensation claims by 360 other Porton Down veterans who had taken part in tests during the Cold War period. [10]

In January 2008 the Defence Minister Derek Twigg announced that he was to award £3m compensation to 360 victims of Porton Down experiments, which amounted to £8,000 each. He added that: 'The government sincerely apologised to those who may have been affected.' He went on to say that there 'may have been aspects of the trials where the life or health of those taking part may have been put at risk.' [11]

Not a full apology and not nearly enough money either, according to Ken Earl, a survivor and founder of the Porton Down Veterans Support Group, but at least it gave closure to his members.

So at least in the Porton Down cases gross negligence by the authorities in question has been established, and a very small amount of compensation paid to the victims, after a protracted battle with the government, but only because of the comparatively small number of cases involved.

The nuclear test victims however are still waiting for their cases of gross negligence to be recognized – almost 60 years since the first atomic test at Monte Bello took place.

Successive British governments in the decade from 1952 to 1962 took advantage of the cream of our young 18-years-old men, by exposing them to two lethal obscenities, exposure to radiation and exposure to nerve gas tests. In both cases the volunteers were used as guinea pigs, and in those days people trusted the authorities to look after them. Those affected either died within a very short time, or endured a shortened lifetime of extreme suffering, exacerbated by seeing their offspring born with terrible deformities, as in the nuclear cases. *How Dared They!*

CHAPTER NINE

Last Thoughts

National Service broke down class and other barriers, giving in some cases lifelong friendships, such as that between Rex Strawson and Jack Turner, serving in the DCLI together in Cyprus in 1948. They still communicate with each other 63 years later, despite living 200 miles apart. Many others regret not keeping in touch with their former comrades after completing their time, and going back to their civilian employment.

This sense of comradeship was confined mainly to other ranks, where young 18-21-years-old men from different social backgrounds, living in different parts of the country, and speaking with diverse accents, were all thrust together, living ten or more to a barrack room. They were united in their intense dislike of the Army and RAF in general, bullying NCOs in particular, and the fact that they were all being paid the same amount of money a week to start with in training.

National Service officers were a different matter. During basic training those candidates considered to be potential officer material (POMs) were taken away from the squads and sent to a unit selection board where they were interviewed by a senior officer. Those selected were put before a War Office Selection Board (WOSBE) where the potential officers were going to be tested. The overall intention was to turn a PO into a 2nd Lieutenant who could command a platoon effectively. These tests consisted of situation challenges, with groups of five, to see who had the best leadership qualities, and included written tests, and giving a five-minute lecture on any subject, followed by final interviews.

Less than 70% of WOSBE candidates passed the examination board, the failures being RTU'd – returned to their units. The successful candidates then went to officer training units (OCTUs), held at Eaton Hall in Cheshire or Mons in Aldershot, where the training was extremely hard. [1]

After being commissioned into one of the Services they found themselves amongst their own social assemblage, but they also found that on their meagre National Service allowance they had great difficulty keeping up with their fellow Regular officers in the officers' mess, because of the great difference in pay, unless of course they came from a privileged background.

For those in the medical profession such as doctors and dentists, it meant an automatic commission into the Royal Army Medical Corps (RAMC), when they joined at a later date after they had finished their degrees. [2] The RAF system of commissions was similar to that of the Army, while the Royal Navy only offered commissions to National Servicemen if they became Regulars.

For most National Service veterans, those former comrades, once so close, have now after between 48 and 64 years, become just faces on dilapidated, very old fading photographs, whose names just will not come back to memory. Others looking back yearn for perhaps an annual reunion of old National Service pals, but rarely get around to actually looking them up.

In a moment of nostalgia some veterans have planned a visit to former Army, Navy and RAF camps both in Britain and overseas, and while some have found something they remember just as it was, the majority have found that the passage of time and natural progress has erased everything they remember, and have gone home disappointed.

After the demise of National Service in 1963, and the need to slim down the manpower in all three Services, many bases were closed down over the years, because they had become redundant and surplus to requirements, and the land was sold off to developers, such as happened at Caterham and Norton camps, and many others all over the country.

Victoria Barracks in Portsmouth, previously used as the Navy's basic training depot is now a museum; RAF Watchett, the main base of the RAF Regiment, closed in 1982, and has now been turned into a holiday camp. Flying operations ceased in 2006 at RAF Coltishall, ex-Battle of Britain station of Douglas Bader fame, and now lies disused and overgrown, and may become a prison. The massive Army establishments at Catterick and Aldershot have been reduced in size; the Grenadier Guards said the last farewell at the Guards' depot at Caterham in 1995 after being home to the five Guards Regiments for over 100 years, as the Regiments' Nijmegen company flag was lowered, and they marched out. The former NAAFI is now a day nursery, while the officers' quarters have been transformed into luxury flats. [3] Norton camp, home of the Worcestershire Regiment, was sold off for housing in the 1990s, and now has over 100 houses on the site. However, Worcestershire Norton Sports Club own the cricket club, football pitches and ranges, and the old depot sergeants' mess is now the club house.

Fenham Barracks, home to the Northumberland Fusiliers until 1962, is now student accommodation, but the Territorial Army Queen's Own Yeomanry holds a presence there. Deerbolt camp, Barnard Castle, is now a young offenders' institution. Strensall Barracks, York, established for over 200 years, is now a training centre for field hospital and medical staff. RAF Padgate is now home to a large housing estate and a high school. [4] RAF Bridgnorth, where Ronnie Corbett did his basic training, was closed in 1963, and is now a country park. RAF Hednesford has been replaced by a large industrial site. However, Devonport naval base is still very much there, being Western Europe's largest naval establishment. [5]

Bill Hubbard and the author arranged a trip to their former RAOC camp at Donnington, in Shropshire, two years ago, and found that the Army camp looked familiar to what they remembered it as. The road leading from the camp to the roundabout was still there, and the bookie's house on the left just before it, a right turn leading to the depot where they once worked. They even found the old cinema, still in good condition, but now being used as a bingo hall. However, Donnington railway station had gone, along with hundreds more all over the country, a victim of the manic Dr. Beeching in 1960. (*See Pic. No. 10*). All that remained was the stationmaster's house and garden which used to run alongside the platform, the scene of their fortnightly Friday 'escape.'

Roger Ramsdale did not bargain for being 'arrested' and interrogated when he paid a visit to the Paderborn guardroom in Germany, almost forty years after he left it in 1959. He was attempting to take photographs of the camp over the wire, but was unaware of recent IRA activity there. Undeterred, Roger returned with his wife the following year, and they were treated like VIPs.

Like so many other National Servicemen serving in the Far East, Stan Hawthorn vowed never to return, but like many others he had the urge to revisit in the 1990s, and went back with his wife to Singapore and Malaya. Howard Duddles had the same feeling, also in the 1990s, taking his wife with him, visiting Ceylon, Cyprus, Singapore and Malaya, and was struck by how much they had all changed since he was last there.

Ron Shaw returned to Korea in June 2010 for the 60th anniversary celebrations of the start of the Korean War in 1950, along with many other National Service veterans. They were guests of a grateful South Korean government for being part of a United Nations peacekeeping force which kept that country free from Communism. During his ten-day visit Ron shared accommodation with Bill Speakman VC, famous for his incredible heroic deeds during the battle of the Imjin River, and went around with him visiting the many hundreds of British war graves. (*See Pic. No. 36*).

However much some advocates would like to see the return of National Service, and young 18-years-old-plus offenders being sent to the front line in Afghanistan, to make decent citizens with some discipline instilled into them, it is unfortunately perhaps, never going to happen. All political parties are against the idea, mostly on a basis of cost, in reply to the occasional request by a Member of Parliament in the House of Commons, for its return.

The three Services are also united in their rejection of their being used as some sort of remedial organization for malcontent young offenders, devoid of any vestige of discipline. The idea is a non-starter in their opinion, however much and however often it is advocated by National Service veterans, as a sort of panacea for all that is wrong with the youth of today. In any case they do not want National Service to return, because since its demise in 1963 their equipment has become too electronically sophisticated for young recruits to learn how to use it in such a short period of time. There are so few Regular personnel in each Service now that they could not deal with thousands of new recruits being conscripted and needing to be trained.

Perhaps the most realistic evaluation of the conscription conundrum was by Lawrence Bell, who points out that things have changed dramatically since the National Service decade. In those days of instant compliance to a command, where discipline was ingrained into young people, both at home, school and work, authority was rarely challenged. As little as 1% of the National Service intake between 1945 and 1963 went absent without leave (AWOL), and had to be tracked down by the Military Police, and in some cases the police. Even this small percentage took up thousands of hours to round them up and take them back to their barracks. Nowadays Lawrence reckons the percentage of young people refusing to submit to actually going into a National Service scenario of one sort or another would be nearer 50%, let alone walking away from it after joining! This mass act of disobedience would in his opinion make it a non-starter, as they would be impossible to track down, requiring thousands of personnel just engaged in trying to find them.

To support this view, the programme on ITV television in 2002 called 'Lads' Army, followed 30 young 18-years-old troublemakers recruited for only a four-week period, as they went through Army basic training at a former military camp in Wiltshire. They were each allegedly paid £1,000 if they completed their four weeks training, (unlike their former National Service contemporaries, who earned just £1 per week to start with, and over a 104-week period, and with a three-month prison sentence if they refused to go). Professional soldiers acted as the NCOs and officers to try to bring some reality to the programme, but it failed to portray the harsh uncompromising reality of National Service basic training in the 1950s, whatever the Service, and wherever situated. [6] By the end of the four weeks only 25 remained out of the original 30 who started, despite the great financial inducement, so just how many would have survived for 104 weeks is open to conjecture.

Time and again in the preceding stories, when the veterans were asked what National Service had done for them, only a few replied negatively, such as Derek Rigby, who although enjoying parts of it, found it a complete waste of time, because the RAF could not find enough work for them to do; it put his studies back a year, and disrupted his career. Albert Lomas, also in the RAF, had the same conclusion, because he lost two years of his professional life, and had great difficulty finding a teaching job when he came out.

However, the reply in 98% of the cases was a positive one, such as Raymond Taylor, RAF, England and Singapore, who thought that National Service had given him two of the most informative years of his life, and asks: *'Why is it not in operation today?'* George Cairns , Green Howards, Berlin, reckons it was one of the best things he has done in his life, and agrees with the previous sentiment. Bernard Cozens, Royal Navy, based in England, learned a lot, became more self-sufficient, has no regrets, and is glad he did it, despite not wanting to go initially. Ivor Thomas, RAOC, thought he had been posted to a holiday camp when he arrived at Shimanzi Barracks in Kenya. By the time he left, after only having to eat, sunbathe, play cards and go out on a night – he *knew* he had been to a holiday camp! George Parry, RAF, Germany, while doing another trade to his own, learned things he would never have done otherwise, and enjoyed the camaraderie. He has since joined ex-servicemen's organizations and has made a lot more friends. Len Dilnot, Yorkshire Light Infantry, in Berlin, enjoyed his National Service, the German beer, and especially the German women, where he saw plenty of action! Last, but definitely not least, Peter Yeates, Royal Navy, serving in Hong Kong waters, found it a great adventure for a young sailor of just eighteen. He reckons that the Hong Kong Flotilla and ML3510 he sailed with were, apart from family life, the best years of his life!

Some National Servicemen had their perceptions on life changed by their experiences during those two years or more, and wanted something different out of life when they returned. Derek Lovemore and Mike Gregson did something about it and emigrated to Australia, and never regretted the move. Raymond Taylor went back to being an instrument maker, but wanted more out of life, so he took management and engineering degrees to enable him to go into management. His National Service experience gave him the confidence to take such a bold step in those days. Malcolm MacGregor went back to his job at ICI, but he was looking for something else, and joined the local police force after a while, his time in the Army standing him in good stead, regarding the discipline, and it was a new challenge.

Many of them realised when they were being posted overseas thousands of miles away by sea that the places they were being posted to would possibly never be seen again by them. This was an age before holidays abroad to far-flung places by charter aircraft had become the norm, and holidays at home to the seaside was about all they could expect; and they were determined to make the most of their situation. A posting to Malaya for example, could include stops at Gibraltar, Aden, Ceylon, Singapore, and take weeks to get there, which included some sightseeing in those exotic places – and it was all time off those two years.

Most National Servicemen came out fitter than when they went in, especially those who had been used to working indoors in civilian life. Although hated by most recruits at the time, those six to ten weeks basic training endured by most conscripts, and even longer for some, were the cornerstone of that new-found fitness. Those recruits who were good at any sport found that all three Services actively encouraged them to train even harder, and travel to compete against other units for the Regiment was encouraged, both home and abroad. This was found by Allan Newman playing rugby in the Far East and Peter Bird and Gordon Duck, using their prowess at football in Germany, England and Egypt. Ken Kirby in Khartoum, carried it a stage further by playing football for the local team and also the Combined Army/RAF team three or four times every week, which did not leave much time for playing soldiers.

Very few would argue against the fact that National Service could be a very boring waste of time for some, with very little to do except fill in the days to go to demob, out of the original 730. This was particularly the case in the latter stages around 1960, when the Army and RAF struggled to find something for them to do, the Navy having dispensed of their services in the late 1950s.

Luck had a large part to do with how a person viewed his lot. For example, Tony Wills was scraping a urinal with a bayonet on a cold January day in Aldershot in 1949, until he volunteered for a posting which could have been anywhere, but turned out to be sunny Bermuda. This was to be a posting to paradise for him, spending afternoons diving into the sparkling coral blue sea at Navy Wells after his morning shift at work.

Derek Lovemore and his pals got up to all sorts of boyish pranks after their Bermuda posting, played soldiers on the Warwick camp ranges, and then made good use of their wonderful location right next to Horse Shoe Beach in 1954.

Conversely, John Scott and twenty thousand others were sent to the war in Korea from 1950 to 1953, to live outside in hoochies cut out of the side of trenches, where the temperature varied between –40 degrees centigrade in winter, when the conditions and food were terrible, living with rats twice the size of any they had ever seen before, and +40 degrees heat in summer. Not to mention the patrols they had to do at night against the Chinese and North Koreans and the severe losses they sustained when the enemy outnumbered them by ten to one.

Eddie Mack fought in the Malayan jungles of Jahore for most of his two years, in 1954, against the Communist terrorists there, with water up to his waist day and night, in the clammy heat of the jungle, and sleeping outside in hammocks. He had to contend with tigers and snakes, and bloodsucking leeches had to be burned off his body with a cigarette many times a day. He fortunately only just escaped a sniper's bullet while acting as lead man on patrol.

After waiting for two years or more for demob to arrive many National Servicemen were strangely quiet when the morning of leaving arrived, however noisily they had celebrated the night before. They realised as soon as they had handed in all their kit into the stores that they were leaving behind comrades they had shared everything with over a long period of time. That closeness and sharing is incomprehensible to anyone who did not do National Service, but it was there. This feeling of loss of comradeship was so powerful that it made many think of signing on, and indeed quite a few actually did, because of it.

Going back to work with people they had not seen for two years was a strange experience, and to many, including the author, they definitely did not compare with the close friends who had been left behind at camp, but commonsense made them try a bit harder to re-establish friendships.

Surprisingly, very few National Service veterans have made a nostalgic return to Bermuda or any of the other Caribbean countries, and fewer still signed on for Regular service in paradise, while those serving in the Far East apparently have an irresistible urge to go back and revisit old triumphs, despite the great distance involved.

One thing which veterans of any age in all three Services have in common is the amazing ability to remember their National Service number. National Service veterans when asked their National Service number rattled it off at machine gun pace, without any hesitation, as if it was ingrained into their memory forever. On phoning Peter Bird and finding he was out for the moment, his wife, discovering what was needed, recited it off just as fast, because she had written it on envelopes containing letters to Peter every day for two years, and still remembered it!

THE VERY LAST TWO!

The very last National Serviceman to be demobbed was 2nd Lieutenant Richard Vaughan of the Royal Army Pay Corps on May 13, 1963. He left his unit in Germany on May 4, and cycled leisurely home to England, so as to claim the distinction of being the last man, instead of Private Fred Turner of the Army Catering Corps, who had been demobbed on May 7. Fred however, had been issued with the very last National Service number – 23819209.

Among the last National Servicemen to be recruited in the Army, Royal Navy and the Royal Air Force were Leonard Teece (Army), William Gardner (Navy), and Robert Collins (RAF). They took part in last year's Remembrance Day Parade at Horseguards' Parade, Whitehall, London, because 2010 was the 50th anniversary of the ending of conscription at the end of 1960. They were traced by the Monica Porter Missing and Found columns in the Daily Mail, on behalf of the National Service (Royal Air Force) Association.

NOTES

Introduction

(1) Hickman, T., *The Call-Up, A History of National Service,* Headline, 2005, p.xi.

(2) Royle, T., *The Best Years of their Lives,* Michael Joseph, 1986, p.158-159.

(3) Ibid, p.167-168

(4) Ibid, p.147

Chapter One: How National Service Started

(1) Royle, T., *The Best Years of their Lives,* Michael Joseph, 1986, p.11.

(2) Ibid, p.14

(3) Ibid, p.16

(4) Ibid, p.18

(5) Ibid, p.22

Chapter Two: What Was It All About?

(1) www.britisharmedforces.org. 'British Army Forces and National Service.'

Chapter Seven: The Far East

(1) As given by Ron Shaw to *The Morning Calm*, April 2010.

(2) Tugwell, M., *The Unquiet Peace*. Stories from the Post-War Army, A. Wingate, London, 1957, p.83.

(3) Ibid, p.84.

Chapter Eight: How Dared They!

(1) 'Reaping the Hurricane,' Paul Lewis, *Saga Magazine*, November, 1998.

(2) Ibid.

(3) Sermon by The Very Revd. Nicholas Frayling BA, LLD, Dean of Chichester, at Portsmouth Cathedral, Saturday February 19, 2005. *Campaign Magazine*, June, 2005, pages 8 and 9.

(4) 'Reaping the Hurricane.'

(5) Ibid.

(6) *Campaign Magazine*, June, 2005, p.9.

(7) *The Sunday Observer*, September 28, 2003. 'Final Agony of RAF volunteer killed by sarin in Britain.'

(8) Ibid.

(9) *The Independent*, Friday, October 29, 1999. Porton Down 'knew tests could be fatal.' John Davison.University of Kent.

(10) 'Cold War at Porton Down.'- Ronald Maddison.' January 8, 2009.

(11) BBC, Friday 1st, 2008, 'Porton Down victims awarded £3m.'

Chapter Nine: **Last Thoughts**

(1) Royle, T., *The Best Years of their Lives*, Michael Joseph, 1986, p.87.

(2) Hickman, T., *The Call-Up, A History of National Service*, Headline, 2005, p.57.

(3) www.footguards.org

(4) www.flickr.com

(5) www.royalnavy.mod.uk

(6) Hickman, T., *The Call-Up, A History of National Service*, Headline, 2005, p.345.

NATIONAL SERVICE INDEX

Clough, Brian, OBE, MA, RAF, 1953-55.

Clough, Joe, Royal Navy, PJX 752427, 1945-47.

Coan, Ken, General Service Corps, 1946-48.

Coy, Kenneth, 18th Hussars, 23753420, 1959-61.

Cozens, Bernard, Royal Navy, C/m 945996, 1954-56.

Crook, Stan., 1st Btn. Royal Warwickshire Regt., 23598185, 1958-60.

Dale, Les, SAC, RAF, 2740384, 1954-56.

Dart, Keith, REME, 22713837, 1952-54.

Davies, Bill, 13/18 Royal Hussars, 1950-52.

Davison, Brian, RAOC, 23561059, 1958-60.

Dilnot, Len, Yorkshire Light Infantry, 1953-55.

Dixon, Gordon, RAF, 5015855, 1956-58.

Duck, Gordon, Green Howards, 22642547, 1952-54.

Duddles, Howard, Cpl, Royal Signals, 23401059, 1957-59.

Edney, Alan, RAF, 3101818, 1952-54.

Ethelston, Mike, Royal Marines, RMFVR 202445, 1955-57.

Fawcett, John, RAF, 2760577, 1955-57.

Ferguson, Thomas, 1st Btn., 'C' Co. Duke of Wellingtons, 22701528, 1951-53.

Forster, John, L/Cpl., Royal Signals, 22378063, 1950-52.

Foster, Michael, L/Cpl RMP, 6 Dog Co., 23793674.

Fulbrook, Michael, Royal Marines, 133258, 1958-60.

Fowle, Peter, Sgt., DCLI School of Infantry, 1946-48.

Gamble, George, RAF Regiment, 4075325, 1951-53.

Gardner, William, H., Royal Navy, P.059192, 1960-62.

Gilbert, Brian, RAF, 3133191. 1949-51.

Goldthorp, Bill, Cptn., RAMC, 1958-60.

Gregson, Mike, 2nd Lt., Queen's Own Royal West Kent Regiment, 1950-52.

Hammond, Mick, Prince of Wales' Own, 23401307, 1957-59.

Hardman, Ken, Royal Signals, 2300154, 1954-56.

Harrison, Stan, REME, 23034651, 1954-56.

Hastings, Edna (Sandy), NAAFI worker, 1945-47.

Hawthorn, Stan, Royal Engineers, 19185687, 1947-49.

Hirons, Philip, RAMC, 22593304, 1951-53.

Hirst, Bryan, RAF, 2324173, 1946-48.

Hornby, Jack, 1st Btn. Northumberland Fusiliers, 21042928, 1947-49.

Hubbard, Bill, RAOC, 23577934, 1958-60.

Hutchinson, George, RAOC, 14158104, 1946-48.

Ives, Leslie, Green Howards, 22139844, 1949-51.

James, Arthur, RAOC, 19194393, 1947-49.

Jennings, Frank, Lincolnshire Regt., 19140897, 1946-49.

Jerome, Ron, Grenadier Guards, 23104529, 1955-57.

Kane, Tom, RAF Bomb Disposal, 23084404, 1946-48.

Kayley, Michael, Northumberland Fusiliers, 23414644, 1957-59.

Keenan, Mick, Royal Army Education Corps, 23094551, 1954-56.

King, Clive, 13/18 Royal Hussars, 23443590, 1958-60.

Kirby, Ken, Royal Army Service Corps, 14057769, 1946-48.

Lipthorpe, Keith, RAF, 4073465, 1951-53.

Lomas, Albert, Cpl., RAF, 2683194, 1947-48.

Lovemore, Derek, Cpl., 1 Btn, DCLI, 22935157, 1953-55.

MacGregor, John, RAF, 2312550, 1956-58.

MacGregor, Malcolm, Royal Engineers, 23512358, 1958-60.

Mack, Eddie, SAS/Royal Hampshire Regt., 23048794, 1954-56.

Maggs, Alan, Signal Ptn., HQ Co., 1st Btn. DLI, 22682442, 1952-54.

Mallows, Ian, RAF, 2442601, 1949-51.

McGouran, Hugh, Cpl., 2nd Btn.Green Howards, 22958613, 1953-56.

Meredith, Roland, Rev. Canon, Ox and Bucks, 22410644, 1950-52.

Miles, Ray, DCLI, 21056272, 1947-49.

Minton, Antony, Royal Signals, 19131157, 1947-49.

Moore, Des, Irish Guards, 2277567, 1956-59.

Morgan, Arthur, RASC, 23108119, 1955-57.

Morley-Jacob, Peter, 2nd. Lt., QORWKR, 429532, 1952-54.

Newman, Alan, Cpl., RASC, 21042893, 1947-49.

Noble, Gordon, RAF, 3147072, 1955-57.

Oliver, Terry, Cpl. RAMC, 22684037, 1952-54.

Parry, George, RAF, 2723344, 1954-56.

Peverley, Stan, RAF Balloon Unit, 4177410, 1954-56.

Pollard, John, REME, 22492532, 1951-53.

Powell, Jack, Cpl., 2nd Btn. Yorks & Lancs, 1945-47.

Prentice, John, Royal Warwickshire Regt., 23455681, 1958-60.

Ramsdale, Roger, 1st Fld. Sqn. Royal Engineers, 23423614, 1957-59.

Rawlings, Derry MM, DLI, 22646443, 1952-54.

Rees, Alun, Royal Engineers, 1946-48.

Rigby, Derek, RAF, 5075040, 1960-62.

Robinson, John, Cpl. Green Howards, 23053496.

Rogers, Charlie, Royal Engineers, 14892884, 1945-48.

Rutherford, Colin, Northumberland Fusiliers, 23328597, 1956-58.

Scott, John, 'A' Co. 2 Pltn. DLI, 22494726, 1951-53.

Scratcherd, Malcolm, AC1, RAF, 1947-49.

Serginson, Alan, Royal Signals, 22618520, 1951-53.

Shaw, Ron, Duke of Wellingtons, 22670824, 1952-54.

Shepherdson, Barrie, Prince of Wales' Own, 23763031, 1960-62.

Shield, Trevor, 15th/19th Royal Hussars, 23761873, 1960-62.

Simpson, Fred, Royal Signals, 14153567, 1946-48.

Sowerby, Rick, RAF, 4176407, 1955-58.

Strawson, Rex, DCLI, 21035429, 1947-49.

Stonehouse, Arthur, Green Howards, 14138142, 1946-48.

Sturgeon, Roy, Royal Engineers, 22624090, 1952-54.

Swanson, Neil, 'A' Co. 1 DCLI, 22920403, 1953-55.

Taylor, Raymond, RAF, 5125289, 1956-58.

Taylor, Ron, L/cpl, DLI, 22583897, 1952-54.

Taylor, Warwick, Bevin Boy.

Tester, Bob, LAC, RAF, 2301987, 1946-48.

Thomas, Ivor, RAOC, 22162501, 1949-51.

Thirkell, Dennis, LAC, RAF, 3100579, 1947-50.

Thompson, John, Queen's Dragoon Guards, 23811765, 1960-62.

Thompson, Sid, RAF, 3078707, 1946-48.

Thurm, Brian, REME, 23408762, 1957-59.

Turner, Jack, DCLI, 19198812, 1946-48.

Unett, Barry, 1st Royal Hampshire Regt, 23648424, 1959-61.

Watson, Arthur, Royal Artillery, 22478508, 1951-53.

Westwood, Peter, RAF, 1955-57.

Wills, Tony, RAOC, 1948-50.

Williams, Fred, DLI, 22606890, 1951-53.

Wilson, Albert, Catering Corps, 23043757, 1954-56.

Wilson, Harry, Green Howards, 23159111, 1955-57.

Yeates, Peter, Royal Navy, C/2952909, 1955-57.

Young, Stan, Scots Guards, 22119162, 1949-51.

BIBLIOGRAPHY

PRIMARY SOURCES:

House of Commons Ministerial Statement, 21st April 2009: Col. 7WS.

AUDIO:

BBC Radio 4, Called Up, *Impressions of National Service*, November 22, 1983.

BBC Radio 4, Charles Wheeler, *The Peacetime Conscripts*, July 23, 2001.

WEBSITES:

National Archives footage of 'Operation Hurricane' at: http://www.nationalarchives.gov.uk/films/1951to1964/filmpage_oper_hurr.htm.

Australian National Archives has primary sources of 'Operation Buffalo' using a keyword search of 'Buffalo Trials.'

'Operation Grapple' video clips on: http://www.tv3.co.nz.

http://www.britisharmedforces.org/ns/nat_history.htm

http://www.dailymail.co.uk/news/article-480432/The-Reality-National-Service-20-ro

UNIVERSITY:

University of Kent Porton Down Project/Maddison, January 8, 2009.

NEWSPAPER:

Porton Down 'knew tests could be fatal,' J. Davison, The Independent, October 29, 1999.

JOURNALS:

Campaign, British Nuclear Test Veterans Association, End of Year, 2004.

Campaign, British Nuclear Test Veterans Association, June, 2005.

Campaign, British Nuclear Test Veterans Association, September 2005.

Campaign, British Nuclear Test Veterans Association, September 2008.

Martell, Lt. Gen. Sir Gifford, 'The Case Against Conscription, Army Quarterly, October 1949.

Tinker, Lt. Col. E., 'National Service Without Tears,' Army Quarterly, April, 1950.

BOOKS:

Baylis, T., *Clock This*, Headline Publishing, 2000.

Blair, J., *The Conscript Doctors*, Pentland Press, Bishop Auckland, 2001.

Catchpole, B., *The Korean War*, Constable, London, 2001.

Charlton, J., *Jack Charlton*, Partridge Press, 1997.

Cobbold, P., *The National Service Sailor*, Quentin Books, Essex, 1993.

Goldthorp, W., *A Two Year Stretch*, Serendipidy, London, 2003.

Hastings, M., *The Korean War*, Michael Joseph, 1987.

Hickman, T., *The Call-Up, A History of National Service,* Headline, London, 2004.

Hollands, D., *The Dead, The Dying and The Damned*, Cassell, London, 1956.

Ives, L., *A Musket for the King*.

Jameson, D., *Touched By Angels*, Eburry Press, London, 1988.

Johnson, B.S., *All Bull,* Allison & Busby, London, 1973.

Lodge, D., *Ginger, You're Barmy,* Penguin, London, 1984.

Monkhouse, B., *Crying with Laughter*, Century Random House, London, 1993.

O'Toole, P., *Loitering with Intent,* Macmillan, 1993.

Royle, T., *The Best Years of their Lives*, Michael Joseph, London, 1987.

Strawson, Rex, *National Service: Officially Unrecognised Service*, 2007.

Thomas, Leslie, *The Virgin Soldiers*, Constable, 1967.

Tugwell, M., *The Unquiet Peace*, Wingate, London, 1957.

Waugh, Auberon, *Will This Do?*, Century, London, 1991.

Wesker, Arnold, *Chips with Everything*, Jonathan Cape, London, 1962.